Blandin de Cornoalha

TEAMS

VARIA SERIES

A list of the books in the series appears at the end of this book.

Medieval Institute Publications is a program of
The Medieval Institute, College of Arts and Sciences

Blandin de Cornoalha
A Comic Occitan Romance

A New Critical Edition and Translation

Edited by

Wendy Pfeffer

Translated by

Margaret Burrell and Wendy Pfeffer

TEAMS

MEDIEVAL INSTITUTE PUBLICATIONS
Western Michigan University
Kalamazoo

Library of Congress Cataloging-in-Publication Data

Names: Pfeffer, Wendy, 1951- editor, translator. | Burrell, Margaret, translator.
Title: Blandin de Cornoalha : a comic Occitan romance : a new critical edition and translation / edited by Wendy Pfeffer ; translated by Margaret Burrell and Wendy Pfeffer.
Other titles: Blandin de Cornouaille.
Description: Kalamazoo : Medieval Institute Publications, [2022] | Series: Teams varia | Includes bibliographical references and index. | Parallel text in Occitan and English on facing pages. | Summary: "The volume makes available for the first time in English an edition of the medieval romance "Blandin de Cornoalha," accompanied by a translation and introduction to the work. Composed in the second half of the fourteenth century by an anonymous author, the story offers an early recording of the Sleeping Beauty folktale, incorporated into the adventures of two knights. Many elements in the romance are comic, suggesting that "Blandin" is not simply a tale of knights in battle, but also a parody of medieval romance in general"-- Provided by publisher.
Identifiers: LCCN 2022024202 (print) | LCCN 2022024203 (ebook) | ISBN 9781580445238 (paperback) | ISBN 9781580445245 (hardback) | ISBN 9781580445252 (adobe pdf)
Subjects: LCGFT: Romances.
Classification: LCC PC3328 .B55 2022 (print) | LCC PC3328 (ebook) | DDC 849/.33--dc23/eng/20220712
LC record available at https://lccn.loc.gov/2022024202
LC ebook record available at https://lccn.loc.gov/2022024203

ISBN hardbound: 9781580445245
ISBN paperbound: 9781580445238
eISBN: 9781580445252

Printed and bound by CPI Group (UK) Ltd, Croydon, CR0 4YY

Contents

List of Illustrations

Figures courtesy of Ministero della Cultura, Biblioteca Nazionale Universitaria di Torino

Acknowledgments

THIS EDITION AND translation has been a long time in the works, and there are a good number of people who have contributed, in one way or another, to its completion. Wendy Pfeffer thanks the University of Louisville Vice President for Research for several internal grants; the University of Louisville College of Arts and Sciences for research funding; the Department of Classical and Modern Languages of the University of Louisville for its Modern Languages Fund; the Fulbright Foundation, whose support for other projects allowed this one to be completed; and the Department of Romance Languages, University of Pennsylvania, which gave her a new home. She thanks librarians at Ekstrom Library, University of Louisville, and at Van Pelt Library at the University of Pennsylvania. She also thanks Dominique Billy, the late Jacques de Caluwé, Roberta Krueger, Walter Meliga, Roy Rosenstein, Patrick Sauzet, Nathan H. Schwartz, Robert A. Taylor, Alessandro Vitale-Brovarone, and all who contributed to this project. The anonymous readers for Medieval Institute Publications made very useful suggestions. To those whose names we have omitted, please accept our apologies.

The authors thank the Ministero della Cultura, Biblioteca Nazionale Universitaria di Torino for permission to publish photos of its manuscript G. II. 34 in this book.

Abbreviations

BnF	Bibliothèque nationale de France
COM	Ricketts, dir., *Concordance de l'Occitan médiéval*
DOM	*Dictionnaire de l'Occitan médiévale*
cm	centimeter(s)
fem.	feminine
FEW	*Französisches etymologisches Wörterbuch*
fl.	flourished
f., ff.	folio, folios
masc.	masculine
ms.	manuscript
PC	number assigned to troubadours by Pillet and Carstens, *Bibliographie der Troubadours*
RlaR	*Revue des langues romanes*
Rom	*Romania*
p.	person
pl.	plural
prep.	preposition
s.	singular
TMAO	Trésor manuscrit de l'ancien occitan

Introduction

THE MIDDLE AGES is a period whose literature is not as well known to American audiences as it should be. We tend to put one thousand years of history (roughly 500–1500 CE) under the header of the Dark Ages, thinking it a period of deep religiosity and general ignorance. Scholars of the period know better—the Dark Ages is a misnomer of the first order, and the second half of that thousand-year span had much more light than it gets credit for.

One approach to the Middle Ages is through its literature, which entertained people then and can entertain us today. Yes, there are literary works that are religious in tone or theme, and there are many works that are light-hearted, with happy endings, that can serve to teach us about human behavior as much as about the medieval period. Into this group, we would put medieval romances, a genre of literature that first appears in France in the middle of the twelfth century and whose descendants include novels of today.

Medieval romances are extended stories that describe the adventures of knights, seeking to prove their valor so as to be worthy of their ladies; these adventures could be exaggerations of daily life of the period (battling other knights) or could involve fantastic creatures. Not only did the hero have to demonstrate his chivalric skills, he also had to demonstrate his knowledge of manners and demeanor worthy of the court. The first romances were composed in verse (often in rhyming couplets); later romances were written in prose. The theme of love and quest for a lady quickly became the dominant driver of romance plots.

In many respects, the plot of *Blandin de Cornoalha* is typical of medieval romances. Two knights, Blandin of Cornwall and Guilhot Ardit of Miramar, set off on adventures. A dog leads them to a cave where two young women are a giant's prisoners. Guilhot stays outside of the cave while Blandin kills the giant and frees the ladies. The three of them rejoin Guilhot and find a castle where two other giants are holding the ladies' family prisoner. Guilhot kills two lions guarding the castle, but is taken prisoner by the giants. Blandin then enters the fray and kills one gargantuan creature. Having escaped from his prison, Guilhot helps Blandin kill a second giant.

The two knights leave the ladies and their family. A talking bird tells them to take different routes when they come to a pine tree. At the pine, they separate, agreeing to meet the day after Saint Martin's Day (November 11). Guilhot kills the Black Knight and his brother, who sought to avenge the death. However, he cannot defeat a group of knights from the Black Knight's family and he is taken prisoner. Meanwhile, Blandin has found a lady leading a white horse; after sharing a meal together, Blandin falls asleep, and the lady steals his horse, leaving him hers. Riding the white horse, Blandin meets a squire who bemoans the death of his lord, killed by ten knights guarding a castle housing an enchanted damsel. With the squire, Peitavin, Blandin arrives at the castle, where he defeats the ten knights.

The damsel's young brother tells Blandin what he must do to break the spell and free her: capture a white hawk guarded by a serpent, a dragon, and a Saracen. Blandin succeeds, and the damsel, Brianda, awakes from her sleep. She and Blandin fall in love, but Blandin must leave her to find Guilhot. Since Guilhot is not at the rendezvous point on the agreed date, Blandin finds the castle in which his friend has been imprisoned. Blandin defeats the lord of the castle, liberating Guilhot. The two knights return to Brianda's castle for a double wedding: Blandin and Brianda, Guilhot with Brianda's sister, Yrlanda.

The romance genre was very popular throughout medieval Europe, with examples found in every literary language of the period. While romances in Old French or Middle English may be better known, the romances composed in Occitan offer interesting vantage points from which to consider medieval literature. The best known Occitan romance is *Flamenca*, whose plot reminds us of the story of Rapunzel. The love triangle involves the heroine, Flamenca, her lover, Guilhem, and her jealous husband, Archambaut. Readers enjoy the cleverness of Guilhem as he plots to see and then meet with Flamenca. Sadly, the sole manuscript for this romance is missing both its beginning and its end, so we cannot know what happens to the lovers.[1] Another Occitan romance, more popular

[1] The eight-line fragment of *Flamenca* in Palma de Mallorca, Biblioteca de la Societat Arqueològica Lul·liana, Codex E represents lines in the middle of the story; we

Figure 1: Turin manuscript, Torino Biblioteca nazionale e universitaria G II 34, folio 40r, the death of Ganelon.

than *Flamenca* if the number of medieval copies, at least eight witnesses, is any indication, is *Jaufre*, a story linked to the court of King Arthur. In this romance, the hero, a knight named Jaufre, accomplishes a series of adventures involving a variety of magical and mythical characters before rescuing the damsel who will become his bride. *Flamenca*, incomplete at 8,095 lines, and *Jaufre*, complete with 10,974 lines, are consistent in length with romances in other vernacular languages. One distinctive feature of *Blandin de Cornoalha* is its comparative brevity.

As a popular genre, medieval romance was open to parody, the culmination of which would be Cervantes' *Don Quixote*. We can see *Blandin de Cornoalha* as a typical romance in its story line, with elements of parody and comedy added for good measure (see below).

Popular romances were copied, that is, put in writing, repeatedly, as happened with the Old French romance of *Perceval*, by Chrétien de Troyes (fl. ca. 1160–1191) which exists in seventeen medieval copies. While some romances exist in hundreds of medieval copies (the *Romance of the Rose* is the best example of this), *Blandin de Cornoalha* was not as fortunate and has come to us in just one unadorned manuscript, now in a library in Turin, Italy. The *Blandin* manuscript is interesting for the other works it contains, mostly historic or geographic accounts, which might suggest that the person who compiled the manuscript may have understood *Blandin de Cornoalha* less as a work of fiction than as another retelling of historic events. The one illustration in the manuscript, for example, shows the death by hanging of the traitor Ganelon (see Fig. 1), a picture

can still describe *Flamenca* as existing in a single copy (see Zufferey's remarks in Fasseur, tr., *Flamenca*, 94).

that accompanies a history of Charlemagne and demonstrates the combination of fiction (Ganelon is a character found in the *Chanson de Roland*, an epic poem) and history. The Turin manuscript's date must be inferred from the watermarks of its paper pages; scholars believe the manuscript was copied at some time between the end of the fourteenth and beginning of the fifteenth century. It appears to have been copied in northern Italy. *Blandin de Cornoalha* is the only work of vernacular fiction in this book whose other works are all in Latin.

We can only guess as to the author of *Blandin de Cornoalha*, an anonymous poem in one manuscript that offers no additional information. The language of the work points to an author whose language was the central dialect of Occitan, Languedocian. The story itself suggests a connection to the Armagnac family of southern France, and a member of that family, John III d'Armagnac may be responsible for the story's travel to northern Italy. The author is very familiar with the literature of his time, as can be seen in his use of analogs and sources. That he calls his work a *dictat*, inventing a new genre in Occitan, ties *Blandin* to literary innovations happening in Middle French during the late fourteenth century and points to the author's creativity.

How does *Blandin* fit into Occitan literary history? Medieval Occitan literature is best known for its lyric poetry, composed by singer-songwriters known as troubadours, who flourished primarily in the twelfth and thirteenth centuries. These individuals invented the idea of romantic love as we know it today; the theme of love pervades their poetry and enters into romances, as can be seen in the case of *Flamenca*, composed in the thirteenth century. Some of those ideas are also present in *Blandin*, composed in the last third of the fourteenth century. There is, of course, much more to Occitan literature than simply the love poems of the troubadours and the romances discussed here—Occitan authors composed epic poems and literary criticism, didactic literature and religious works as well. Troubadours were very capable of criticizing their colleagues, of laughing at and with them. *Blandin* finds its place in this corpus as a comic romance, an Occitan text that is willing to poke fun at the literary history that precedes it, even as its author seeks to demonstrate his own literary talents and creativity.

The romance of *Blandin de Cornoalha* is worth reading today for a number of reasons. It serves as an example of medieval Occitan literature, a work that is manageable because of its relative brevity and enjoyable because of its plot. We can learn about perceptions of medieval knighthood from this tale and try to understand what a medieval audience might have found comic, both in the story and about knights in general. The only English translation of *Blandin* is not widely available and was not based on a new edition of the text. Not as well known as other Occitan romances, particularly in the English-speaking world, *Blandin* is a good read and deserves better press.

This study, edition, and translation began as the doctoral dissertation of Margaret Burrell, research she defended in 1974. For a variety of reasons, she decided not to publish her dissertation at that time, and her ideas lay dormant for several decades. In 2010, she offered her work to Wendy Pfeffer, in hopes that Pfeffer would be able to complete what Burrell had begun. They did a good deal of collaboration on the translation by email and polished it over the course of a two-week meeting in Louisville, Kentucky. The translation is by Burrell with assistance from Pfeffer. Pfeffer has developed the linguistic analysis based on the language of the text, not on some perfect vision of fourteenth-century Occitan; she composed the introductory material with assistance from Burrell.

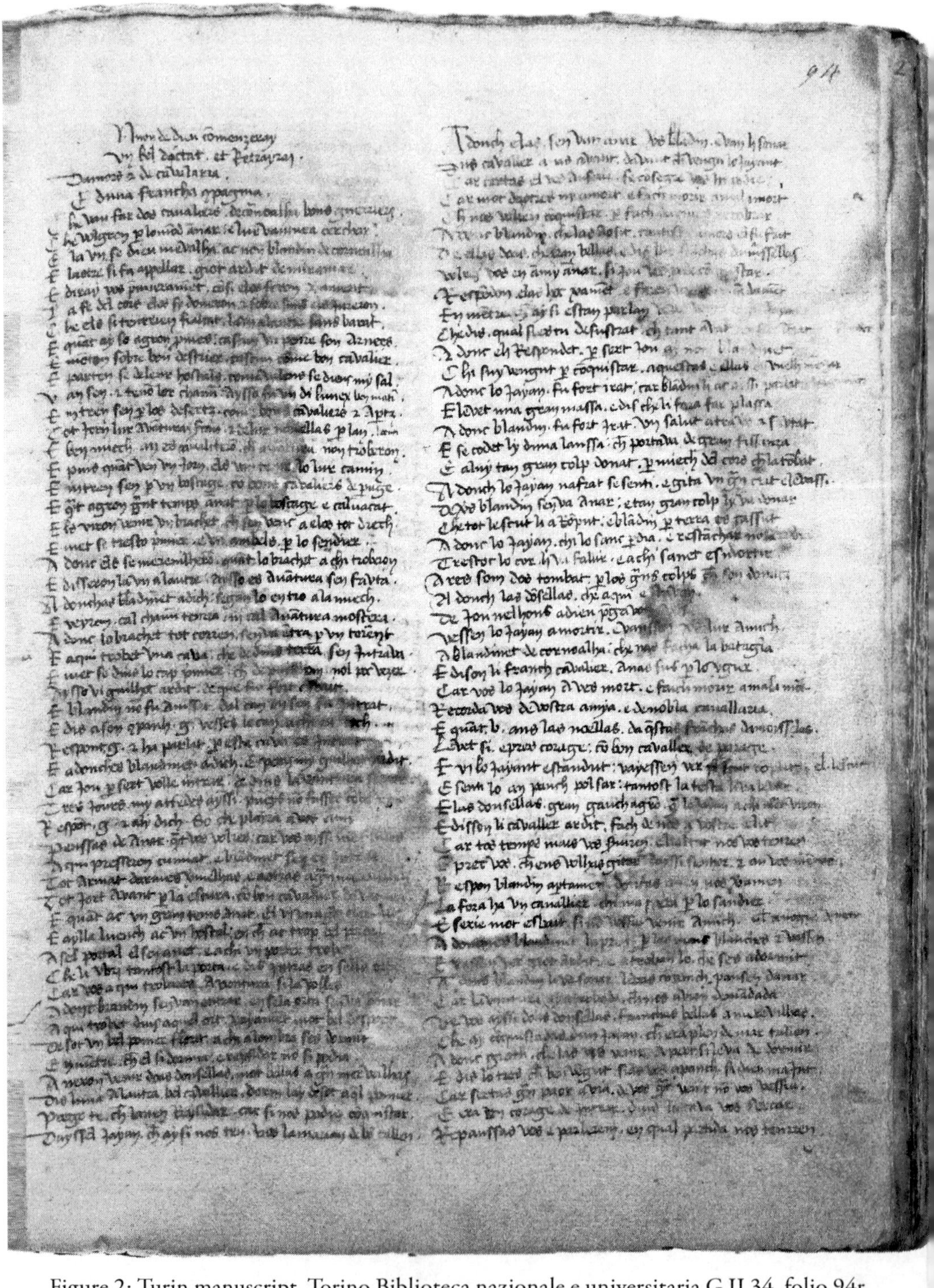

Figure 2: Turin manuscript, Torino Biblioteca nazionale e universitaria G II 34, folio 94r, the opening lines of *Blandin de Cornoalha*, showing water damage on all outside edges.

The Manuscript

B*LANDIN DE CORNOALHA* is preserved in a single manuscript, a volume that has resided in Turin since at least the beginning of the eighteenth century, when the first catalog of what was then a royal library was completed.[1] A number of scholars consulted the text over the course of the nineteenth century. In January 1904, the Turin library was severely damaged by a major fire which destroyed thousands of volumes in five of the library's thirty-eight rooms;[2] many precious manuscripts in the collection were lost forever. The volume containing *Blandin*, which Jean Gorrini claimed was the only Occitan manuscript in the collection, survived, with water damage, because it was housed with Latin, rather than with vernacular works.[3] Following the fire, the codex was repaired and rebound; the damage sustained is still visible (see Fig. 2), but does not render the text illegible.

The manuscript is cataloged as Torino Biblioteca nazionale e universitaria G II 34 (formerly DLXXXIX. 1. III. 5 in Giuseppe Pasini's catalog[4]). The book is written on paper and is currently composed of 133 folios measuring 29 or 30 cm by 22 cm. Its contents are as follows:

— Introductory material, genealogical trees of the biblical families of Adam, Abraham, Jacob, and Jesse, folios i–vii.

— The following folio is completely blank and numbered by a modern hand, folio 0.

[1] See Pasini, Berta, and Rivautella, *Codices manuscripti bibliothecae regii taurinensis*, 2:151. It is a reality of medieval Occitan studies that a good number of the texts exist in unique manuscripts (cf. *Flamenca*).

[2] Gorrini, *L'incendie*, 29.

[3] Gorrini, *L'incendie*, 169n.

[4] Pasini, Berta, and Rivautella, *Codices manuscripti bibliothecae regii taurinensis*, 2:150.

- Jacobus de Aquis (Jacopo d'Acqui, died 1334), *Secunda pars Cronice libri imaginis mundi*, the *Second Part of a Chronicle of the World*, folios 8r–91v. Jacobus was a Dominican friar who may have been associated with the community in Saluzzo. His *Chronicle* is rich in northern Italian events, incorporates the *Song of Roland* into that history, and does not mention the 1334 election of Pope Benedict XII, which serves as a *terminus ad quem* for the work and suggests a year for Jacobus's death.[5]
- *Conspectus, sive mirabilia urbis Romae*, the *Miracles of Rome*, author unknown, folios 92r–92v. This text, composed in the twelfth century, exists in numerous manuscripts. In general, editors of the *Conspectus* have ignored this witness.
- Folio 92 is followed by two completely blank folios, numbers 93a and 93b.
- *Blandin de Cornoalha*, folios 94r–99v. The text of *Blandin* is copied in two columns, each roughly 8.5 or 9 cm wide. The scribe left room for an initial majuscule (see Fig. 2), a capital letter; the text opens in expected fashion, one octosyllabic verse per line. At verse five, however, the scribe changed his *modus operandi*, writing two lines of verse for each line of the manuscript column. This method of copying a romance is fairly exceptional and almost never seen in manuscripts of French or Occitan texts. The few examples of this practice that we have been able to locate are found in transcriptions of Anglo-Norman texts or in Anglo-Norman manuscripts, almost all located today in England,[6] which makes the Turin manuscript all

[5] Chiesa, "Iacopo da Acqui."

[6] See Careri, Ruby, and Short, *Livres et écritures*, for details. They provide these examples: Cambridge, University Library, Ii.1.33, f. 120, "trois proverbes en couplet d'octosyllabes ajoutés dans la marge inférieure, chaque couplet est copié sur une ligne," 34; London, British Library, Harley 4733, "*Roman de Brut* anonyme en couplet d'octosyllabes, fragment: une seule colonne de texte, disposition du couplet sur une seule ligne, avec les deux vers separés par un point," 92; Oxford, Bodleian Library, Rawlinson D 913 (S.C. 13679), "recueil de fragments; deuxième fragment, Benedeit, *Voyage de Saint Brendan* en couplet d'octosyllabes (fragment): deux octosyllabes par ligne," 146. We can add London, British Library, Cotton Nero A.V., the *Comput* de Philippe de Thaon; Oxford, Bodleian Library, Selden Supra 38, an Anglo-Norman version of the *Évangile de l'enfance*. There exists another Occitan example, parts of Bertran Boysset's copy of the *Roman d'Arles*, Aix-en-Provence, Musée-Bibliothèque Paul Arbaud, 63; see Hasenohr, "Le rythme et la versification," 236–37.

the more curious, especially as it is clear from spelling in the *Blandin* transcription that the scribe was an Italian (see below), someone who may not have known all the conventions of how to copy a romance. While one might hypothesize that the scribe was seeking to save parchment by copying two lines of verse per line, there are blank sheets in the *Blandin* gathering, so this hypothesis does not hold very well. With all other editors of this text, we do not follow the scribe's practice in our presentation.

— A table to accompany the following text, folio 100r.

— Jacques de Vitry (born between 1160 and 1170; died in 1240), *Historia Hierosolymitana* or *History of Jerusalem*, folios 102r–129r. Jacques de Vitry composed the work while he was in the Middle East, serving as bishop of Acre (he began the *Historia* in 1219); it is a contemporaneous account of the Fifth Crusade. This text seems a late addition to the codex, copied over three columns rather than two and using Arabic rather than Roman numerals; it was certainly part of the book by the early eighteenth century.[7]

— An unidentified Latin text, folio 130r, probably added to the codex when it was rebound.[8]

— Various ownership marks, folio 131r, again probably a folio added to the book after the fire.

— Random notes, along with one line of music, folio 131v.

— Notes, in a very modern hand, on the watermarks and a study of the gatherings, certainly added when the volume was rebound, folio 132.

As is clear, the volume includes texts that are historical in nature—a chronicle of the world, the *Miracles of Rome*, a history of Jerusalem—and *Blandin*. In other words, one Occitan romance among historical and/or geographic texts all in Latin.[9] There are other medieval manuscripts with a related composition, the mixing of fiction and nonfiction, of which one

[7] Pasini, Berta, and Rivautella include it in their description of the book, *Codices manuscripti bibliothecae regii taurinensis*, 2:151.

[8] Pasini, Berta, and Rivautella reported 129 ff. in the volume, *Codices manuscripti bibliothecae regii tauinensis*, 2:150.

[9] Busby suggests that in fifteenth-century northern Italy, there was a "continuing co-existence of three literary vernaculars" (Italian, French, and Occitan), *Codex and Context*, 2:631.

example is a twelfth-century manuscript in Durham, Cathedral Chapter Library C.iv.27, which contains Wace's fictional *Brut*, alongside Geoffrey Gaimar's *Estoire des Engleis* and Jordan Fantosme's *Chronicle*, these last two nonfiction. "The *Brut* is used ... as part of a sequence of historical works"[10] though without the mixing of languages found in the Turin manuscript. A thirteenth-century manuscript, Bern Burgerbibliothek 113, includes, *inter alia*, romances, didactic works, texts relating to Palestine, and historical works relating to France—another collection with similarities to the Turin manuscript. Keith Busby says of the Bern codex, "There seems to be a desire to provide coverage of an area corresponding to actual political domains."[11] Perhaps the insertion of *Blandin* into the Turin volume represents an attempt to situate the adventures of our heroes either in Italy or in real time.

The manuscript's date of composition must be inferred from internal evidence. Based on the watermarks of its paper pages,[12] scholars believe the manuscript was copied at some time between the end of the fourteenth[13] and beginning of the fifteenth century;[14] it appears to have been copied in northern Italy.

Pfeffer consulted the manuscript in Turin in 2014, taking digital photos, which allow easy enlargement. Careful reading of the text and review of the photographic evidence have allowed her to confirm readings that were hypothetical in earlier editions or to refute some readings (the edition of *Blandin* by Paul Meyer was given special consideration, as the work was copied for Meyer before the manuscript was damaged in the 1904 fire). She noted the marginal comments (first spotted by Giulio Bertoni[15]) while on site, a feature that earlier editors had not incorporated in their editions, and studied them carefully in the photographs. The margins of the manuscript suffered more water damage than the middle of each page, and the notes are particularly hard to read (see Fig. 3); her transcriptions of these notes were confirmed by Alessandro Vitale-Brovarone,

[10] Nixon, "Romance Collections and the Manuscripts of Chrétien de Troyes," 20. See also Short, "L'avènement du texte vernaculaire," 12.

[11] Busby, *Codex and Context*, 1:432.

[12] See Briquet, *Les filigranes*, numbers 691 and 11087.

[13] Galano, ed., *Blandin di Cornovaglia*, 35.

[14] Burrrell, "A Critical Edition," 3.

[15] Bertoni, "Correzioni al testo di *Blandin de Cornouailles*," 409.

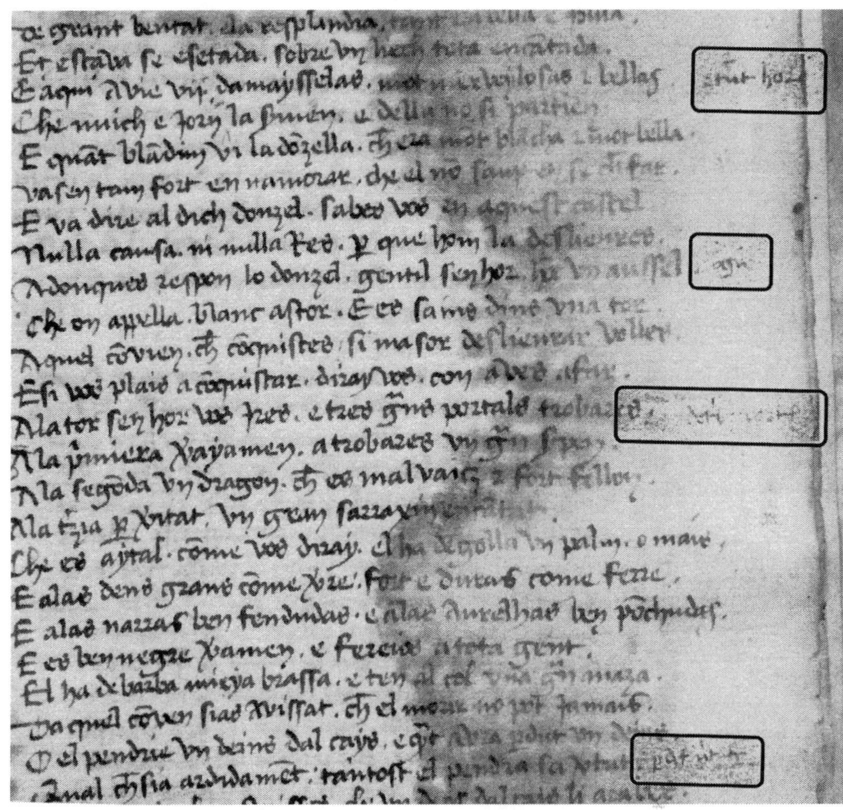

Figure 3: Turin manuscript, Torino Biblioteca nazionale e universitaria G II 34, folio 97r, lines 1393–433 of *Blandin de Cornoalha*; marginal notes marked.

who examined the Turin manuscript under ultraviolet light.[16] This is the first edition to include these marginal notes, composed by a medieval reader who offered commentary and explanation of the text. These notes have been printed alongside the lines they accompany, both in the Occitan text and in the English translation.

The edition presented here retains as many of the manuscript readings as possible, based on the principles that the author had solid linguistic and artistic skills and that the scribe was competent. This attitude is

[16] See Pfeffer, "À la marge d'un roman à la marge," for a detailed discussion of these notes.

very different from that of Meyer, the first editor, who felt that neither the *Blandin* author nor the manuscript's scribe knew Occitan especially well. Sabrina Galano was more willing to credit the author and the scribe with skill, but her edition, with its consistent effort to create a regular octosyllabic line, still implies distrust of the author.

Versification and Genre

Versification

The meter of *Blandin de Cornoalha* has led scholars to ask, was the poet simply a poor versifier or is there some other explanation for the inconsistency of meter in the text? We argue here that the anonymous author took liberties with the not-yet-written rules of Occitan romance by varying line length. The greater part of *Blandin* is written in octosyllabic couplets. There are, however, any number of lines that are not octosyllabic in the manuscript; we have chosen not to emend these lines, though we do signal the irregularities in the notes. Burrell demonstrated "how easily most of the seven- and nine-syllable lines can be regularized by a simple spelling change,"[1] and Galano incorporated many such changes into her edited text. For those lines that the manuscript presents as particularly long, we have, on occasion, broken these long lines into two, creating thereby at least one octosyllabic line. One very successful emendation of this nature is at the end of the romance (2403–4) where, by breaking a long line and considering its meaning, we have arrived at a conclusion that is very satisfactory for meaning, meter, and context.

Burrell observed in 1974 that most scholarly discussions of Occitan meter and rhyme had been concerned with the usage of troubadour poets of the twelfth and thirteenth centuries, that very little had been said about Occitan courtly romances.[2] Even after the publication of Frank M. Chambers' *Introduction to Old Provençal Versification* in 1985, her statement retains validity—Chambers states explicitly that his real interest is the lyric.[3] The recent publication of a number of Occitan romances as

[1] Burrell, "A Critical Edition," 76.

[2] Burrell, "A Critical Edition," 76.

[3] Chambers, *Introduction to Old Provençal Versification*, 1.

editions and/or translations (*Jaufre* and *Flamenca* come quickly to mind) has expanded the discussion, though the authors of these two romances consistently used an octosyllabic couplet for their stories.

Chambers reminds us that the thirteenth-century *Canso de la Crosada* is built on laisses of alexandrines (a twelve-syllable line) followed by a single line of six syllables; throughout, we have a laisses of long lines, each concluding with a shorter line.[4] Chambers also offers the better example of the *Vida de sant Honorat* by Raimond Feraud, "The versification of this poem is a chaos of alexandrines, octosyllables, and hexasyllables, riming for the most part in pairs."[5] The most recent editors of the *Vida de sant Honorat* argue that Raimond Feraud used a variety of meters and rhyme schemes though he eventually settled down to one meter per chapter.[6] There is also the example of the *Breviari* of Matfre Ermengaud, whose understanding of octosyllabic verse was idiosyncratic. As Chambers explains, "Each verse, whether its ending is masculine or feminine, contains exactly eight syllables. This of course is normal for lines with masculine rimes; but for those with feminine rimes the result is not what we could call octosyllables, but paroxytonic heptasyllables."[7] This combination of octosyllables with a masculine ending and heptasyllables with a feminine ending is frequent in troubadour lyric. In sum, medieval narratives in Occitan do not all conform perfectly to a supposed octosyllabic norm. Furthermore, Ricketts and Hershon speak of the syllable count of words ending in *-ia*: towards the end of the thirteenth century, the two letters were being counted as a single syllable in verbs, even though this practice was discouraged by the *Leys d'amors*, a fourteenth-century Occitan rulebook for poetic composition.[8] Raimond Feraud counts *ia* as one syllable or two depending on the number of beats in a given line of poetry.[9] We believe that the author of *Blandin* follows the model of his contemporaries.

[4] In the first part of the *Canso*, the short, final line connects to and rhymes with the following laisse. The second part of the work, by a different author, follows a slightly different pattern: the short final line's rhyme word links to the following laisse by being repeated at the caesura of the first line of the next laisse.

[5] Chambers, *Introduction to Old Provençal Versification*, 263.

[6] Ricketts and Hershon, eds., Raimond Feraud, *La vida de sant Honorat*, 140.

[7] Chambers, *Introduction to Old Provençal Versification*, 265.

[8] Ricketts and Hershon, eds., Raimond Feraud, *La vida de sant Honorat*, 141.

[9] Ricketts and Hershon, eds., Raimond Feraud, *La vida de sant Honorat*, 141.

We can also consider the use of the caesura by the *Blandin* author, a break frequently found but not mandatory in an octosyllabic line.[10] In his use of the caesura, our poet followed no particular pattern. For Guilhem Molinier, author of the *Leys d'amors*, there should be a tonic accent on the fourth syllable if there is to be a caesura. The *Blandin* poet occasionally observes this rule, most notably when he begins a line with an adverb such as *apertamén(t)* (accent marked here),[11] but his use of the caesura is not regular enough to see in it any regular pattern. One might say the author did follow the advice of the *Leys d'amors* concerning this poetic device, for the *Leys* grants something of an exception to longer rhymed *novas* (see below) with regard to the caesura.[12] We observe, moreover, that the sections dealing with the adventures of Blandin flow more smoothly than those dealing with Guilhot, a phenomenon directly attributable to increased use of the caesura as dictated by the *Leys d'amors*.

Blandin's author has been criticized for many "failings" as a poet, inconsistent use of the caesura being only one. Arne-Johan Henrichsen considered the use of the *anar* + infinitive construction as a crutch used by poor poets in order to fill an octosyllabic line: "One has the impression that poets whose style was imperfect and unartistic used it as a peg, for the needs of the verse."[13] It is true that the anonymous author uses this construction very often, but we see no reason to criticize the poet for telling his story as he saw fit.

Another criticism of the author of *Blandin* is his perhaps excessive dependence on filler vocabulary, notably the conjunction *e*. Such use of this conjunction is, however, not exceptional in any fashion; Jules Ronjat observed similar usage in a number of Occitan regions and in French.[14]

[10] Burrell points to Lote, *Histoire du vers français*, 1:222–23. But see Marquèze-Pouey, "Les 'grands vers' dans la poésie occitane des XIIe et XIIIe siècles," 286–90; Marquèze-Pouey suggests a variety of caesura options.

[11] *Apertamen*, *apertamens*, and *apertament* are used forty-two times in the story, nineteen of these times in initial position in the line of verse, that is, 45% of their occurrences.

[12] Guilhem Molinier, *Las Leys d'amors*, ed. Anglade, 1:97.

[13] "On a l'impression que des poètes dont le style est négligé et peu artistique l'emploient comme une cheville, pour les besoins de la versification," Henrichsen, "La périphrase anar + infinitif," 363.

[14] Ronjat, *Grammaire istorique des parlers provençaux modernes*, §776.

Rhyming couplets, the norm for medieval romances, are called by the *Leys d'amors rims caudatz,* "those rhymes when two or three lines accord at the end."[15] Meyer dismissed the rhymes of *Blandin* in a few terse sentences, saying of the author, "This text includes rhymes which, if they are attributed to the author, ... lead us to doubt that he was really 'Provençal,' though they do not suggest an Italian origin for him."[16] Meyer thought the author was Catalan.

Because we believe the author of *Blandin* was a competent versifier, we have tended to assume, when pairs of lines in the manuscript did not rhyme, that the rhyming line had been lost; we have edited the text accordingly, inserting blanks for missing rhymes and missing rhyme lines (lines 222, 262–63, 592, 700, 806, 1324, 1427, 1434, and 1893–94). Burrell analyzed all the rhymes of the work, based on her reading of the manuscript. She noted the relative lack of assonance and concluded that "the majority of the lines are in poor rhyme, yet this is not a mark of disapprobation against the author."[17] It should be added that the most common rhyme in the text is built on infinitives ending in *ar* (the most common infinitive ending in Occitan) such as *intrar* : *sercar* (207–8). Based on our calculations, of all the perfect rhyming pairs in *Blandin*, roughly 65 percent use a rhyme in *ar*. We observe further, that the author was capable of leonine rhymes (where two syllables rhyme) on occasion, such as *verament* : *comandament* (123–24), *trebalhat* : *batalhat* (1713–14), *astre* : *pastre* (1971–72), or *corage* : *parage* (169–70), a rhyming pair repeated in the romance (533–34, 677–78, 1209–10).

The author is capable of enjambment, where the meaning of a line continues without break to the following line (see lines 131–32, 251–52, 587–88), which suggests a somewhat capable poet.

We think the author of *Blandin* was influenced by traditions more familiar to authors of medieval epic poetry, *chansons de geste*, in which genre the use of verbal formulas and of caesura is usual. Galano believed

[15] "Aquel rims cant duy verset almens o trei al mai s'acordo en la fi ses tot meja d'autre bordo principal o biocat de diversa acordansa," Guilhem Molinier, *Las Leys d'amors*, ed. Anglade, 2:100.

[16] "Il y a en effet dans ce texte des rimes qui, si elles doivent être imputées à l'auteur, comme je le crois, conduisent à douter que celui-ci ait réellement été provençal, sans donner à croire pourtant qu'il ait été d'origine italienne," Meyer, "Le roman de *Blandin de Cornouailles*," 171.

[17] Burrell, "A Critical Edition," 95.

that our author followed the traditions of the Italian *cantare* tradition—oral performance of a story by professional singers or storytellers, often working from memory—though she does not use that technical term; she emphasizes the idea of performance of the text.[18] The earliest extant French epic, the *Chanson de Roland*, was composed using assonance rather than rhyme, and this reality may also have influenced our author. Scholars of French epics have shown that these long stories were composed using the techniques identified by scholars of Homer, notably the use of formulas and repetition, markers of oral composition and presentation. Paula Leverage argues convincingly that oral techniques of repetition represent a conscious rhetorical effort on the part of the author of a medieval text.[19] Furthermore, as Raymond Cormier has shown, the use of formulas is not restricted to epic verse; his study of the Old French romance of *Eneas* demonstrates that the author, composing a written, rather than oral text, still used formulaic language to tell his story.[20] Elements of formulaic composition can be seen in *Blandin*, such as the repeated use of *verayamen* or that Blandin is often described as "lo bon Blandin." Even the refrain of the tale, behaving "com bon cavallier de parage" (first used at line 170), suggests a formula. The freedom to repeat may explain any number of verbatim repetitions in our story. Compare

Els cavalcheron tot apert
tant che atroberon lo desert.
Apertamen es calvacheron
tro che lo pin trobat agheron.
Adonc dis lo bon Blandin,
"Guihot Ardit, ve vos lo pin!
Ayssi coven ayan conselh
de so che nos a dich l'ausel. (571–78)

with

Nos cavalchen trestot apert
tant che atroben aquel desert.
E apertament nos entren
tro che lo pin trobat agem.
E aqui nos tenghem conselh
de so che nos a dich l'aussel. (1921–26)

[18] Galano, "Indizi di oralità."

[19] Leverage, *Reception and Memory*, 294.

[20] Cormier, "Indications d'oralité dans l'expression poétique du *Roman d'Éneas*."

In these two excerpts, the language is almost identical, an example of repetition that may suggest elements of oral composition and a conscious rhetorical strategy.

The Genre of Blandin

Another possible explanation for the metrical liberty of the *Blandin* author may come from his familiarity with fourteenth-century northern French *dits*. Even before the publication of *Blandin* by Meyer, the text had been considered a romance, parallel to Occitan stories such as *Flamenca* and *Jaufre* or Old French romances such as those composed by Chrétien de Troyes. This descriptor is logical, as the narrator tells a story with a beginning, a middle, and an end; the theme of chivalric behavior is key; the tale ends with a double wedding. It should be added that Lucia Lazzerini has called *Blandin* not a romance but rather a fairy tale in verse.[21]

Medieval Occitan authors created their own terms for the genres of their literature, one of which is *novas*, meaning a kind of story or *récit*, perhaps implying something different than a romance. The word (always plural, with an -s) also means "news" as in our text (see line 1122). Scholars have not yet fixed the literary definition of *novas*, used with works of varying lengths and a variety of natures. The term is used with shorter works such as the *Novas del papagai* (312 lines long), though brevity itself may not be a distinguishing factor of the genre.[22] *Flamenca*, 8,095 lines long and incomplete, reads like a romance and is called a *novas* by its author (line 250).[23] Two other works, *Jaufre* (complete with 10,974 lines) and *Daurel e Beton* (incomplete, only 2,198 lines extant), also call themselves *novas* (*Jaufré* at line 21, *Daurel* at line 2), so it would appear that brev-

[21] Lazzerini, *Letterature medievale in lingua d'oc*, 225; Martínez would disagree, "Una entesa ben interessada," 49.

[22] See Fasseur, tr., *Flamenca*, 82–84.

[23] Limentani made the designation clear in the title of his edition: *Las novas de Guillem de Nivers ("Flamenca")*. Fasseur understands *novas* as signifying a new attitude vis-à-vis older works, "un génie du présent dont la nouveauté s'affirme," *Flamenca*, 91; she calls *Blandin* a *novas* in "La matière bretonne," 324. Huchet argues that the term represents "mettre en fiction la pluralité des voix de la littérature," "*Jaufré* et *Flamenca*, *novas* ou romans?," 297.

ity does not define the genre. The *Leys d'amors* uses *novas* and *romans*, "romance," as synonyms.[24]

The anonymous *Blandin* author took a different approach in naming the genre he chose to use—he wrote a *dictat*: "[E]n non de Dieu commenzeray / un bel dictat et retrayrai ..." (lines 1–2), though he did not explain exactly what a *dictat* was. At no point does the author call his work a romance nor a *novas*. We believe that the generic term of *dictat* should be connected to the Middle French genre of the *dit* and that the anonymous author could have used his familiarity with contemporary French literature to create his own genre in Occitan.

In Old and Middle French legal language, the technical term *dit* is synonymous with "sentence" or "verdict." Outside the realm of the law, *dit* can be used to mean "proverb," as a description of the words of a song, as a synonym for a love letter or *salut d'amour*, and finally as a generic descriptor.[25] These French terms and meanings have cognates in Occitan.[26] Monique Léonard summarizes a description of the genre in these terms, "The *dit* is a work in verse, not sung, on the short side, and constructed using various metrical schemes, among which some seem preferred, notably rhymed octosyllabic couplets."[27]

Numerous *dits* were composed in Old French throughout the thirteenth century, demonstrating the flexibility of the genre. *Dits* range in type from moralistic to satiric, from religious to historical; they can be seen as personal poetry; some can best be described as shopping lists.[28] All *dits* seem to share certain characteristics: they are short, to the point, exhibit elements of oral composition. By the fourteenth century, some *dits* approached publicity pieces[29] or offered edifying or amusing stories for listeners.

[24] Guilhem Molinier calls Matfre Ermengaud's *Breviari d'amors* (34,597 lines) both a romance and a *novas*; *Las Leys d'amors*, ed. Fedi: "... no·y fam gran forsa cant es pauzatz en novas rimadas, maiormen can son longas, coma·l romans [del *Breviari*] *d'Amors* e d'autres gran re," 254.

[25] Léonard, *Le* dit *et sa technique littéraire des origines à 1340*, 37–42.

[26] See *FEW* s.v. DICERE III 67, and DICTARE III 71.

[27] "Le dit est une pièce en vers, non chantée, plutôt brève et construite selon de multiples schémas métriques parmi lesquels certains semblent privilégiés, notamment l'octosyllabe à rimes plates," Léonard, *Le* dit *et sa technique*, 73.

[28] Léonard, *Le* dit *et sa technique*, 219.

[29] Jeay, *Le commerce des mots*, 243.

As the fourteenth century progressed, French authors pushed the genre in a new direction, adding narrative content and taking care to name themselves in the story. A prime example of this development can be seen in the works of Guillaume Machaut (ca. 1300–1377), who named a number of his pieces *dits*. His *dits* range in length from 350 to more than 9,000 lines—clearly Machaut abandoned the idea of brevity as a generic feature. In each of his *dits*, Machaut expressed his thoughts vis-à-vis the world and praised his patrons. According to Georges Becker, Machaut and his contemporaries fused reality and fiction, the personal and the ideal, "with a mastery which respects the unity of composition, tone, and style with each poem."[30] Machaut identifies himself clearly as the narrator, often recounting a story that may well resemble a courtly romance (the *Dit du lyon* serves as a good example). Machaut uses the pedagogic properties of the *dit* in his *Dit d'alerion*, again naming himself as the narrator and explaining the theme of love by means of the language of the hunt. Above all, the narrator seeks to teach the reader how to live in a courtly world.[31] The masterpiece of Machaut, his *Livre du voir-dit*, recounts a tale of love, offering a lesson as to how to love, how to approach the lady. The story appears true, complete with allusions to contemporary historic events (the work was composed between 1362 and 1364). William Calin argues that Machaut did, indeed, invent a new genre:

> Machaut's greatest triumph as a realist, and as a narrative poet, may well be the new literary style he created or, at least, made his own: the inept, blundering narrator, who is also an inept, blundering lover. This pseudoautobiographical character is prone to cowardice, sloth, snobbery, misogyny and pedantry.[32]

This new genre, still called the *dit*, has been described by Jacqueline Cerquiglini in these terms: "1. The *dit* plays with discontinuity; 2. It presents a speaker using 'I' in the present tense; 3. The 'I' ... is a clerical author, in other words, the *dit* instructs."[33] Furthermore, "The law of distancing ...

[30] "Avec une maîtrise qui respecte l'unité de composition, de ton et de style avec chaque poème," Becker, "Guillaume de Machaut," 357, quoted by Léonard, *Le* dit *et sa technique*, 58.

[31] Calin, *A Poet at the Fountain*, 108–9.

[32] Calin, *A Poet at the Fountain*, 241.

[33] "1. Le 'dit' joue avec la discontinuité; 2. Il relève une énonciation en je et du temps présent; 3. Le je en question est celui d'un clerc-écrivain, autrement dit, le 'dit'

can refer not only to the composition of the text but to its meaning as well. We see therefore the privileged relation between the *dit* and parody."[34] She concludes that Machaut's *dits* suggest a change in audience, that the text is no longer heard, but read; it has become a visual object.[35]

Machaut was an incredibly popular author in the second half of the fourteenth century, popularity seen in the number of manuscripts that remain, in the desire of noblemen to possess copies of his works, and in the number of authors who copied or imitated him, Chaucer, for one.[36]

As for the travels of Machaut's works, we know that Gaston Febus (1331–1391), count of Foix and Béarn, owned a copy of several of Machaut's *dits*. Gaston was an uneven supporter of the literary arts; Jean Froissart, for example, was unsuccessful in his attempts to sell the prince a copy of his romance of *Melyador*, despite the many evenings Froissart spent at the count's court in Orthez, reading the work aloud. It is believed that a collection of Machaut's works, now called the Ferrell-Vogüé manuscript, was owned by Gaston Febus and that he loaned this book to Yolande de Bar, wife of the king of Aragon, John I; she never returned it. The story of this manuscript, in itself, points to awareness of Machaut in Occitania, certainly at the court of Gaston Febus and perhaps at the Armagnac court in Rodez as well. It is not beyond reason that the anonymous author of *Blandin* would decide to borrow some of the novelties exploited by the French author, starting with the genre assigned to *Blandin* in its opening lines.

Dictat is not a rare word in the corpus of *COM*, but its meaning tends not to be that of a specific genre. For example, Guiraut Riquier describes poetry in general:

en vers et en cansos et en autres dictatz c'avem desus nomnatz	[In verse and in songs and in other *dictatz* which we named above] Guiraut Riquier, Letter 11, lines 300–302[37]

enseigne," Bazin-Tacchella, Hélix, and Ott, *Le livre du voir dit de Guillaume Machaut*, 49, quoting Cerquiglini, "Le clerc et l'écriture," 158–63.

[34] "La loi de distanciation ... peut renvoyer, non seulement au principe de composition du texte, mais à son sens. On saisit alors le rapport privilégié du dit à la parodie, ou tout simplement à la traversée des modèles littéraires," Cerquiglini, "Le clerc et l'écriture," 159.

[35] Cerquiglini, "Le clerc et l'écriture," 159.

[36] Chaucer's *Monk's Tale*, the *Canon's Yeoman's Tale*, *Sir Thopas*, recounted by Chaucer the pilgrim, all rely on an author/narrator as seen in Machaut's models.

[37] Guiraut Riquier, *Les épîtres de Guiraut Riquier*.

where it is clear that *dictatz* refers to any genre, as opposed to one in particular. The anonymous *De doctrina de compondre dictats*, from the second half of the thirteenth century, uses the word "dictat" only in its title, the term covering a number of different lyric genres.[38]

Zulema Jiménez-Mola is the only scholar to have sensed that *dictat* might be a descriptive generic term, but she thought that the author of *Blandin* did not have a clear sense of the meaning of *dictat*[39] and concluded that *Blandin de Cornoalha* falls between a romance and a *novas*. She did not make the connection between this Occitan example and the northern French models.

We believe we can attach *Blandin de Cornoalha* to the development of the *dit* and that the anonymous author is the first to compose a *dictat*, that is, a *dit*, in Occitan. The author could have heard *dits* recited at the court of Gaston Febus. He chose to compose *Blandin* in a genre that was very popular at the time. Martínez recognized the novelty of *Blandin*, pointing to a new literary genre,[40] but he did not see the technical evidence presented in our text.

One element that Léonard noted in the *dits* she studied is the pride that authors took in their works; they would often describe their efforts as beautiful, "beaux," especially if the works were pleasing, though under two conditions: the work had to be appealing and the author had to maintain a certain distance vis-à-vis what he had written.[41] These two conditions are certainly met in *Blandin*. That thirteenth-century *dits* are relatively short is an element continued in the *Blandin* story, at 2,405 lines much shorter than the average for Occitan or Old French romances.

This aspect of the creativity of the *Blandin* author has not been considered in the past. Other editors of the story understood the second line with its simplest meaning. Cornelius van der Horst translated *dictat* as a work in verse, "une pièce en vers";[42] Sabrina Galano suggested composition, "componimento";[43] Ross Arthur used the term

[38] Marshall, ed., *The* Razos de trobar *of Raimon Vidal*, 95–98.

[39] Jiménez-Mola, "Un género para 'Un bel dictat,'" 1034.

[40] Martínez, "Una entesa ben interssada entre la realitit i la fantasia," 49.

[41] "Il est necessaire que l'œuvre soit plaisante, ... mais il faut aussi que l'auteur observe une certaine distance vis à vis de ce qu'il écrit," Léonard, *Le* dit *et sa technique*, 82.

[42] Van der Horst, ed., *Blandin de Cornouaille*, 216.

[43] Galano, ed., *Blandin di Cornovaglia*, 43.

"poem";[44] Jordi Tiñena[45] and Arseni Pacheco,[46] who published *Blandin* in Spanish and in Catalan translation, both translated *dictat* as "dictat," which is neither a translation nor an explanation. Espadaler resorted to "relato," story, and said *Blandin* was a romance.[47] Not one of these scholars perceived that *dictat* was a technical term for a genre.

By calling his work a *dictat*, the *Blandin* author sought to connect his effort to Machaut's works, as well as to the works of other French authors (Jean Froissart and Guillaume de Degulleville, for example). Granted, the anonymous author does not name himself, nor does he insert himself into the story as forcibly as did Machaut. He chose to use elements that come out of an oral tradition of storytelling, to remind the audience that an author was present, that an author/performer was recounting this tale of two knights.

We conclude that the author of *Blandin* has not deserved the bad press he received over the course of centuries. The author was inventive and capable of telling a good story, using various techniques of versification and composition at his disposal.

[44] Arthur, tr., *Blandin de Cornoalha*, 12.

[45] Tiñena, tr., *Blandín de Cornualla, anònim*, 29.

[46] Pacheco, *Blandín de Cornualla i altres narracions en vers dels segles XIV i XV*, 27.

[47] Espadaler, "Las *novas*, un territorio sin fronteras," 107.

Language of the Author and of the Text

TRYING TO IDENTIFY the characteristics of the scribe and the author is difficult, but some important details can be observed. Given that the author of *Blandin de Cornoalha* is unknown, we cannot compare this work to others by the same individual. The author's language is clearer in the rhymes, on the assumption that these words are less likely to change significantly as a text is copied. The language of the scribe is clearer in the lines of the work, as the scribe can choose spellings and perhaps also grammar usages familiar to him. Furthermore, it is obvious from the orthography of the text in its single manuscript that the scribe who copied the text into what is today Turin Biblioteca nazionale e universitaria G II 34 was as familiar with Italian spelling conventions as with those of Occitan (see below).

Paul Meyer and others were convinced that the author of *Blandin* had little poetic and less grammatical skill. We believe, however, that the anonymous author knew his language well, even if he did not perfectly conform to grammatical norms established in medieval and modern grammars.[1]

One of the key attacks by Meyer, in the first publication of the text, was the author's mother tongue. After considering varying aspects of the text including idiosyncratic words such as *caysal*, "molar" (line 1550), which the French scholar connected to the Catalan *caixal*, Meyer concluded that the poet was Catalan, "a Catalan who tried his best to write in 'Provençal',"[2] a conclusion attacked by other scholars. Julien-Bernard Alart rebutted the Catalan hypothesis in detail and concluded that

[1] See Lewent, "Three Little Problems of Old Provençal Syntax," 167, for a similar thought.

[2] "Je n'induis pas absolument que le poëme de *Blandin de Cornouailles* soit proprement Catalan: je ne crois pas qu'il y ait assez de traces de l'idiome catalan pour autoriser cette conclusion; mais j'admettrais volontiers que l'ouvrage a été composé par un

Blandin was composed in Languedoc, perhaps specifically in Montpellier, a city with close connections to Catalonia in the mid-thirteenth century, his date for the work. In his lengthy article on the language of *Blandin*, Alart concluded that the only place where a possible Catalan rhyme might be detected was in the couplet of lines 47–48, *dich* : *nuech*.[3]

Camille Chabaneau maintained that the language used was acceptable Provençal (as Occitan was generally called in Chabaneau's time) and that the faults seen by Meyer as the result of Catalan provenance could all be attributed to the fact that the author was not a literary sophisticate. As Chabaneau noted,

> Of all the Provençal texts I know, *Blandin de Coroalha* is the one where the vernacular speech is most marked. The author was probably ... from the Languedoc, not well versed in the classical language or uninterested in respecting its forms, substituting the forms of his dialect and, moreover, a poet distant from tradition and rhyming not according to spelling or rules, but according to the pronunciation of his region, which was already that of today. Almost all the false rhymes that Meyer identified are precise, if not rich rhymes, if pronounced as they are today.[4]

An article by Pere Bohigas on "La matière de Bretagne en Catalogne" also investigates the possibility of Catalan authorship of the poem. He agreed with Meyer's conclusion, but also said that the equivocal rhymes could simply be due to the author's lack of sophistication. Bohigas concludes that the author's language is Occitan, from the second half of the thirteenth century:[5]

Catalan qui s'est efforcé d'écrire de son mieux en provençal," Meyer, ed., "Le roman de *Blandin de Cornouailles*," 172.

[3] Alart, "Observations sur la langue du roman du *Blandin de Cornouailles*," 287.

[4] "*Blandin de Cornouaille* est, de tous les textes provençaux que je connais, celui où l'influence du parler vulgaire se marque le plus sensiblement. L'auteur était probablement, comme le suppose M. Alart, un homme de Languedoc, peu versé dans la langue classique ou peu soucieux d'en respecter les formes, et y substituant à tout instant celles de son dialecte; de plus, versificateur également très-dégagé de la tradition et rimant, non d'après l'orthographe et les règles, mais d'après la prononciation de son pays, qui était déjà sur bien des points celle d'aujourd'hui. Presque toutes les rimes fausses que M. Meyer a signalées deviennent exactes, sinon riches, si on les prononce à la moderne," Chabaneau, "Notes critiques sur quelques textes provençaux," 31.

[5] Bohigas, "La matière de Bretagne en Catalogne," 89–90. "Cependant, la langue

> The language of this poem, despite the alterations made by a poor copyist, is Provençal and different from the hybrid language of poets of the second half of the fourteenth century and of the first quarter of the fifteenth. That is why I think we should place this poem towards the end of the period of the troubadours, the time of Cerveri and of Jofre de Foixà, author of the *Regles de trobar*, the last authors to write the language of the troubadours during the last half of the thirteenth century.

While Meyer's Catalan thesis has been generally discredited, it had the merit of tossing the tale to scholars in the Iberian Peninsula who were happy to claim it as their own. For this reason, there have been multiple publications of *Blandin* in Catalan and in translation, especially towards the end of the twentieth century. One purpose of these publications was to claim the work for Catalonia or for Spain.

North of the Pyrenees, Cornelius van der Horst published a careful linguistic analysis and diplomatic edition of the text in 1974. He concluded that the anonymous author was a native of the region east of the Rhône River, that the romance was probably composed in the Rhône Basin or in the department of the Alpes-de-Haute-Provence,[6] using the evidence of his own study. Sabrina Galano, who completed a critical edition of the text with Italian translation, argues that the anonymous author hailed from the southwest of modern-day France, specifically the area within Languedoc and Catalonia.[7] Galano continues, and we agree, that the author composed his work using the *koiné* of Occitan in the second half of the fourteenth century. This common language shared features of all dialects of Occitan, along with, in *Blandin*, elements of Catalan and French.

To support this statement, we offer below some linguistic observations relating to the language of the author and of the scribe. In most cases below, only the first example as found in this edition is identified by line number.

de ce poème, en dépit des altérations dues à son mauvais copiste, est encore provençale, et assez différente de la langue hybride de nos poètes de la second moitié du XIVe siècle et du premier quart du XVe. C'est pourquoi je suis d'avis qu'il faut placer ce poème vers la fin de l'époque des troubadours, au temps de Cerverí et de Jofre de Foixà, l'auteur des *Regles de trobar*, les derniers auteurs à écrire chez nous la langue des troubadours durant la deuxième moitié du XIIIe siècle."

[6] Van der Horst, ed., *Blandin de Cornouaille*, 64.

[7] Galano, "Nuove congetture sulla lingua del *Blandin de Cornoalha*," 109.

1. Orthography

1.1. Double Consonants

Many consonantal phonemes are represented by both single and double consonants: /t/ in *gitar* (181), *gittar* (481); /l/ in *gola* (1480), *golla* (1418); /r/ in *garier* (866), *garrier* (1980); /p/ in *apella* (1679), *appella* (662); /m/ in *comanset* (1596), *commanset* (334); /n/ in *anar* (73), *annar* (7); *eschinna* (1590), *esquina* (1202); *penna* (482) for *pena*.

1.2. Spelling of Initial /dž/ + e- or i-

The scribe uses both *g* and *j* to represent /dž/: *gita* (144), *jetan* (1825), *ges* (387), *gentils* (513) and *gens* (1180). Note, however, that the scribe also used *g-* when representing /g/, see *gerier* (for *guerrier*) (2184) and *gera* (for *guerra*) (2396).

1.3. Spelling of Intervocalic /dž/

The scribe consistently uses g to represent intervocalic /dž/. Examples include *dampnage* (410), *parage* (220), *mesageria* (641). The use of *plassa* for *plaga* (136) would seem to indicate that *ss* represents /dž/ here,[8] especially given *plages* (301, 2099, 2305) and *plagas* (798).

1.4. /tʃ/

The phoneme /tʃ/ may be represented by *ch* in words with palatalized *t*, as in *nuech* (48), *nuich* (228), *nuch* (498). We also find *estregia* (1916), where *gi* represents /tʃ/.

1.5. /g/

The phoneme /g/ is represented as *g*, *ga*, *ge*, *gh*, *gi*, *go*, *gu*: *garde* (1006), *goardon* (1131); *gerier*, "warrior," (2184),[9] *gera*, "war" (2396),[10] *gherier* (1780), *guerriers* (6); *poges* (352), *poghes* (326), *porghes* (1764) for *pogues*.

[8] Bourciez says that this may be a feature especially of the south-west, Bourciez, *Éléments de linguistique romane*, §269(a). Ronjat notes that intervocalic g frequently disappears or becomes a /y/ or an *-i-* (*Grammaire istorique*, §278).

[9] As early as line 6, where we find *guerriers*, we know the scribe was aware of the convention of g + u to represent /g/ before *-e-*.

[10] This is the only instance in our text where the word for "war" is used; however,

We also find *Giot* (12). While some of these forms may be found in medieval Catalan,[11] they are hardly unique to that language.

1.6. /k/

The phoneme /k/ is represented by *c*, *ch*, and *qu* in both initial and medial position: *pesquier* (682), *peschier* (784), *boscage* (35), *boschage* (219), *che* (5), *que* (58). It is represented by *ch* and *c* in final position: *fuoch* (1196), *fuoc* (2158), *loch* (62).

1.7. Final /ts/

The verbal ending *tz* is never found in conjugated forms in this text but is rendered by *s*, so that one finds *as* for *atz* in the imperative, as in *annas* (552); similarly, *es* is used for *etz* for second person plural present indicative in *vesses* (62), *aves* (163) and present subjunctive in *annes* (1719). The orthography *tz* does occur in the text, for example, in the word *malvaitz* (1414), *malvatz* (1515); we also have *-is* for *-tz*, *vois* (2189) for *votz*, a spelling that may reflect French influence.

1.8. Intervocalic /ñ/

The palatal phoneme /ñ/ in medial position is represented by *gn*, *nh*, *ngn*, *n*, *ng*: *lignage* (265), *linhage* (484), *lingnage* (818), *linage* (488); *senhor* (182), *sengor* (649), *sengnors* (820). In final position, /ñ/ is represented by *nh*, *nch*, *gn*, *hn*: *companh* (61), *companch* (194), *compagn* (239), *compahn* (1729).

1.9. Separation of Syllables after /m/

The scribe appears to use a silent consonant to separate syllables when the first ends with /m/ and the second begins with /n/, choosing either *g*, *damgnage* (822), or *p*, *dampnage* (410). The word for "sleep" also presents an interconsonantal *p*, *sompn* (1066), perhaps to insist on pronunciation of the final *n*. Pierre Fouché notes that *mpn* occurs in Occitan as well as in Catalan;[12] he believes these spellings represent partial differentiation of *mn*.[13]

the comments relevant to the word "warrior" hold for this term as well. See the preceding note.

[11] Bourciez, *Éléments de linguistique romane*, §269(b).

[12] Fouché, *Phonétique historique du roussillonnais*, 211.

[13] Fouché, *Phonétique historique du roussillonnais*, 150.

1.10. Internal *l*

The most striking examples of metathesis are found with *calvacar* (243, 569, 609) for *cavalcar* (544, 1761, 2004) and *descalvacar* (695, 1955; there are no examples of this second infinitive spelled correctly in the text). This "spelling error" is also seen in the conjugated forms of these two verbs.

1.11. Palatal /j/ or /lj/

Palatal /j/ is represented by *lh, l, ll*: *molers* (2401), *molhers* (2393); *asallir* (318), *asalhir* (338), as well as the Italianate *gl*: *assaglir* (1470) (see §1.17, below). We also find *fils* (385), alongside *filh* (336); the spelling *fils* could come from French as well as from Catalan.[14]

1.12. Sibilants

The phoneme /s/ is represented initially and medially by *s, ss, z, x* and sometimes *c*: *sorre* (1326), *ssor* (1358); *sella* (216), *ssela* (1092); *basinet* (1195), *bassinet* (2157), *bacinet* (752); *corrosat* (1232), *corrosses* (1773), *corrozar* (1529); *Sarraxin* (1416). At line 1500, a marginal note suggests the alternate spelling of *Sarrazin*. There is one instance of *tz* for /s/ in final position in *ensentz* (2386).

The spelling *x* in the text usually has some connection with *s*: *cx* represents *s* in *diluncx* (26); *x* represents *ts* in *servixi* (1652); *iss* in *crexon* (1574) and *s* in *dix* (779) and *luxent* (1484); compare *lussant* (1582).

The phoneme /z/ is most often represented by *z* though also by *s*; there is one example of *ç* as well: *donzella* (993), *donsella* (215), *donçella* (1752).

1.13. Variation between *ent* / *en*

One consonant whose use fluctuates is final *t*. This loss of *t* is familiar in Languedoc, where *t* tends to disappear, particularly after a consonant, especially *-n*.[15] Examples are found in adverbs, as in *apertamen* (183), *apertament* (307), *apertamens* (1255); *fortmen* (566), *fortment* (1088); also

[14] Fouché observes that in the Catalan dialect of Roussillonnais, final *-l* can disappear or be palatalized, depending on the community and/or the presence of *s*. His examples are VALLE > *vall* > *val* against *colles* > *colls* > *cos*, *Phonétique historique du roussillonnais*, 226b.

[15] Compare Zufferey, *Recherches linguistiques*, 243.

in present participles: *cantan* (1306); *caminant* (1950); *sercan* (29), *sercant* (829); in adjectives such as *gran* (78), *grant* (37); *valen* (319), *valent* (339); and nouns, *Orien* (517), *Orient* (545); *talen* (346), *talent* (1854).

1.14. Internal *r*

Rhotacism (*r* > *l* or *l* > *r*) is found in *marvais* (1350), *erme* (2188), *Brandin* (91). Metathesis with *r* may be found in *broden* (374), *pordom* (2050) for *prodom* (2051), and *frem* (1477), *fremasses* (2309).

1.15. Final Nasals

There are fluctuations in the use of *-m* and *-n*; many examples are found in verb conjugations; we have generally chosen to retain the manuscript orthography throughout the edition. Examples include: *sum* for *son*, adjective (910), *som* for *son*, verb (153); first person plural *farem* (1824) and *faren* (124, 226, 496, 595, 1267, 1274, 2378). A similar phenomenon can be observed in the spellings of the word "with": some forty times as *an*, eight times as *am*, twelve times as *amb*, and once as *ambe*.

1.16. Final *ch*

Van der Horst noted a significant number of rhyme pairs where one of the terms ended in *ch*, inter alia: *aossit* or *aussit* : *dich* (563–64, 1919–20, 2107–8), *brachet* : *drech* (39–40), *dich* : *amy* (499–500), *dich* : *complit* (1799–1800), *esbaït* : *amich* (187–88), *gauch* : *saut* (441–42), and the most frequent of all, *dich* : *ardit* or *Ardit* (65–66, 225–26, 303–4, 363–64, 495–96, 1447–48, 2089–90, 2201–2, 2217–18, 2299–300, 2313–14, 2371–72, and 2399–400). We agree with van der Horst that the most logical explanation of these pairs is that *ch* and *t* had so softened in pronunciation as to be interchangeable.[16] Van der Horst uses this linguistic development to situate the author of *Blandin* in one of four departments: the Gard, the Bouches-du-Rhône, the Vaucluse, and the Var.[17]

[16] Van der Horst, ed., *Blandin de Cornouaille*, 27.

[17] Van der Horst, ed., *Blandin de Cornouaille*, 29.

1.17. Particularities of the Scribe

The scribe prefers, by far, the use of *che* to *que*, using the first spelling 432 times versus twenty-eight times for the second, one clear marker of the scribe's Italian origins. Another possible Italian marker is the spelling *-gl* for palatized /j/, as in *batagla* (160), *mereviglar* (561), *pavaglon* (683), *acuglit* (852), *toagla* (1037), *taglar* (1244), *assaglir* (1470), and *Cornoalgla* (1857).

That there is sometimes confusion between the phonemes /k/ and /t/ may be seen in the use of *aubert* (2163) for *auberc*, although this may be imputed to scribal confusion between *c* and *t*.

The scribe almost always spells the first person singular subject pronoun *Jou* (93 occurrences)—the initial capital letter *j*[18] is very clear; there is one instance of *Jeu* (891), one of *hieu* (881), and one of *ieu* (lower-case *i*, 2230). We have chosen to retain the *jou* spelling whenever used by the scribe, recognizing the issues involved (Meyer and van der Horst printed *iou*; Galano printed *jou*). By the same token, the scribe appears inconsistent in his spelling of the verb "to liberate." With other editors, we have consistently adopted the *-u* spelling for all forms of *deslieurar*/*deslievrar*.

1.18. French Influence

A fair number of words suggest French influence, though in almost every case, the Occitan term or spelling is more prevalent. Burrell considered the use of *fils* (385) as well as the expected *filh* (336) as not surprising and representing French influence.[19] We observe *bo* (270) (French *beau*) as another suggestion of French vocabulary. Doublets such as *andos* (546), *andous* (389); *dos* (5), *dous* (315); *dolor* (258), *dolour* (1118); *jorn* (29), *jort* (494), *jour* (2026) might suggest additional evidence of French influence,[20] though again, in each case the Occitan form is dominant. Alart states that the spelling *hostel* (1608) as well as the forms *joly* (1696), *jollia* (1386), *joliamen* (997), *tresque* (1102), and *hostet* (2187) come from French.[21]

[18] Or *I-*, as the distinction between *i* and *j* was not yet established.

[19] Burrell, "A Critical Edition," 104.

[20] Bourciez, *Éléments de linguistique romane*, §263(c); Bourciez and Bourciez, *Phonétique française*, §73.

[21] Alart, "Observations sur la langue du roman du *Blandin*," 292. *Hostel*, at 1608, is a poor example, as it represents a scribal error.

Line 352 is interesting for the formulaic "res dou monde," particularly in comparison with the same formula, "ren del mont," and "ren dal mont" in lines 326, 536, and 1570. Is the spelling of *dou monde* the copyist's error as van der Horst suggests?[22] It may be an additional example of French interference.

Van der Horst suggests the rhyme pair *gorja* : *forja* (753–54) is composed of French loan words.[23] In truth, the Dutch scholar's list of French words or words with French influence[24] points to a good deal of interaction between French and Occitan, especially insofar as the lexemes in his collection suggest first occurrences in Occitan before a first occurrence in French.[25]

The adjective *cortois* (2329) is clearly a French spelling for a word more often seen in this text as *cortes* (2078) or *corteis* (931), *corteys* (1696).

The orthography *deusent* (1168) suggests the pronunciation of modern French *descend*, "he descends," /dɛsã/, in place of the Occitan *descent*, /desen/. This is the only appearance of this verb in *Blandin*.

We have offered a number of examples of French influence on the language of *Blandin de Cornoalha*, from spellings, to expressions, to the occasional example of morphology. How or where this influence came into the text remains an open question. Van der Horst thought the presence in Avignon of the papacy, under French influence, might explain the phenomenon.[26] We would suggest that the interactions of the Armagnac family with the French court are an equally plausible explanation. We know, too, that French was one of several languages in use at the court of Gaston Febus.

2. *Phonetics, Vowels*

2.1. Diphthongs *-au* and *-ai*

Spelling suggests that some Latin diphthongs followed by /k/ retained the diphthong. We have *pauc* (1062) and *pauca* (288), from the Latin PAUCUM, expected Occitan forms, alongside forms such as *paoch* (946), *pauch* (173) with no examples of *poco*, the Italian form.

[22] Van der Horst, ed., *Blandin de Cornouaille*, 101n.

[23] Van der Horst, ed., *Blandin de Cornouaille*, 110n.

[24] Van der Horst, ed., *Blandin de Cornouaille*, 58–60.

[25] Van der Horst, ed., *Blandin de Cornouaille*, 59.

[26] Van der Horst, ed., *Blandin de Cornouaille*, 64.

2.2. Treatment of *-ariu*

The Latin suffix *-ariu* is represented in our text by *-er* and by *-ier*; *cavalier* (22), *cavaller* (109), *cavaler* (767); *escudier* (1966), *escuder* (1115); *pomer* (95), *pomier* (102); *porter* (86), *portier* (2087). The majority of these words are in an *-ier* form, as in *guerrier* (656) and its variants; *esparvier* (1310), *mestier* (360), *vergier* (162). The *-ier* form is found in both French and Occitan. Although Levy does not list any forms in *-er*, Édouard Bourciez sees this as a development of the south of France.[27] Ronjat identifies the region around Foix and areas in the Quercy as localities where the two forms exist concurrently.[28]

2.3. *-a* and *-ay/ai*

Rhymes suggest that these two spellings may represent the same sound. Particularly with the verb *plaire*, "to please, to be pleasing," Meyer consistently suggested emending the *-ay* or *-ai* spelling to *-a*. However, the number of times that the scribe accepts a word ending in *ays* or *ais* as rhyming with *as* is significant, leading to rhyme pairs such as *plays* : *prenas* (1659–60); *ayas* : *plais* (1669–70); *agias* : *plays* (1861–62); *plais* : *aotrias* (1937–38); *plais* : *fassas* (2355–56).

2.4. *ay* and *ai*

These two spellings are used in rhyme, starting in the opening lines (*commenzeray* : *retrayrai*, 1–2) and as alternate spellings of a same word, such as *frayre* (five occurrences) / *fraire* (three occurrences). They represent variant orthographies and cannot be used to establish phonetic conclusions.

2.5. *-e* before *n* or *m*

There are two forms developing from open *e*: the expected monophthong as with the adverb *ben* (203) and the French form *bien* (1476, 2040). We observe that *ben* is also used adjectivally (26, 106).

[27] Bourciez, *Éléments de linguistique romane*, §264(b) p. 294: "Le Midi hésite entre *er*, *ier*, *eir*."

[28] Ronjat, *Grammaire istorique*, §114.

2.6. Closing of /e/

Free ẹ also shows two forms. As well as the expected forms *conven* (516), *convench* (2167), the text has the French forms *convien* (1405) and *convient* (1890).[29] Possibly by analogy, blocked ẹ gives *ei* as in *deins* (1430) from DENTE.

The *Blandin* author pairs open /ɛ/ and closed /e/, marked here as ẹ, creating imperfect rhymes, as Alart preferred to call them, rather than to see them as Catalan as Meyer had done.[30] We find, for example, *donzel* : *consẹlh* (2349–50), *aquẹl* : *castel* (381–82), *donsellas* : *mervẹilhas* (99–100), *consẹlh* : *ausel* (577–78, 1925–26), and *castel* : *consẹlh* (2297–98). These rhymes do suggest that the distinction between open and closed *e* was uncertain for the author of *Blandin*.

2.7. /o/

There are various causes of diphthongization of *o* in the text. The action of /k/ on tonic *o* has produced the following results. IOCUM produces *joc* (1488), unaffected, but from FOCUM, the text has *fuoch* (1196) and *fuoc* (2158); from LOCUM, *loch* (657), *luoch* (249), *loech* (828), and *luench* (83); from NOCTEM, *nuech* (48), *nuich* (228), and *nuch* (498). Joseph Anglade suggests that the *ue* form developed in the fourteenth and fifteenth centuries.[31]

The triphthong in *grueyssa* (1466), found also in Catalan, is formed from GROÍSSA < GROSSÍA and is caused probably by the freeing of yod from the following palatalized consonant which then combined with yod.[32] The marginal note, *de gratitudine*, seeking *grasitudine* to translate *de grueyssa*, suggests that the meaning of *grueyssa* was not obvious.

[29] Bourciez, *Éléments de linguistique romane*, §266(a); Bourciez and Bourciez, *Phonétique française*, §60,1; also Pope, *From Latin to Modern French*, §448.

[30] Alart, "En admettant comme fondées les déclarations de M. Meyer, et pour ma part j'ai quelques doutes en ce qui concerne les rimes en *el*, je ne présume pas qu'on puisse voir ici, au lieu d'influences catalanes, autre chose que des licences habituelles d'un mauvais rimeur provençal qui, le plus souvent, se contente d'une simple voyelle pour établir ses rimes," "Observations sur la langue du roman du *Blandin de Cornouailles*," 286–87.

[31] Anglade, *Grammaire de l'ancien provençal*, 73.

[32] Anglade, *Grammaire de l'ancien provençal*, suggests a comparative form *grueysser* for the adjective *gros*, though he tagged *grueysser* with a question mark (233).

3. *Phonetics, Consonants*

3.1. Initial *sc* and *st*

Prosthetic *e* has occasionally been omitted, as in *scut* (1240; compare *escut* 1186), *scuder* (1125; compare *escuder* 1115), *spassa* (399; compare *espassa* 1581), *strenna* (2404).

3.2. Intervocalic /g + a/

The text is consistent in the spelling of *jayan* or *jayant* (105) < *GAGANTEM.

3.3. Intervocalic /c + a/

The text offers *pagaras* (357) < PACARE and *pregar* (1356) < PRECARE, both typical examples of Occitan evolution.

3.4. Initial /k + a/

Initial /k + a/ results in two responses, with or without palatalization: CANIS > *can* (60) and *chins* (785); CAMMINUS > *camin* (34, 240) and *chamin* (25); CABALLUS > *caval* (691) and *chival* (1016). The palatalization may represent a Northern Occitan pronunciation,[33] though this text is unlikely to have received much Northern Occitan influence.

3.5. /j/ and Palatalized *l*

The fact that *donsella* rhymes regularly with *meravilha* (for example, 99–100, 993–94) suggests that *lh* may have been pronounced without palatalization by our author, as had been observed by Chabaneau.[34] In her edition, Galano suggests that the question was not pronunciation of *meravilha*, which she suggests clearly had a palatalized /l/, but rather that of *donsella*.[35] Something similar occurs with *companilha* : *avia* (1085–86), where it is implausible that *companilha* represents anything other than *compania*. Here, the *lh* spelling does not represent a palatalized /l/ at all.

[33] Bourciez, *Éléments de linguistique romane*, §166, §269(a); Ronjat, *Grammaire istorique*, §244.

[34] Chabaneau, "Notes critiques," 36.

[35] See Galano "Nuove congetture" 105, and Galano, ed., *Blandin di Cornovaglia*, 53n.

There is a related example in *Guilhem de la Barra*, where we find *donzelh* : *parelh* (1275–76); the palatalized /l/ in *donzel* seems very clear, though this is a highly unusual pronunciation of the word—it may simply be an example of eye rhyme.

3.6. Vocalization of /l/

We find *otrage* (821) and *outrage* (2304), revealing a fluctuating *u* and complete vocalization of *l*; the manuscript presents *saut* (442) and *salut*, emended to *sault* (138); the presence of *l* here is meaningful. Latin MULTUM is represented in our text more often by *mot* (thirty times, never abbreviated) than by *mout* (nineteen times, frequently written *mot* with a stroke indicating an added letter). On two occasions, however, *mout* is spelled out (994, 1741). Lastly, the text presents one example of *beutat* (1385), showing vocalization of *l*.

3.7. Final Consonants in General

Chabaneau observed that the author tended not to pronounce final consonants as a general rule; he offers numerous examples, including *gauch* : *saut* (441–42); *colp* : *tolc* (1533–34); *amic* : *Ardit*[36] (see §§1.16 and 3.8).

3.8. Loss of Final /n/

Based on rhymes, we know that orthographic *-n* was not always pronounced. We find these examples in our text: *ayssi* : *matin* (269–70, 283–84, 497–98); *ayssi* : *camin* (2205–6); *camin* : *vi* (1991–92, 2027–28). Similar rhymes are found in the fourteenth-century Occitan *Romance of Esther*. Galano suggests that certain words, *matin* and *camin* among them, maintained spelling with a final *n* that was no longer pronounced.[37]

[36] Chabaneau "Notes critiques," 437–38.

[37] Galano, "Nuove congetture," 104.

3.9. Examples of Final /r/

The *Blandin* author rhymes *ors* : *os*, a rhyme acceptable in Occitan.[38] Chabaneau noted that disappearance of the *r* conforms "à la prononciation languedocienne actuelle."[39] Galano offers an example from *Jaufre* whose anonymous author rhymed *ves* : *fers* (lines 1123–24).

3.10. *nuich*/*nuech*/*nuch*

Our text offers three different spellings for the Occitan word derived from NOCTEM; *nuich* (228, 293, 1391, 1952, 2293, plus *anuich*, 2246) is the most frequent, followed by *nuch* (498, 539, 542, and *anuch*, 2230); neither of these orthographies is found at the end of a line. *Nuech* is found only once (48), in position to rhyme with *dich*. Galano observed rightly that the rhyme pair *dich* : *nuech* (47–48) has solicited the most lengthy linguistic discussions among scholars of *Blandin*.[40] An inventive explanation, first offered by Meyer, was to see Catalan influence in the spelling of *nuech*, for only in Catalan can the words for "[he] said" and "night" rhyme, though the Catalan spellings would be *dit* : *nit*.[41] Chabaneau proposed reordering line 47 to read "Adoncas a dich Blandinet / Segon lo entro a la nuech," creating the rhyme pair *Blandinet* : *nuech*.[42] Chabaneau sees *nuech* as related to *nuet*, a perfect rhyme in his re-ordered couplet. *Nuech* is, however, a straightforward spelling, found in the regions of Provence and Languedoc,[43] whereas *nuich* seems to be a cross between the French *nuit* and the Occitan *nuech*. Galano suggests that *nuech* should be considered a copyist's error or one more example of French influence.[44]

[38] Anglade, *Grammaire de l'ancien provençal*, 195, cites Bertran de Born "S'ieu fos aissi" [PC 80, 40]; Paden, Sankovitch, and Stablein, eds., treated *r* before *s* as inaudible, *The Poems of the Troubadour Bertran de Born*, 96.

[39] Chabaneau, "Notes critiques," 39.

[40] Galano, ed., *Blandin di Cornovaglia*, 37n.

[41] See also Alart, "Observations sur la langue du roman du *Blandin*," 287–88. Fouché's examples support this statement, *Phonétique historique du roussillonnais*, 169 and 224–25.

[42] Chabaneau, "Notes critiques," 33.

[43] Meliga, "Osservazioni sulle grafie della tradizione trobadorica," 786.

[44] Galano, ed., *Blandin di Cornovaglia*, 38n; Alart, "Observations sur la langue du roman du *Blandin*," came to the same conclusion regarding this word (287).

4. Morphology

4.1. Declension System

The two declensions of earlier Occitan have lost their formal utility in this text. Though the scribe continues to use the occasional subject/object endings, word order is a more useful method for understanding the text, as the declensional endings are no longer functional. For example, the noun *donsel/donzel* never adds a declensional ending, regardless of its use in a sentence. However, mastery of the new system is imperfect. Compare "come bons cavaliers e apertz" (28) to "com bon cavaliers et apertz" (2210). In the two examples, both Blandin and Guilhot are referenced as subjects of the preceding verb, but in the first case, we have *-s* marking *bon* as plural; in the second case, one can feebly argue that *bon* demonstrates maintenance of the two-case system; note that *apertz* maintains the objective form in both samples.

4.2. Masculine Article

The manuscript suggests some confusion concerning the masculine article. There are a few instances of *le* for *lo* (*le matin*, 284; *le bon Blandin*, 1069; *le quart matin*, 1113) and of *los* (pl.) for *lo* and vice versa (*los feges* s. [699]; *totz lo cavaliers* pl. [963]). However, for the most part, the masculine article *lo* is used correctly; these few exceptions may suggest French influence or scribal fatigue.

4.3. Plural Feminine Article

The expected form, *las*, is used consistently throughout.

4.4. Demonstratives

There is the occasional use of *ayssel* (105, 564) and *esta* (64, 1016, 1130, 1317) as demonstrative adjectives. Ronjat considers forms of *este* as literary, though he acknowledges that the form is used in the mountains of Bigorre.[45] There is one Catalan instance of demonstrative use of *esta* recorded in *Medieval Catalan Linguistic Texts*, no. 20.[46]

[45] Ronjat, *Grammaire istorique*, §519 and note.

[46] Russell-Gebbett, ed., *Medieval Catalan Linguistic Texts*, 89.

The text also uses *la un* as a demonstrative/indefinite pronoun (9, 18, 45, etc.) and its feminine form *la una* (213, 254) as well. Burrell thought that this usage is not found elsewhere in Occitan,[47] though it seems to appear fairly often in *COM*. Chabaneau considered this demonstrative typical of the Languedocian dialect;[48] it is also common in Old Catalan.

4.5. Pronouns

The frequency of personal pronouns as subjects of verbs is noteworthy. In theory, Occitan is a zero-pronoun language, a group of languages that do not require use of a subject pronoun with each verb. Given that fact, the frequent use of subject pronouns in our text is remarkable. *Jou* is found 93 times, *tu* 24 times; *nos* and *vos* are both used 49 times; *el* occurs 118 times; *ela* is used 4 times, *elas* 9 times. Galano observed that the verb *respondre* followed by direct discourse was always accompanied by an expressed subject noun or pronoun.[49] Ronjat noted that some areas of the Occitan-language area used subject pronouns even when verb endings would suffice to identify the subject, an observation intensified by David Heap.[50]

The use of relative pronouns to introduce clauses is uneven. Occasionally the pronoun is omitted, as in line 944, but more often the pronoun is expressed pleonastically as in lines 192, 1131, 1144, 2302. There are far more instances in the text where the whole relative clause serves no other purpose than to lengthen the narrative; Kurt Lewent discusses this matter in his note, "Three Little Problems,"[51] suggesting that pleonastic relative clauses push the reader or listener to focus on the noun and its emotional value.[52]

[47] Burrell, "A Critical Edition," 110.

[48] Chabaneau, "Notes critiques," 32.

[49] Galano, ed., *Blandin di Cornovaglia*, 67n.

[50] Ronjat, *Grammaire istorique*, §771; Heap, *La variation grammaticale en géolinguistique*.

[51] Lewent, "Three Little Problems of Old Provençal Syntax," 167–69.

[52] Lewent, "Three Little Problems of Old Provençal Syntax," 171.

4.6. Verbs

Present

Some verbs show unusual forms, developed probably by analogy. Galano pointed to consistent use of *-e* for the first person singular indicative present in almost all verb groups;[53] in this edition, we can point to *jou presse* (707); *jou ame* (1689, 2303, 2345); *jou perdonne* (1794); *jou prege* (1836), *preghe* (1983, 2019, 2078); *jou torne* (1187); *jou sente* (833); *jou tene* (1808, 2117); *jou volle* (67, 2324); *jou pode* (122); [*jou*] *crese* (336), *jou creze* (1371); *jou sabe* (1619). This use of an *e* ending has been observed in the Auvergne and Rouergue regions of Occitan.[54] Furthermore, from the fourteenth century on, Catalan developed an *-e* in the first person of *ar* verbs, which also became *-o* towards the end of the fifteenth century. Burrell thought that the use of *-e* might equally be seen as evidence of French influence.[55]

Van der Horst thought the alignment of endings of irregular verbs with those of regular verbs occurred by analogy with the regular verbs. Van der Horst sees these forms as authorial; the Dutch scholar observes that these endings, especially in the first person singular, were noted in literary Occitan by Ronjat, among others.[56]

The first person singular present indicative of *pregar* has various forms in the text: *prego* (103, 761), *prec* (181, 782, 2114, 2349), *prege* (837, 1836, 2057, 2331), *preg* (1006, 1044, 1316, 1653, etc.), found eleven times in all, and *preghe* (1063, 1983, 2019, 2078, 2333). In light of the rarity of *-o* in the text, which more often uses *prec* or *preg*, Burrell suggested that *prego* might be Catalan or a reflection of the Italian scribe.[57]

The first person singular present indicative of *voler* shows a good number of variants: *volle* (67, 1667, 1889, 1903, 2324), *vuelh* (212, 1015, 1761, 2080), *vol* (594, 1364), *volc* (1675, 1904), *volho* (2094). This last spelling suggests Italian pronunciation.

53 Galano, "Nuove congetture," 106.

54 Pfister, "La localisation d'une scripta littéraire en ancien occitan," 261.

55 Burrell, "A Critical Edition," 110.

56 Van der Horst, ed., *Blandin de Cornouaille*, 53, citing Ronjat, *Grammaire istorique*, §650.

57 Burrell, "A Critical Edition," 110.

The author uses various spellings of *plazer*, third person singular present indicative (*plai, plais, play*). These forms would not be acceptable in Catalan, which has only one form available: *plau*. Examples of *plazer* conjugated at the rhyme include: *demandas* : *plais* (1325–26), *plays* : *prenas* (1659–60), *ayas* : *plais* (1669–70), *agias* : *plays* (1861–62), *plays* : *aotrias* (1937–38), *demandas* : *plas* (2105–6), *conselhas* : *plas* (2315–16), *sapias* : *plas* (2323–24), *plais* : *fayssas* (2331–32), *plais* : *fassas* (2355–56), and a similar rhyme with *plas* : *faray* (2347–48). These examples support the observation made above (§2.3), that *ai* and *a* were perceived by the author as rhyming.

Imperative

The form *sapias* (823, 1671, 1775, 2323) as a polite imperative has been formed by analogy with *sapchatz*, which can be both second person plural imperative and present subjunctive, hence the subjunctive form used in this text as an imperative.

Preterite and Periphrastic Perfect

The periphrastic perfect tense is formed with auxiliary verbs *aver* and *anar*, as well as with *estre*. Meyer considered this an indication of possible Catalan origin,[58] but Bourciez accepts this usage as normal in both French and Occitan.[59] The periphrastic perfect tense is also occasionally expressed by the use of *va* + gerundive, as in *va(n) sercant* (829, 856). Henrichsen cites *Blandin de Cornoalha* as a prime example of the use of *anar* + infinitive, a verbal form capable of expressing both preterite and simple future.[60] *S'en anar* + infinitive can play the same role.[61] Henrichsen sees this usage as gaining force in the fourteenth and fifteenth centuries[62] and considers it proof of the vitality of the preterite form in Occitan, both medieval and

[58] Meyer, ed., "Le roman de *Blandin de Cornouailles*," 201.

[59] Cf. Grévisse, *Le bon usage*, §715(i).

[60] See Bras and Sibille, "Lo futur perifrastic de tipe *anar +infinitiu,*" for discussion of the use of *anar* to express the future.

[61] Henrichsen, "La périphrase anar + infinitif en ancien occitan," 361.

[62] Henrichsen, "La périphrase anar + infinitif en ancien occitan," 362.

modern.[63] Though Catalan offers a similar structure, there is no need to see Catalan influence in the use of *anar* + infinitive in our text.

A number of verbs form the third person plural preterite with *-gheron* rather than the expected Occitan *-oron* or *-eron*. These include *agheron* (574, 982), *pogheron* (728), *tengheron* (2298) alongside *tengeron* (582) and *tencheron* (2206) (the expected form would be *tengron* [545]),[64] and *vengheron* (335, 466, 2381), which José Ramón Fernández González reports as expected, though with the spelling *venguèron*.[65] The *gh* spelling probably represents an Italian's representation of /g/; the added *e* serves as a support vowel.[66]

Future and Conditional

The conditional of *vezer* is found as *vigra* (236), third person singular, and *vigras* (418), second person plural.

We regularly find an interconsonantal support vowel in future forms of *rompre*: *rumpiray*, *rompiray* (708, 711); *romperon* (740). Meyer suggested emending *saveran* (823) to *savran*,[67] which implies that he thought the *e* was a support vowel, perhaps inserted for the rhyme. A similar case occurs with *prometeray* (1047), rhyming with *serviray* (1048); see too *meteray* (2124), not at the rhyme. We also have *defandares* (1188), rhyming with *nulla res* (1187) and *renderay* (968), rhyming simply with *ay* (967); in this case, the *e* is needed neither for rhyme nor for meter.

Subjunctive

The author's use of the subjunctive mood seems to follow Occitan norms. Curiously, we find what appears to be a subjunctive form of the verb *voler*, *voch*, where clearly an indicative is indicated (1237, 1256, 2253). These examples may not represent the subjunctive mood at all, but a continuation of the practice of *-ch* for *-c* (see §1.6, above).

63 Henrichsen, "La périphrase anar + infinitif en ancien occitan," 363.

64 Fernández González, *Gramática histórica provenzal*, 403.

65 Fernández González, *Gramática histórica provenzal*, 409.

66 Fernández González calls *aguèron* the normal modern form, *Gramática histórica provenzal*, 374.

67 Meyer, ed., "Le roman de *Blandin de Cornouailles*," 183; his line 821.

Participles

The *Blandin* text makes no distinction between gerundives and present participles, except insofar as the author has expressed *en* before the verbal form. Sometimes, as with *corren* (51), the word may be used adverbially as well.

4.7. General Morphological Issues

We find in *Blandin* "per lo castell a batalhar" (298) which parallels examples found by Lewent of what he called "a special use of the preposition 'a.'"[68] Lewent suggests that "the construction *a* with infinitive belonged to a more popular way of speaking—as in epic poetry";[69] he cited a good number of examples from the story of *Jaufre* (not an epic, but a romance or *novas*), repeating the observation of Breuer that "In *Jaufre*, the infinitive, where it follows its object, is always accompanied by *a*";[70] Lewent continues that "Such consistency has not always been observed by other writers,"[71] though we can find one other example of this use of double prepositions in our text with "an la gola per mal a far" (1480). Van der Horst commented very briefly on the use of two prepositions, referring to Else Wehowski's study of the *Vida de la benaurada sancta Doucelina* where the same practice is observed.[72] The *Blandin* author did not feel obligated to use two prepositions, as can be seen in "e per faich d'armes recobrar" (1782).

5. *Vocabulary*

5.1. Arms and Armor

Though *Blandin de Cornoalha* is a comparatively short story, with relatively few descriptions of any sort, one can find in this text a remarkable collection of terms relating to arms and armor. Below, some of these terms for *matériel de guerre*:

[68] Lewent, "Three Little Problems of Old Provençal Syntax," 171–80.

[69] Lewent, "Three Little Problems of Old Provençal Syntax," 179.

[70] Lewent, "Three Little Problems of Old Provençal Syntax," 177, quoting Breuer, ed., *Jaufre*, 371n.

[71] Lewent, "Three Little Problems of Old Provençal Syntax," 177.

[72] Van der Horst, ed., *Blandin de Cornouaille*, 56, citing Wehowski, *Die Sprache der Vida de la benaurada sancta Doucelina*, §216.

armes (77, 116, 418, 434, 696, 1642, 1782), *armar* (435, 1277, 2133, 2138), the author uses *armes* for arms of battle and as a more general term for the activities of a good knight.

arnes (20, 673, 692), the term means harness, but can also represent arms and armor, an example of synecdoche.

aubert (2163), "the quintessential armour for the ... Middle Ages, a mail tunic."[73]

bacinet (752, 1195, 1213, 1226, 1693, 2157), "a helmet to fit the skull."[74] Charles Henry Ashdown offers this description, "Acutely pointed at the apex, ... It descended on both sides well over the ears, and was carried round to the back of the neck, as a rule, in a straight line."[75] Sylvain Vondra adds that the bascinet's design protected not only the head, but the temples, forehead, and back of the neck.[76] Stefano Asperti argues that the bascinet with visor comes into use circa 1360–1370 in Catalonia and that this innovative form of head protection is what is meant when the *Blandin* author refers to a *bacinet*. Asperti therefore dates *Blandin* to the last third or last quarter of the fourteenth century.[77]

beroyer (457), Meyer suggests a kind of dagger, perhaps made in the Berry region,[78] an explanation accepted by the editors of the *FEW*.[79] Asperti argues convincingly that the word represents a piece of armor, usually worn by foot soldiers, used to protect the head.[80] *Blandin de Cornoalha* is the only medieval Occitan verse narrative to use this term.

73 Bradbury, *The Routledge Companion to Medieval Warfare*, 256; Ashdown, *European Arms and Armor*, 169.

74 Bradbury, *The Routledge Companion to Medieval Warfare*, 253.

75 Ashdown, *European Arms and Armor*, 169–70.

76 Vondra, "Le bacinet de Banyels," 107.

77 Asperti, "Bacinetti e berroviere."

78 Meyer, ed., "Le roman de *Blandin de Cornouailles*," 201.

79 *FEW* s.v. Berry I 336.

80 Asperti, "Bacinetti e berroviere," 22–23.

camalh (1226), chain mail protecting the neck area,[81] often attached to the bascinet by laces;[82] *Blandin de Cornoalha* is the only example in *COM* narrative texts.

coltel (748, 1545, 1592), a knife or dagger,[83] "well adapted for close fight of foot against foot."[84]

daga (1547), a dagger, "a small knife for stabbing, usually a reserve weapon, often carried in a belt, [with] two sharp edges and a sharp point."[85] Steven Muhlberger considers the dagger a "weapon appropriate to [a warrior's] calling."[86] J.-F. Finó states that it comes into use at the end of the thirteenth century.[87] It would seem to be a fairly common word, though it does not appear frequently in *COM*, which records but one other example, from a lyric by Peyre de Ruppe, dated to 1468.[88]

destral (1195), an ax, as per *FEW* III 62b.

escut or *scut* (147, 172, 343, 445, 721, 725, 1186, 1204, 1216, 1221, 1230, 1240, 1246, 1261, 2153), a shield.

espassa or *spassa* (399, 1211, 1484, 1581, 2153, 2157, 2161, 2172), a sword, "the weapon *par excellence* of the later medieval knight ... with strong symbolic value."[89]

jusarma (1221), "Staff weapon with a long blade, sharpened on both sides and ending in a long point, up to eight feet in length."[90] Following the editors of the *FEW*, van der Horst calls the word a

[81] Finó, "Les armées françaises lors de la Guerre de cent ans," 11.

[82] Ashdown, *European Arms and Armor*, 176; the *FEW* suggests the term appears in Occitan in the twelfth or thirteenth centuries (*FEW* s.v. MACULA VI.1 14b) and cites *Blandin*.

[83] Bradbury, *The Routledge Companion to Medieval Warfare*, 242.

[84] Hewitt, *Ancient Armour and Weapons in Europe*, 154–55, 314.

[85] Bradbury, *The Routledge Companion to Medieval Warfare*, 242.

[86] Muhlberger, *Deeds of Arms*, 8.

[87] Finó, "Les armées françaises lors de la Guerre de cent ans," 13.

[88] The title of this piece is "Vers sobre Patz e Guerra," *incipit* "Entre la Patz e Guerra s'es moguda," published by Jeanroy, ed., *Les joies du gai savoir*, LV, 243–46.

[89] Bradbury, *The Routledge Companion to Medieval Warfare*, 249.

[90] Bradbury, *The Routledge Companion to Medieval Warfare*, 244.

hapax in the fourteenth century,[91] but there are several uses of the term contemporary with *Blandin*.[92]

lansa or *lanssa* (139, 374, 451, 724, 896, 945, 1186, 1201, 1238, 1475, 1517, 1527, 2148), a lance or "a cavalry weapon with a long wooden shaft and metal head."[93]

malha (1179), mail, "body defence throughout the Middle Ages … usually consisting of metal rings joined together."[94]

massa or *maza* (135, 349, 391, 1426, 1504, 1520, 1523), a cudgel or club *FEW* VI.1 508a; "initially an infantry weapon, its prime use was by cavalry."[95]

ponhals (742), poniard or poignard *FEW* IX 512b. *Blandin de Cornoalha* is the only medieval Occitan verse narrative to use this term.

5.2. *amia* (439)

In context, this term clearly means "amity, friendship" (French *amitié*), though van der Horst understood the word as meaning "amie," "girlfriend," at this point in the story.[96] In Occitan, the suffix *-ia* was used to form abstract nouns and could also be used to form verb stems.[97]

5.3. *beres* (704)

Burrell suggested that *beres* relates to a word found in Honnorat, *barras*, "nom de l'espace vide qui se trouve dans la mâchoire inférieure du cheval, entre les dents canines et les molaires, dans lequel le mors de la bride appuie."[98] Van der Horst translated it simply as jaws, "mâchoires."[99]

[91] *FEW* s.v. *WISARM XVII 598; van der Horst, ed., *Blandin de Cornouaille*, 57.

[92] The *FEW* cites the use of *gizarme* "sorte de hallebarde" in the 1343 cartulary of Mirepoix, *FEW* XVII 598. Other examples include the 1358 *Coutumes de l'Agenais* and Joan de Castelnou's 1375 "Glosari al Doctrinal"; see TMAO, s.v. *gizarm**.

[93] Bradbury, *The Routledge Companion to Medieval Warfare*, 244.

[94] Bradbury, *The Routledge Companion to Medieval Warfare*, 257–58.

[95] Bradbury, *The Routledge Companion to Medieval Warfare*, 245.

[96] Van der Horst, ed., *Blandin de Cornouaille*, 153. s.v. *amia*.

[97] See Adams, *Word-Formation in Provençal*, 201.

[98] Burrell, "A Critical Edition," 211, citing Honnorat, *Dictionnaire provençal-français*, 1:237.

[99] Van der Horst, ed., *Blandin de Cornouaille*, 180.

5.4. Blandin / Brandin

The scribe is very consistent in the spelling of the hero's name, a name which is, moreover, almost never fully abbreviated. The name *Blandin* appears 140 times in the text; only at lines 167, 395, and 565 is it abbreviated to *B.* in the manuscript; the scribe does shorten the name by using strokes for the letter *n*, writing *Blādī*; *Blandinet* is shortened in the same fashion. The only exception to this observation occurs at line 91, where the scribe clearly wrote *Brandin*. We retain this spelling in the interest of presenting the text as medieval readers might have seen it.

5.5. *freid* (1120)

The manuscript is very clear as to the spelling of this word which occurs in rhyme position, though its rhyme is now missing; we have supplied *seid*. *Freid* clearly means "cold"; *fred* is found in Gascon dictionaries, identified particularly with the areas of Bigorre and the Gers.[100]

5.6. *freit* (900)

The manuscript is very clear in its spelling, and the word appears in rhyme position. We understand *freit* as a past participle of *fregir*, *frir*, "to fry," though the rhyme with *contrent* is imperfect and other solutions could be proposed. *Fregir* and *frir* are both Gascon infinitive forms, cited in several dictionaries of the dialect.[101] The first could give a past participle with loss of intervocalic /dž/; the second would easily give *freit* as well. There is also the form *f[e]rit* (118), which we understand as a past participle of a different verb, *ferir*.

5.7. *jounelhons* (156), *enjunenhols* (1604)

Burrell proposed that the use of *jounelhons* < GENUCULUM, instead of the expected Occitan *genolh*, was likely due to displacement of the tonic and atonic vowels in the diminutive *genolhon* > **gonelhon*.[102] Under

[100] See Grosclaude, Nariòo, and Guilhemjoan, *Dictionnaire français occitan*, http://www.locongres.org/, s.v. *froid*.

[101] For example, Grosclaude, Nariòo, and Guilhemjoan, *Dictionnaire français occitan*; Rei Bèthvéder, *Dictionnaire français/occitan*, http://www.locongres.org/, s.v. *frire*.

[102] Burrell, "A Critical Edition," 109.

GENUCULUM, the *FEW* (IV 113a) offers examples of vocalic metathesis or assimilation, in areas such as the Béarnais (*jonolh*), the Creuse (*dzonwe*), the Périgord (*janoueis*), and in the Hautes-Alpes (*janouilh*).[103] These examples suggest that our forms, while unusual, need not be emended. Related words in this text are *enjunenhols* (1604) and *s'anjounelhet* (1648), built on the same root. We understand a conjugated form of infinitive *enjunenhar*, "to kneel down," parallel to the Middle French infinitive *engenouillier*. The *FEW* gives the examples of *ajunilhar* (Marseilles) and *enjulhá* (Béarnais) which are close to our term;[104] *en genolhons* is found in the *Mystère de Sanct Poncz*, line 3808.

5.8. *pueys*, *puissas*, *puisses*, *puyes*, *puyesses*, *puys*, *puysses*; *plus che*

We find multiple forms for "thus, then"; *puys* is the most frequent, used twelve times in *Blandin* and frequently in Old Occitan (225 times in the *COM* corpus). The form *pueys* (70) is a spelling variant of this and used even more frequently in Old Occitan (1,032 times in the *COM* narrative corpus); *puyes* (970) may look like a scribal error, though the spelling is found in other texts (specifically, *Rollan a Saragossa* and the *Vie de Sainte Marguerite*, according to *COM*), so we do not emend. The form *puissas* (2027, 2289) is also found in *Flamenca* (6596) and in the *Canso de la Crosada* (laisse 127, line 6). Only two forms, *puyesses* (465) and *puysses* (1054, 1493, 1827, 1833, 2201) are unique to *Blandin*.

There is also the matter of *plus*. The scribe consistently offers *plus che* for "since" or "after" (French *puisque*, Italian *poiché*) where the expected form would be *pus que* or, for this scribe, *pus che*. Meyer and Galano tended to emend; van der Horst appears not to comment. We believe that the spelling as found in our text was intended and do not emend, though the *plus che* form is rare. We note that Bertran Boysset, a fourteenth-century native of Arles, used this spelling at least once in his works on surveying.[105]

[103] *FEW* IV 113–15.

[104] *FEW* IV 114.

[105] See the *Traités d'arpentage* in Portet, *La vie et les oeuvres de Bertran Boysset*, 2:171. Jean Sibille considered *pus* and *plus* interchangeable in his article on use of the term, see "Fidelitat a la lenga vernaculara," passim.

5.9. *la serp, lo serpent*

The text presents *la serp* with a feminine article (1487), modified by adjectives in feminine forms (1488) as expected. The text also presents *lo serpent* with a masculine article (1462) modified by feminine adjectives (1464). An explanation for the shifting gender of the snake is gender confusion between *serpent* and *serp*, though one may doubt that a native speaker of Occitan would confuse gender in this fashion. Other Romance languages observe related gender distinctions (compare, in French, *le vase*, "the vase" and *la vase*, "the mud"), so one should not attribute this confusion to an Italian scribe. Van der Horst suggests that the text used feminine forms for reasons of rhyme,[106] which is plausible but not fully convincing.

[106] Van der Horst, ed., *Blandin de Cornouaille*, 125n.

Literary Analogs and Possible Sources

THERE ARE MANY more romances written in Old French than in Occitan, and it is not surprising that most of the analogs for *Blandin* concern the literature of the north of France. As will become clear, *Blandin* is not the reworking or *remaniement* of an earlier tale; its author draws elements from a variety of sources. We find references from a range of traditions, as is common in late medieval romance. The discussion below follows the plot of the story to consider literary analogs and possible sources.

Prologue: Relationship between the Two Knights and Their Origin

The inseparable friendship between Blandin and Guilhot Ardit is a commonplace of medieval literature. An early model is found in the *Chanson de Roland* where "Rollant est proz e Oliver est sage, / Ambedui unt merveillus vassalage" [Roland is worthy and Oliver is wise / Together they have a wondrous faithfulness] (lines 1093–94).[1] Many examples are found in the *chansons de geste*, epic poems, probably because the warrior community of epics celebrates friendship between comrades-in-arms. The ethos of the epic ensures that such friendships are fostered by the martial prowess of the heroes.

When knights move into the realm of the *roman courtois*, it is their chivalric and courtly manners which determine their merit. In the romances of Chrétien de Troyes, for example, it is Gauvain who functions as the epitome of chivalric and courtly conduct[2] and who often befriends the hero. In the *Chevalier de la charette*, Gauvain and Lancelot ride off in

[1] Segre, ed., *La chanson de Roland.*

[2] See Busby, *Gauvain in Old French Literature*, for a detailed discussion of this character in medieval romance; Badel, *Introduction à la vie littéraire du Moyen Âge*, ch. 11.

search of the abducted Guinevere, Gauvain motivated by chivalry alone (line 234), but Lancelot by love (lines 372–77).[3] In the *Conte du Graal*, Gauvain and Perceval ride off in search of the meaning of the Grail (line 4718), and in the *Chevalier au lion*, Gauvain persuades his friend Yvain to take leave of Laudine for one year in order to attend tourneys and to win fame for his prowess in arms (line 2540). In *Blandin*, the opening statement of intent by the author makes clear that Guilhot epitomizes chivalry and Blandin love; this seems to be borne out by the structure of the story. Guilhot would then seem to be a Gauvain-type, while Blandin is the overall hero, an interpretation seen in the different episodes.[4]

The names of the two knights have special significance and emphasize the difference in their characters. Guilhot Ardit is a less complex character; his second name—Ardit—reflects his rash nature. He has the Rolandian trait of being brave but not foolhardy. The author of *Blandin* may have been acquainted with *Le Bel Inconnu*, where, in a list of persons expected to attend the tournament in that romance, *li Lais Hardis de Cornouaille*, "The Ugly Hero of Cornwall," is mentioned (line 5489); the epithet was perhaps borrowed for Guilhot.[5]

Blandin's name has wider implications, appropriate for a more complex character. The first of these is a possible identification as a Bran-type character, although we admit that supporting evidence is slight. At line 91, the scribe wrote "Brandin" for "Blandin";[6] this might be indicative of an earlier Bran-identification confused by a previous scribe, but the characteristic features of the legend found in the plot are few. In *Bran the Blessed in Arthurian Romance*, Helaine Newstead lists some of the characteristics of Bran which are found in the romance.[7] However, it is clear from her study that the only connections between Blandin and Bran are the similarity in name and the feast at the end of Brianda's enchantment. Newstead sees a basic pattern in each of the versions of the legend: "The hero undertakes a perilous adventure in an enchanted *pallais*, he beholds worship of a

[3] See also Kelly, *Sens and conjointure*, 66.

[4] Guilhot is a debased Gauvain-type; thirteenth-century non-Grail romances tend to discredit Gauvain. Cf. Loomis, *Arthurian Tradition and Chrétien de Troyes*, 147, 399–407. See also Busby, *Gauvain in Old French Literature*, 400–402.

[5] Renaut de Bâgé, *Le Bel Inconnu*.

[6] But see §1.14 in the linguistic discussion.

[7] Newstead, *Bran the Blessed*, 18–24.

cor (transformed into a *tor* or vessel) which produces abundance and fights with or is attached by a fiery gigantic adversary."[8]

In *Blandin*, the hero does undertake a perilous adventure, not in an enchanted palace but for an enchanted woman; his perilous adventure involves taking an *astor* after fighting both a fiery adversary and a quasi-gigantic figure (see below for discussion of the Saracen). However, it is difficult to see how the *cor/tor* confusion could extend as far as to include an *astor*.

The fact that there is an abundance of food and wealth (Brianda's feast and treasury) does not indicate any supernatural agent, as in the usual Bran-type stories. Rather, these elements could be explained as the usual feast-after-hardship motif found in all romances. We must therefore conclude that *Blandin* is not linked directly with the Bran tradition, although a fortuitous combination of certain features and hints of this tradition would suggest that some of its elements found their way into the store of commonplaces.

A more tantalizing remark made in the story is found at line 77, where Blandin is described as "tot armat d'armes vermelhas." The hero as a Red Knight features in two traditions, the defense of a spring and the quest for the Grail; Red Knights appear in a large number of Old French romances, Gerard Brault calling the character "one of the most popular figures in Arthurian literature."[9] Although Blandin does not encounter any such "water adventure," his companion Guilhot does have an adventure with a knight defending a pond. It is possible that the author has used duplication of character as a means of amplification, that he has divided adventures traditionally associated with one hero between two in his *dictat*. The tradition of the Red Knight at a spring is so persistent that it cannot be ignored. In his study of *Yvain*, Charles Bertram Lewis made the following observations:

> It is impossible not to regard the antagonists of our heroes as identical. They all defend a spring or some other spot, and are nearly all clad in red armour or mounted on steeds caparisoned in red. Thus Esclados le Roux, as his name alone indicates. Iweret had a red shield and red lions on his armour .... Mabonagrain is clad in vermillion ..., the horse of Malgier le Gris is covered with a vermillion

[8] Newstead, *Bran the Blessed*, 106.

[9] Brault, *Early Blazon*, 33.

> cloth .... Sir Gareth's adversary is called the Red Knight of the red lawns. Marigart le Roux bore a crimson shield, Bréhus sans Pitié a crimson ensign .... Crimson or vermilion apparel would thus seem to belong to the office of the defender of the spring, and from this point of view it is important to note that as soon as Yvain becomes the official champion of the spring he is clothed by Lunete in a vermilion mantle (line 1883).[10]

Lewis adds that Yvain is again clothed in a scarlet mantle in the episode of the castle of Pesme Avanture at lines 5420–23,[11] and Alfred Adler also points to the fact that Yvain is clothed in scarlet by Lunete, "Thus making him coincide with Esclados in his quality as a Red Knight."[12]

Besides being traditionally the defender of a spring or place, the Red Knight is also connected with the quest for the Grail. In the Vulgate *Lancelot*[13] Bohors is clothed by the daughter of King Brangor in red samite. In Chrétien's *Perceval*, the hero defeats the Red Knight who had stolen the cup from Arthur's court and takes the Red Knight's armor (line 1174), and in the *Queste del Saint Graal*, Galaad, after being conducted to Arthur's court by an old man in a white robe, passes tests to prove that he is the one who will be the hero of the quest. He, too, is wearing vermillion arms.[14] It is possible to see a connection between the Red Knight as the defender of a spring or custom and the Red Knight as the hero of a Grail quest. In most of the romances where the knight is obliged to defend a spring, there is a chapel nearby,[15] and by implication, the Red Knight becomes the defender of a faith or religious custom.[16] By a process of analogy, the Red Knight also becomes associated with the quest for the greatest symbol of faith, the Grail.

Blandin, armed in vermillion, has only a tenuous connection with the Grail romances; his connection with a defender of a spring is even more distant. It is interesting that we have here an example of a hero, wearing ver-

[10] Lewis, *Classical Mythology and Arthurian Romance*, 121–22.

[11] Lewis, *Classical Mythology and Arthurian Romance*, 144n1.

[12] Adler, "Sovereignty in Chretien's *Yvain*," 290.

[13] Cited by Newstead, *Bran the Blessed*, 52.

[14] Frappier, "The Vulgate Cycle," 302.

[15] For example, *Yvain*, lines 393–94.

[16] Lewis, *Classical Mythology*, explains the religious significance of *Yvain* by linking it with the cult of Zeus at Dodona, passim.

million arms, who does not appear to be connected with either a defense adventure or a Grail quest. Michel Pastoureau notes that red was the most popular color for arms and armor throughout the medieval period, seen in literary and historic documents.[17] As the French scholar observes, "red is the sign of nobility, of beauty, and of courage."[18] He specifically mentions "strange Red Knights" who appear in Arthurian romances, representing a metaphoric, dream world.[19] *Blandin*'s author may well have been invoking the general symbolism of red, "noble birth, honor, valiance, generosity, and strength ... justice and charity,"[20] without necessarily connecting the color to the spring or the Grail.

The origin of the two knights is said to be Cornwall: they are "dos cavaliers / de Cornoalha bons guerriers" (lines 4–5) and yet later on, it appears that only Blandin comes from Cornwall, while Guilhot is from Miramar, perhaps implying that it is in a separate region (lines 10–12). Furthermore, they introduce themselves at the conclusion of the first adventure as "cavalliers d'Orien / sercans avantura veramen" (lines 517–18). How can we reconcile these apparent differences?

The mention of the East can be seen as an attempt to inject exoticism and perhaps also military valor into the tale. We should remember the great influence that the Crusades had on the literature of the twelfth and thirteenth centuries to explain why romance heroes were said to have come from the East. Examples may be found in the literature of the North—Chrétien's *Cligès* is divided between the Arthurian court on the one hand and the empires of Greece and Constantinople on the other[21]—and there is a complete category of adventure romances which have a Greco-Byzantine setting,[22] including the Spanish *Libro del caballero Cifar*, a fourteenth-century romance, whose hero, Cifar, claims that he comes from the East.[23] Thus, in *Blandin*, two knights claiming to come

[17] Pastoureau, *Rouge*, 74.

[18] Pastoureau, *Rouge*, 78.

[19] Pastoureau, *Rouge*, 78.

[20] Pastoureau, *Rouge*, 79.

[21] Chrétien de Troyes, *Cligès*, line 47.

[22] Holmes, *A History of Old French Literature*, ch. 15.

[23] The *Libro del caballero Cifar* has been dated between 1299 and 1305 by Northrup in *Introduction to Spanish Literature*, 92. It is but one example that shows authors seeking to connect their heroes with the East.

from the East, perhaps a reference to a recent journey, does not prevent the heroes from also hailing from Cornwall.[24]

The location of Cornwall as the origin of the heroes presents some geographical difficulty. At first, both are said to be from Cornwall; then it is Blandin who comes from Cornwall and Guilhot from Miramar. While there is no Miramar in either Cornwall or northern France, it is a fairly common place-name in Spain, and was especially known in the thirteenth century as the site of the monastery built by the Catalan philosopher and mystic, Ramon Llull.[25]

The form given in Jehan de Nostredame's account of the origin of *Blandin*, however, is *Myremas*; this was explained by Meyer as the attempt by Nostredame to impose his own place of origin onto his biography.[26] There is a town called Miramas at the northern end of the Étang de Berre in Provence, and it is also possible that the *Blandin* author has this town in mind, but changed the form to agree with the more famous city.

The first mention of Cornwall could be seen to refer to the whole realm of the "matter of Britain" or tales relating to King Arthur; it is the reference to Cornwall which accounts for the romance being included by some critics in the category of Arthurian romance, even though there is no mention of Arthur or of his court.[27] Thus, the knights are two of that vast crowd of characters who populate the general Arthurian landscape called here, by the author, Cornwall. Within this vast imaginary region lies the geographical area of Cornwall and the community of Miramar, which might be physically located in Spain or Provence.[28]

[24] It is also possible to read this as a compliment to Richard of Cornwall (see First Sightings) and an indirect reference to Richard's journey to Syria in 1240.

[25] Alcover and Moll, *Diccionari català-valencià-balear*, vol. 7, s.v. Miramar.

[26] "*Miramar* est un nom de lieu assez fréquent; mais la forme que lui a donnée Nostre-Dame, *Myremas*, c'est un village voisin de Salon, la ville où était établie la famille du peu scrupuleux biographe," Meyer, ed., "Le roman de *Blandin de Cornouailles*," 173.

[27] For example, Nelli and Lavaud, eds., *Blandin de Cornouailles*, 450; see Fasseur, "La matière bretonne," 322–24.

[28] There is a theory that *Cornoalha* and especially its variant *Cornevalha* could refer to a place in northern Spain. In the German *Parzival* we find the place *Kornvaleis*, which has generally been accepted as Cornwall. However, much of *Parzival* is set in Spain, in particular in Toledo, Castille, and Galicia, and, in particular, in an area around La Coruña, which could be corrupted into *Kornvaleis*. This error would then lead to the assumption that the whole *dictat* is set in Spain.

The Combined Adventure (lines 13–609)

The tripartite structure of this episode offers Blandin's adventure in what may be considered a form of the Otherworld, followed by the encounter between Blandin, Guilhot, and the giant at the castle, and then the separation of the two heroes.

Blandin's Adventure

The most significant element is the presence of the little dog, sent as a messenger to guide the knights towards the entrance to the cave.[29] The subsequent rescue of two maidens from the giant is set in an Otherworld landscape, and the little dog as messenger can be considered part of it. The most obvious example of a dog connected with the Otherworld is Cerberus, guardian dog at the entrance to the world of the dead in Virgil's *Aeneid*. In medieval romances, a dog was sometimes used as a messenger either in purely courtly situations or from the Otherworld.[30]

The dog in *Blandin* is clearly sent to guide the hero to the aid of the maidens, although no mention of it is made once Blandin has traveled through the cave. The animal may fit the category of Guiding Beasts, established by Arthur Gilchrist Brodeur, who divided useful beasts in medieval literature into three categories, of which the first is

> guiding beasts, which render assistance to the hero, and show him the way to his goal, in order to attain their own ends or the ends of those who sent them, and because upon the hero's success their own success—disenchantment of themselves, of the *fée* or other distressed personage whose messenger they are, etc.,—depends.[31]

In courtly romances, a dog was also used as a messenger. The best example is perhaps Husdant, the dog Tristan gives to Iseut in Béroul's *Tristan*. When Tristan, dressed as a fool, comes to the court of King Mark, Iseut will not recognize him; it is only after the dog which he had given her greets him with affection that she will acknowledge that the fool is her lover, Tristan. In the *Chastelaine de Vergi*, the heroine uses a little dog to

[29] See Pfeffer, "Canes virumque cano: *Blandin de Cornoalha*."

[30] Paton, in her *Studies in the Fairy Mythology of Arthurian Romance*, notes that the dog is often accompanied by a white stag in most fairy-type stories, and that the hero is led into the presence of a *fée* or *fées* while in pursuit of these two animals, 229.

[31] Brodeur, "The Grateful Lion," 518.

tell her lover that he can see her (lines 30–39).[32] Some critics have seen in this romance elements of the fairy mistress theme,[33] although Frederic Whitehead sees it simply as a stylized situation:

> In fact, the orchard and the castle, so strangely deserted by everybody except the lady and the little dog, are scarcely real places at all, but rather the stylized features of a décor demanded by a type of romance in which amorous encounters invariably take place *sotz ram* or *dins cortina* [under a branch or in a garden].[34]

A dog as a messenger is then a commonplace of romance, with evidence to suggest overtones of the Otherworld.

Not only the use of the dog as messenger hints at the presence of the Otherworld, so too does Blandin's passage through a waterfall to enter the cave (line 52). In *The Other World according to Descriptions in Medieval Literature*, Howard Patch maintains that "the approach to the region is sometimes underground, down a well perhaps, and sometimes under the sea. It may also be by a path through a desolate tract or by a flight up through the skies. Sometimes there is a water barrier, a river, perhaps, or the sea."[35] In most of the fairy romances, there is explicit mention of some form of water barrier that the hero has to cross before coming to the fairy's dwelling. In *Lanval*, the hero finds his fairy mistress beside a running brook;[36] in *Partenopeus de Blois*, as in *Guigemar*, the hero finds himself in a boat which takes him to an unknown destination. Arthur C. L. Brown explains this as a Celtic element, saying that fairy mistresses "are nearly all first seen near a spring or river or lake or by the seaside. Especially is this the case in Celtic fairy stories, because of the belief, strongly held by the Celts, that the approach to fairyland lay across the sea or beneath the waves."[37]

Otherworld features are also discernible in Blandin's journey through a dark cave until he eventually reaches a place of great light, where he is asked to defend two damsels from the giant who holds them prisoner.

[32] Stuip, ed., *La chastelaine de Vergi*.

[33] Brown, *Iwain*, 20.

[34] Whitehead, *La châtelaine de Vergy*, xxxiv.

[35] Patch, *The Other World*, 3.

[36] Marie de France, *Lais*, lines 45 and 54–56.

[37] Brown, *Iwain*, 21.

Patch gives an account of Walter Map's story involving the Otherworld, called here the underworld.

> The underworld, too, appears in Walter's famous story of King Herla, who, to carry out his contract with the pygmies, goes to their home and enters "a cavern in a lofty cliff" where "after a space of darkness they passed into light." This came not from the sun or moon but from lamps, and the mansion was "like the palace of the sun in Ovid's descriptions." On Herla's return he is warned to let none of his company dismount until the dog with which they have been presented shall leap from the arms of the man who carries him. Some of the retinue disobey the order and are changed to dust. King Herla learns that although he supposed his stay to have been but three days, he has in reality been there for well over two hundred years.[38]

In this story, there are many correspondences with *Blandin*; one might presume that the author of *Blandin* used either this account or a derivative as a source for Blandin's descent into the cave. Not only is there a dog in Walter Map's account, but the mention of the three days' stay has a parallel in *Blandin*, whose hero tells Guilhot to wait at the entrance three days for his return (line 69).

Patch enumerates other examples of access to the Otherworld through a cave.[39] For example, Marie de France's *Yonec* offers a similar geography. The heroine follows a path into a hill which has only one entrance, and after walking in the dark she comes to a fair meadow where she sees a city enclosed by a wall.[40] With such examples found plentifully in medieval romances, it can be assumed that in *Blandin*, there is an Otherworld landscape in the first adventure.

Blandin emerges from the cave and meets a gatekeeper who tells him to go into a garden to find adventure. There, he is asked by two damsels to deliver them from the giant who holds them captive. It would be impractical to enumerate the examples of maidens delivered from the hands of giants by heroes, because it is a commonplace of romance. What is interesting in this example is that the maidens or damsels offer themselves to

[38] Patch, *The Other World*, 232, quoting from Walter Map, *Master Walter Map's Book De Nugis Curialium*.

[39] Patch, *The Other World*, 233–34, 237.

[40] Marie de France, *Yonec* in *Lais*, lines 345–56.

Blandin for having defeated the giant (lines 177–80). They offer their loyalty, and earlier, they had said that they would offer their love (lines 104–6). This scenario has some slight similarity to the account of Yvain's adventure at the castle of Pesme Avanture, where, after defeating two *filz de netun*, sons of a demon, the hero is supposed to marry the daughter of the lord of the castle (lines 5468–72, 5482–83), as a reward for his services. However, *filz de netum* are not necessarily monsters, and this parallel may link more firmly with the next adventure.

Defeat of the Giants by Blandin and Guilhot

Once Blandin and Guilhot are reunited at the entrance to the cave, they ride off with the two damsels, until they come to the castle which originally belonged to the family of the two ladies. It is here that the similarity with Chrétien's *Yvain* and the castle of Pesme Avanture becomes striking. Earlier, Yvain fought with a giant, Harpin de la Montagne (lines 3852–57), and then Yvain has to fight with the two demonic characters mentioned above. It would seem that two adventures have been combined into one in *Blandin*, so that the heroes have to fight three enemies—all giants—a father and his two sons. The giant killed by Blandin in the first part of this adventure is the brother of the two who had captured the damsels' castle (line 278). It seems quite a family gathering of giants: there is the mother of the giants and her two lions, which Guilhot kills, the father giant, the son who was earlier killed by Blandin, and the other son, Lionet. The reason for the presence of the two lions with the giants' mother may explain the name Lionet. Because of Yvain and his lion, the animal is most noted as the companion of heroes, perhaps as befits the "king of the beasts."[41] It is difficult to explain why the *Blandin* author considered the animal fit company for the giants, one of whom may have been named for the animal. The analogies with Chrétien's *Yvain* also include the weapons used by the giants, who all fight with huge clubs (lines 5509–15), a common weapon for giants and other adversaries.

Where *Blandin* differs most noticeably from *Yvain* is that there are two heroes to combat the giants, whereas in *Yvain* there is only the eponymous hero, not permitted the assistance of his lion. Once Yvain

[41] McCulloch, *Medieval Latin and French Bestiaries*, 137. See also Hershon and Ricketts, eds., *Elucidari de las proprietatz de totas res naturals*, 540.

has defeated the monsters, three hundred captive maidens are released; in *Blandin*, it is the male members of the household who are freed once the giants are defeated. The deliverance of persons from the hands of giants or other besieging figures is a commonplace of medieval literature.[42] The capture of Guinevere in Chrétien's *Lancelot* is only part of a larger captivity, for Meleagant had several of Arthur's people from the kingdom of Logres as captives in his land. When Lancelot rescued the queen, he also freed the people of Logres. In Chrétien's *Erec*, the hero and Enide are riding through the forest when they hear the cries of a damsel in distress. After Erec leaves his wife to go to the rescue, he learns that two giants have seized the damsel's lover; he overtakes the giants, slays them, restores the lover to his lady, and then rejoins Enide.[43] Similar scenes are found in the Occitan romance *Jaufre*, whose hero combats a devil with magical powers. *Blandin* is no exception to the pattern.

Separation of the Heroes

After this adventure, Blandin and Guilhot ride along; when they are some distance from the castle, they hear the song of a bird (line 550). The message that the bird gives in its song leads to their separation and to Blandin's rescue of Brianda. It is therefore possible to see the talking bird as a messenger sent by Brianda, in much the same way as the *donzella d'otra mar* (see below) is a messenger. This would make Brianda a type of fairy mistress who summons her lover by indirect means.[44] The fact that the knights are to find the two roads beneath a pine tree recalls the central fountain episode in *Yvain*, where the fountain is found beneath a miraculous tree

[42] Cf. Newstead, "The Besieged Ladies in Arthurian Romance." Also Loomis, in speaking of the deliverance of a damsel from giants in *Arthurian Tradition*, 85: "Quite possibly this is no peculiarly Celtic theme, but was a *lieu commun* of storytellers, which was picked by the Breton *conteurs* and grafted upon the Arthurian cycle."

[43] Chrétien de Troyes, *Erec*, lines 4280–4537.

[44] Cf. Paton, *Studies in the Fairy Mythology of Arthurian Romance*, 15, "The induction to the story resembles many another that recounts the entrance of a mortal into fairyland. In the Celtic stories ..., the fairy mistress in person summons the hero whom she loves to the other world. But she is not limited to one method in accomplishing her ends, and we have a variety of inductions to our fairy episodes, recounting the means by which the fay draws the knight to her presence. A very ordinary form represents her as sending out a fairy messenger disguised as some tempting victim for the huntsman's dart, usually a stag, a boar, or a bird, which lures the young knight to her domain."

whose leaves never decay;[45] Lewis's study confirms that the pine tree figures prominently in the scenes of fairy marvels.

The mention of the two roads is significant in view of what happens to each of the knights. Blandin takes the narrow path, while Guilhot takes *lo gran camin* (line 594), supposed to lead to great adventure. There are biblical overtones here, particularly of the distinction between the two roads in St. Matthew (7:13–14).[46] But given that there are numerous examples in medieval romances of choices between two or more routes, it would be rash to posit direct biblical symbolism, equating Blandin with the righteous and Guilhot with the damned. Patch thinks the poor road theme is developed from the wasteland motif and offers these examples:

> A very poor road, thorny and full of briars, takes the hero along its dark way through mountains, valleys, and forests, and ultimately to the pine which stands beside the spring and the stone in Chrétien's *Yvain*. This avenue of approach would seem to derive from the *terre gaste*. The scene in such a journey to the Other World recalls a little what we have found in the *Mule sans Frain*; and indeed it has been compared with that and with a corresponding part of the *Wigalois* and the *Chevalier de Papegau*.[47]

The most notable parallel of the separation of two knights along two different paths occurs in Chrétien's *Lancelot*, where Lancelot and Gauvain set off to find the abducted Guinevere. Gauvain takes the water bridge path, while Lancelot takes the sword bridge path (lines 689–99). In *Lancelot*, however, the two knights have a definite goal, whereas in *Blandin*, the heroes are in search of some undefined adventure.

[45] Lines 384–85. See Lewis, *Classical Mythology*, 78–86.

[46] "Intrate per angustam portam: quia lata porta, et spatiosa via est, quae ducit ad perditionem, et multi sunt qui intrant per eam. Quam angusta porta, et arcta via est, quae ducit ad vitam: et pauci sunt qui inveniunt eam!" (Enter by the narrow gate. The gate is wide that leads to perdition, there is plenty of room on the road and many go that way; but the gate that leads to life is small and the road is narrow, and those who find it are few.)

[47] Patch, *The Other World*, 296. For a further account of the Wasteland motif, see Nitze, "The Waste Land," 58–62.

Guilhot's Adventures (lines 609–985)

This section divides into three episodes, dominated by the second, Guilhot's combat with the Black Knight at the pond. The tripartite structure consists of a preliminary episode with the shepherd, the central episode at the pond, and the concluding episode where Guilhot is overcome and imprisoned.

Encounter with the Shepherd and Messenger

After riding into a plain, Guilhot sees a shepherd eating mutton; the knight more or less invites himself as a dinner guest. There is the famous similar account of an interaction with shepherds in *Aucassin et Nicolette* (sections XXI and XXII), definitely idyllic in tone with touches of irony or parody, whereas Guilhot's encounter is extremely practical. A similar picnic occurs in the Occitan story of *Jaufre* (lines 4201–44). While Guilhot is dining with the shepherd, he is issued, indirectly, a challenge by the Black Knight. A messenger tells him that the Black Knight wants to fight two knights from Cornwall, presumably Blandin and Guilhot (lines 647–48). Guilhot accepts the challenge and rides to meet the Black Knight. That there is a form of challenge is important: in *Yvain*, Calogrenant is accused by Esclados le Roux of having destroyed his land without a formal challenge (lines 491–92), and to do so was considered unchivalrous. But Guilhot is within his rights in challenging the Black Knight since he has heard the knight's intentions from the messenger.

The Combat with the Black Knight

In several medieval romances, there are ingredients which are found in Guilhot's adventure: a Black Knight, guarding a spring or some other spot, challenges all who pass or is challenged by the hero and defeated. The hero then usually takes his place as the defender of the place or may ride away. Some earlier scholars saw in this type of adventure traces of the Arician Diana myth as revealed in J. G. Frazer's *Golden Bough*,[48] and Lewis has seen it as part of the rain-making ceremony of the cult of Zeus at Dodona.[49] Pastoureau observes that "A black knight was almost always a character of

[48] Especially Nitze, "A New Source of the *Yvain*," 269–80. Cf. Frazer, *The Golden Bough*, chs. 1 and 2.

[49] Lewis, *Classical Mythology*, 54–55.

primary importance (Tristan, Lancelot, Gawain) who wanted to hide his identity,"[50] though such is not the case in *Blandin*. More significant is that black was a very rare color in the heraldry of medieval Occitania,[51] so for *Blandin*'s audience, this character stands out.[52]

Whatever its primary source, the custom of defending a spring or other venue had become a commonplace of romances by the thirteenth century. And, as Norris Lacy cogently observed, "It is a custom of romance that custom must be respected. ... One cannot ignore a custom because romance convention requires that customs be obeyed."[53] Lewis enumerates some of the instances where a custom is found, including Huon de Méry's *Tournoiement Antécrist*, the *Livre d'Artus*, the *Roman en prose de Tristan*, *Claris et Laris*, and *Brun de la Montagne*; these last two "even mention some traits which are not in Chrestien—traits, too, which bear the stamp of genuine traditions relating to the spot."[54]

What these romances have in common is the defense of a spring, whereas *Blandin* has a pond covered by a tent. Guilhot's formal act of defiance is to break this tent-like structure (line 714), whereupon the Black Knight who *era in garda del paschier* (line 716) strikes Guilhot, and the combat begins. The fact that he is a Black Knight also has great significance for the defense custom. In the Welsh *Owein*, the hero is obliged to do battle with a Black Knight;[55] this story is closely dependent on Chrétien's *Yvain*. In *Fergus*, the hero fights a Black Knight, and, again, there are elements similar to *Yvain*.[56]

Perhaps the most interesting analogy of all is found in the Occitan *Jaufre*,[57] where Jaufre meets a Black Knight who seems enchanted. He is a devil,[58] pressed into the service of defending a chapel by an old hag, whose

[50] Pastoureau, *Black*, 73.

[51] Pastoureau, *Black*, 72.

[52] Brault offers a list of Black Knights, in *Early Blazon*, 31–32.

[53] Lacy, "On Customs in Medieval French Romance," 982.

[54] Lewis, *Classical Mythology*, 50–51.

[55] Loomis, *Arthurian Tradition*, 279.

[56] Lewis, *Classical Mythology*, 100: "The fight between Fergus and the Black Knight (lines 2035–2441) ... seems to be a reminiscence ... of some traits in *Yvain*."

[57] Lee, ed. *Jaufre*. Nelli and Lavaud, who also edited *Jaufre*, follow Rita Lejeune's dating of ca. 1180 (Nelli and Lavaud, eds., *Le roman de Jaufre*, 34).

[58] See Pastoureau on the long association of the devil with the color black, *Black*, 51–58.

husband was a terrible giant. When that giant was killed, the hag called upon the devil to protect her and her two children. One of the children was now a leper, the other is about to return. Jaufre waits for the return of the devil (lines 5170–660). In this episode of *Jaufre*, there is not only a combat with a Black Knight, but this foe has a brother, a mother, and a father who was killed. Given that Guilhot learns from a messenger that the Black Knight is sending to his brother Leonet for a horse (line 650), it is possible to equate this Leonet with the Lionet (line 380) killed earlier by Blandin. This could mean that the giants' mother with the lions is the same person as *Jaufre*'s old hag. It is obvious that the adventures of Jaufre were familiar to the author of *Blandin*; the *Jaufre* romance was known throughout medieval Europe.[59] This episode in *Jaufre* would seem to have furnished the material for Guilhot's encounter at the fishpond and the earlier adventure at the castle of the imprisoned family of the damsels.

As well as from *Jaufre*, the author of *Blandin* probably drew from another source for the exact nature of the object defended. As Lewis indicates, the object is usually a spring, and *Blandin* is the only known example where the object is a fishpond. Because this seems so incongruous, we may ask if the author had some ironic intent in making a pond so important. Guilhot embodies the realistic, practical aspects of life and since his appearances often occasion some comedy, it is possible that the fishpond is part of the ironic humor associated with him.[60]

The duration of the defense of the pond has many analogs. The hermit tells Guilhot that the Black Knight has been the guardian of *lo bosch e lo vergier* for seven years (lines 814–15), and this is the traditional length of time between challengers of a custom. In *Yvain*, Calogrenant relates an

[59] Nelli and Lavaud, eds., *Le roman de Jaufre*, 17: "La popularité de *Jaufre*, qui a dû être très grande, est attesté par un fait significatif: son histoire était peinte à fresque sur les parois de la chambre ... du palais des rois d'Aragon à Saragosse." Ross Arthur's description of the spread of the story includes adaptations in French, Spanish, and Tagalog (*Jaufre: An Occitan Arthurian Romance*, x).

[60] See Lacy, "Halfway to Quixote." Loomis has an interesting comment on the name of Esclados in *Yvain*, which may have some bearing on the name of the pond. The messenger tells Guilhot that the Black Knight may be found in a plain called Claus Cubert (line 662). Perhaps the place has been confused with the man, for Loomis says of Esclados, "If we subtract the *es* from Esclados, the remaining element suggests the name of a king hostile to Arthur in the *Vulgate Lancelot*, Claudas de la Terre Deserte" (*Arthurian Tradition*, 282). Claudas might then become the Claus, which, instead of being applied to the Black Knight, was applied to the place he defended.

adventure which had happened to him seven years before, when he had unwittingly challenged and been defeated by the keeper of a magic fountain (line 173); whereupon his cousin Yvain avenges the family honor by defeating the keeper, thereby continuing the seven-year pattern. In the *Joie de la Cort* episode of *Erec et Enide*, Mabonagrain has successfully defended an orchard against all comers for seven years prior to Erec's arrival, because of a pledge he made to his mistress (lines 6059–74). Gauvain claims that he would rather die or languish in prison for seven years than break his faith (*Perceval*, line 6176),[61] and in *Le Bel Inconnu* there are two seven-year customs mentioned. The first concerns Blioblïeris who has defended the Perilous Ford for seven years but who is at last defeated by the hero as a test of prowess; his prowess is again tested by another custom, reminiscent of the *Joie de la Cort* episode in *Erec*. Elie explains that the knight who can successfully defend a *pavillions* for seven years may, at the end of that period, marry the *Pucele as Blances Mains*.[62] Given the similarities with *Blandin*, Renaut de Beaujeu's *Le Bel Inconnu* is most likely to have been close to the source of this episode.

Healed by the Hermit, Retribution Befalls Guilhot

Guilhot meets a hermit who heals the wounds sustained in his fight with the Black Knight. Hermits are also a commonplace of romance; instances of special interest are the hermit in *Yvain*, the hermit in the *Conte del Graal*, and the hermit in *Jaufre*. In *Yvain*, the hermit does not really heal Yvain but provides him with bread and water (line 2838); it is the lady of Noroison who heals him with the salve she sends. Nevertheless, the hermit does look after Yvain's needs to some extent. The *Conte del Graal*'s hermit helps Perceval understand his family history and reminds the hero of his mission, a different kind of healing. In *Jaufre*, it is the hermit who explains the nature of the Black Knight, whom the hermit dismisses, since he is a holy man and the other is a devil. The hermit expresses fear for Jaufre's

[61] While most *Perceval* manuscripts present a seven-year period, the manuscript known as the Guiot text (Paris, BnF f.fr. 794) reads eight years (see Chrétien de Troyes, *Le roman de Perceval*, ed. Busby).

[62] Lines 1955, 2009–24. The line references are given for the texts previously cited. A reign of seven years rather than the traditional eight (cf. Frazer, *The Golden Bough*, 369) has been explained by Graves in *The White Goddess*, 128, as originating in the primitive Thessalian religion.

safety (lines 5608–9) in case the brother of the demon should appear, and the hermit in *Blandin* does exactly the same (lines 819–22).

Having been healed by the hermit and having stayed eight days (lines 2026), which is the same as the time spent by Jaufre at the dwelling of his hermit (line 5653), Guilhot rides out and encounters the second Black Knight, whom he slays. He is dining in a meadow when the family of the Black Knight rides up and challenges Guilhot. This incident is strongly reminiscent of the *Chanson de Roland*, where Roland is beset by Saracens who seem to be inter-related. This, indeed, is not the only echo of *Roland* to be found in the episode. Earlier, Guilhot had gone to fetch water for the dying knight, in much the same way as Turpin does for Roland (laisse CLXV), and when the knight dies, Guilhot puts him in the pond so that wild beasts will not eat his body (lines 783–84). Similar sentiments are expressed in *Roland* when the heroes are buried (laisse CLXXVIII), although this practice would have been common in the Middle Ages.

Blandin's Adventures (lines 985–1865)

This section can also be divided into three episodes. There is, first, Blandin's encounter with the *donzella d'otra mar*, the overseas damsel. No sooner has he left her than he meets Peytavin and becomes involved with the rescue of Brianda, which comprises the second major episode, the combat with the ten guardian knights. His success leads to the third, the release of the enchantment, with its three attendant perils.

The donzella d'otra mar

We noted earlier that *romanciers* used the term *outremer* in its Crusading sense to refer to the East; it might be supposed that the damsel whom Blandin meets in the wood is from that part of the world. René Nelli takes a different view in this extract from the *dictat*, for he considers that *oltra mar* "is without doubt Great Britain."[63] Since he has assumed that the *Conivalha* of line 1038 refers to the French region of Cornouaille, whose principle city is Quimper in Brittany,[64] his theory is plausible. However, given that the damsel is sent to the spot by Brianda (cf. line 1777), and

[63] "L'outre-mer, c'est sans doute ici la Grande-Bretagne," Nelli and Lavaud, eds., *Blandin de Cornouailles*, 453n1.

[64] Nelli and Lavaud, eds., *Blandin de Cornouailles*, 451n2.

that Brianda retains some of the traits of Morgain (see below), it can also be assumed that *otra mar* refers to the Otherworld or the fairy world, of which Brianda may be a part.

The damsel's role as a messenger for Brianda is similar to that of a damsel in a story told by Andreas Capellanus, especially because Blandin, in greeting her, asks for her love (lines 999–1002).[65] As Andreas recounts:

> A knight met in a forest a beautiful damsel sitting on a caparisoned steed. She had preternatural knowledge of his errand, for she informed him that his lady had imposed as a condition of her favor that he should win a hawk in Arthur's court and prove in combat that he enjoyed the love of a damsel more beautiful than any at the court. He recognized that he needed the damsel's assistance to complete the adventure. She gave him the kiss of love and offered him her own steed, declaring that it would take him to his destination. After surmounting various trials of his prowess, the knight won the hawk and returned to find the damsel at the same place. She rejoiced over his victory and promised that whenever he, alone, sought her in that place, he would find her there.[66]

The correspondences with Blandin's adventure are so many that it may be presumed that the author of *Blandin* used Andreas Capellanus as a source for this part of this story. Blandin requests the love of the unknown maiden, and she provides him with a horse to accomplish the next part of his adventure, though it must be admitted that she does this in a far more roundabout way than the maiden in Andreas's story. Blandin is not aware that he has been chosen to deliver Brianda from her enchantment by capturing the hawk, but the damsel knows (cf. lines 1776–81) for it is she who has chosen him. There is no doubt that she corresponds to the lone damsel in Andreas's version; the details are so similar that it must have been the source of the episode in *Blandin*.[67]

The fact that Brianda causes Blandin to ride a horse which she has provided would indicate that she is linked with the fairy tradition and with Morgain in particular. It is one of Morgain's attributes that she fur-

[65] This is also a stock situation found in the *pastourelle*: a knight espies a maiden or peasant singing a love song and requests her favors or even rapes her (Gravdal, *Ravishing Maidens*, 104–21; Paden, *The Medieval Pastourelle*, 1:ix).

[66] Andreas Capellanus, *De amore*, ed. Walsh, summarizing pages 270–81.

[67] In most versions similar to this incident, the hero is aware of an adventure concerning a hawk, cf. Loomis, *Arthurian Tradition*, 90.

nishes her lover or protégé with a magnificent steed which is usually white. Newstead cited the example from the *Roman de Troie* and other examples from romances which show that this was a common motif.[68]

Because of these two elements—the meeting with the *donzella d'otra mar*, who, in Andreas Capellanus's version, has been identified as a fay and the provision of a horse—it may be concluded that Blandin's adventure involves the fairy Otherworld and has its source in Andreas and in the Celtic Arthurian tradition.

Defeat of the Knights

It is only after Blandin has met Peytavin that he learns of the enchanted woman and the knights who must be slain before she can be released. Whoever can defeat them in combat wins the hand of Brianda (lines 1133–35). This episode completes the later form of the custom, begun by Guilhot earlier with his defeat of the Black Knight at the pond. Lewis has recorded all the instances in romances where this custom appears and concludes that the main theme is "the defence of the spring—the single combat between the challenger and the strong man who defends the spring, the defeat of the defender and the marriage of the wife of the latter to the victor, who then succeeds to the dead man's domains and becomes in his turn the guardian of the spring."[69]

Even though there is no spring in the episode of the castle of Pesme Avanture in *Yvain*, this has been seen as a form of the defense of a custom; the same is true of the *Joie de la Cort* episode in *Erec*.[70] In these two

[68] Newstead, "The Besieged Ladies in Arthurian Romance," 817. "The gift of a fine steed and white armor by the queen of Meideland to her mortal protégé Lanzelet is another link to the traditions of Morgain, for Morgain's gift of a wonderful horse to her favourite is one of the most distinctive motifs in her legend. According to the *Roman de Troie*, Morgain la Fée bestowed such a horse on Hector, for whom she cherished an unrequited passions. ... In *Floriant et Florete*, Morgain, like the queen of Meideland, gives her foster son a horse, 'le plus biau destrier / Qui soit el mont,' and white armor. And in the English *Sir Launfal*, a cognate of the Breton lais of *Graelent* and *Lanval*, a fay whose characteristics identify her with Morgain gives the hero her own marvellous white steed. These are a few examples, among many that can be cited, of a widespread motif traceable to early Celtic tradition." For an almost complete survey of instances where Morgain has supplied the hero with arms and a horse, see Loomis, "Morgain la Fée and the Celtic Goddesses," 183–92.

[69] Lewis, *Classical Mythology*, 87.

[70] Lewis, *Classical Mythology*, 91–92.

examples, mention is made of the valiant knights who tried the test and failed; in *Erec*, the heads of the vanquished are impaled on stakes. It is perhaps from this tradition that the ten guardian knights originate, entrusted with their task by Brianda's father (lines 1333–34), for there is also what Lewis describes as the romantic version of the custom. "These lines [*Le Bel Inconnu*, lines 2013–17] undoubtedly contain the essential feature of the 'custom': the châtelaine was bound by the 'custom' to marry the slayer of her lover. In other words, she passed into the possession of the victor as the prize of victory."[71] He goes on to give later examples, adding, "This romantic version of the 'custom,' as we may call it, the version as it exists in the episode of La Joie de la Cort and in the *Livre d'Artus*, became most popular, for it occurs again in *Meraugis de Portlesguez*, in the prose *Merlin*, and in Malory's *Morte d'Arthur*, book VII."[72]

The mention of the failure of many good knights to achieve this test in both *Yvain* and *Erec* provides the link with *Blandin*, along with the fact that Brianda is the prize for whoever can defeat the knights. We note that Peytavin makes no mention of the other three tests which will secure Brianda's release. It may be assumed that only the knight who passed the first test and defeated the ten knights could proceed to the next stage.

Sleeping Beauty and Brianda's Release

This episode of the story is the most interesting in terms of analogies, for the combination of the tests and the enchantment seems to exist only in *Blandin*. There are many medieval examples of enchantment of places, but relatively few of persons. One notable case is in *Le Bel Inconnu*, where Blonde Esmeree is transformed into a snake by two enchanters, Madon and Evrain, until the hero Guinglain accomplishes the adventure of the *fier baiser*, kissing her in her monster form so that she can regain her human form. Guinglain eventually marries her.

A closer model for Brianda's enchantment may be found in the early thirteenth-century prose romance of *Perceforest* (Book 3, chapters 50, 52, 59, and 60[73]). In this story, dated to roughly 1320–1340 and composed in the Picard dialect of Old French,[74] we learn of three goddesses, invited

[71] Lewis, *Classical Mythology*, 115.

[72] Lewis, *Classical Mythology*, 116.

[73] We follow the chapter numbering in Roussineau's edition.

[74] Oster, "Les six réveils de la Belle au bois dormant," 231; Taylor sets the dates as

to a meal in honor of a girl named Zellandine. The first goddess gives the child good health; the second goddess, insulted because of a social error, curses the child, promising that a piece of flax caught in her finger will make her fall asleep and stay asleep until the flax is removed; the third goddess, Venus, prophesizes that all will turn out well in the end.

As would happen, one day when Zellandine was spinning, she fell into a mysterious sleep from which no one could wake her. For her protection, her father put Zellandine in a room in a high tower, sealing all but one window; the tower was surrounded by a moat. Troylus, who had fallen in love with Zellandine earlier in the story, manages to get across the moat, but cannot enter the tower. Abetted by a magical bird-shaped messenger, Troylus is transported to the window sill of Zellandine's bedroom. Encouraged by Venus, he rapes the sleeping princess and then exchanges a ring he had received from her earlier with one she is wearing. Troylus then escapes from the castle on the back of the magical bird. Nine months later, Zellandine gives birth. Sucking on his mother's finger, the infant removes the splinter of flax, and Zellandine awakens. She and Troylus are reunited and depart for Britain.

Sleeping Beauty has become a well-known story, cataloged by scholars as Stith Thompson number D1960.3, folktale number ATU 410.[75] Jeanne Lods argues that the complete Sleeping Beauty *récit* has five elements:

1. the cause of the enchantment,
2. the accident that caused it,
3. the arrival of the prince,
4. the princess's awakening,
5. the fate of the prince, the princess, and eventually their children,[76] all seen in the version found in *Perceforest*.

In *Blandin*, the precise nature of Brianda's enchantment is never specified, though we know that her father is responsible for the spell, casting it after

slightly later, 1330–1350, *Le roman de Perceforest*, 29.

[75] Neemann, "Schlafende Schönheit"; see Thompson, *Motif-Index of Folk-Literature*; Uther, *The Types of International Folktales*; and Barchilon, "L'histoire de *La Belle au bois dormant*."

[76] Lods, *Le roman de Perceforest*, 84–85.

he had lost his lands. Given that she has seven maidens to attend to her needs, we can assume that she is in some form of deep sleep. *Blandin*'s version of Sleeping Beauty has the all elements that mark the folktale except the accident that leads to the sleep; it certainly includes the travails of the prince who will break the spell—the most creative activities in the *Blandin* retelling—and the happy ending. Truly unique in *Blandin* is Brianda's agency, even while under the spell: she will claim it was she who sent a damsel to seek help (lines 1775–82), exactly how we do not know, unlike her more passive brother, who simply waited for help to arrive.[77] Interesting in the *Blandin* version is the beauty's position, seated rather than lying on the bed. Emese Egedi-Kovács suggests that the Sleeping Beauty episode is the most original element of our tale,[78] and that the *Blandin* author knew his audience would be very familiar with a "*donna encantada* enfermée dans une tour," an enchanted lady imprisoned in a tower.[79]

There exists yet another medieval version of Sleeping Beauty, the plot of *Frayre de Joy e Sor de Plaser*, a Catalan story that also dates from the fourteenth century. *Frayre de Joy* shares more elements with the *Perceforest* version of the folktale than with the *Blandin* author's recounting.[80] Gilles Roussineau sums up well the relations between the three roughly contemporaneous texts, observing that they represent the oral tradition of Sleeping Beauty in literary form.[81] With Esther Zago and Emese Egedi-Kovács, we think the *Blandin* author developed his Sleeping Beauty motif independently of *Perceforest* and of *Frayre de Joy e Sor de Plaser*.[82] Though

[77] Brianda appears to be the dominant figure in this household; note that Blandin asks her if Yrlanda can marry Guilhot (lines 2323–26), before their brother, the only male in the family, is brought into the conversation (lines 2349–50).

[78] Egedi-Kovács, *La "morte vivante,"* 200.

[79] Egedi-Kovács, *La "morte vivante,"* 204.

[80] See Roussineau, "Tradition littéraire et culture populaire," 35–37.

[81] Roussineau, "Tradition littéraire et culture populaire," 38: "Les trois textes représentent, sous une forme organisée et littéraire, un conte spécifique—la Belle endormie—où se retrouvent des motifs communs qui appartiennent à la tradition orale. Ils sont à la fois une élaboration de lettrés et une expression de la culture populaire."

[82] Egedi-Kovács, *La "morte vivante,"* 204, citing Zago, "Some Medieval Versions of Sleeping Beauty," 424. See also Roussineau, ed., *Perceforest*, 1:xxiii: "Il serait vain, en effet, de vouloir établir des rapports de filiation entre les trois récits." Roussineau is speaking of *Perceforest*, *Frayre de Joy*, and Giambattista Basile's *Sole, Luna e Talia* and does not include *Blandin* here; his observation stands for our text as well.

Blandin and *Perceforest* both rely on a bird to break the spell, the birds function very differently in the two versions.

In *Perceforest* and in *Frayre de Joy e Sor de Plaser*, the Sleeping Beauty is raped while sleeping, associating fecundity with unconsciousness.[83] Roussineau asks where Charles Perrault may have found the source for his virginal Beauty, to which one answer might be *Blandin*, whose heroine is not attacked before she is awakened, a unique element in the medieval versions of the folktale.[84]

The three adversaries which Blandin has to defeat before capturing the white bird do not appear frequently in that combination in medieval romances. A serpent, associated with the devil and all things evil (from Genesis), is a common foe. In *Yvain*, the hero comes across a lion caught in the coils of a serpent, and Yvain rescues the lion. As well as the serpent, the dragon was associated with the devil and with evil; the double combination which occurs in *Blandin* is uncommon in the romances.[85]

According to Newstead, a commonplace of romances associated with Bran or Bran-type figures is the combat with a fiery foe, though the dragon in *Blandin* does not really constitute a fiery foe. Medieval bestiaries do not associate dragons with flames—that weapon is assigned to the basilisk.[86] Occasionally authors of romances would distinguish between a dragon and a fire-drake; presumably the latter roared fire while the former did not.[87]

The enchanted Saracen is a new element insofar as can be ascertained, although his general description (lines 1418–26) is similar to that of the Giant Herdsman in *Yvain*, without the details of color. The Saracen

[83] Roussineau, ed., *Perceforest*, 1:xxv, citing Soriano, *Les contes de Perrault*, 129.

[84] Léglu notes the differences between Brianda's chastity and the rapes in the parallel narratives, *Multilingualism and Mother Tongue*, 109.

[85] Cf. Brodeur, "The Grateful Lion," 510. "The antithesis of lion and dragon, a ready inference from scriptural symbolism, received wide currency from early Christian times, and enjoyed increasing popularity during the Middle Ages, through the *Physiologus* and the Bestiaries in many tongues. In these documents—the origin of much mediaeval beast-lore—the lion is invariably the symbol of Christ, or of God; and the serpent or dragon commonly represents Satan."

[86] McCulloch, *Medieval Latin and French Bestiaries*, 93 for the basilisk and its association with fire; 112–13 for the dragon. The *Elucidari* does not mention fire in connection with the basilisk (Hershon and Ricketts, eds., 513).

[87] Cf. Newstead, *Bran the Blessed*, 98, 102, 153.

is black, and the Giant Herdsman resembled a Moor, so the details correspond in general fashion.[88] The loss of the Saracen's strength, a unique Achilles' heel, would seem to be a variant of the Samson story (Book of Judges: 13–16), and it is strange that his magic fortitude should reside in his teeth. The only reference to teeth in the romance literature is found in *Huon de Bordeaux*, where the young hero is condemned by Charlemagne to the impossible quest of demanding an enormous tribute from the emir of Babylon, including a handful of hairs from his beard and four of his greatest teeth. Huon is helped in this task by Auberon, identified as the son of Morgain and Julius Caesar. Perhaps the *donzel*, Brianda's brother, who is such a help to Blandin, could be identified with Auberon, although it does seem rather remote. Usually it is a dragon that is the fiercest trial for a medieval hero, so *Blandin* is exceptional is giving the Saracen final position.[89]

The importance of the white hunting bird to the release of Brianda is not found elsewhere, although there is a tradition involving a quest for a hunting bird, usually a sparrow-hawk.[90] Roger Sherman Loomis has compiled evidence to show that Morgain is traditionally the heroine of the sparrow-hawk adventure, in which her beauty enables her champion to carry off the prize,[91] but he also comments that

> Chrétien's account of the sparrow-hawk contest and its eleven analogs in romance reveal on close scrutiny that they constitute merely one group in a much larger class of *contes* concerned with a testing talisman which is displayed, usually in Arthur's court, and which serves to prove the hero and his lady-love superior to all others.[92]

Andreas Capellanus's *récit* is in this mold.[93] In *Blandin*, Arthur's court is never mentioned, but the capture of the hawk serves a definite function in

[88] Colby, *The Portrait in Twelfth-Century French Literature*, maintains that "If ... the individual were said to be ugly, the listener had good reason to suspect that he would play an important but unpleasant role in the story and that, being wicked, he merited no sympathy at all. A deliberate exception such as the Giant Herdsman must have been a very effective means of surprising the listener" (99).

[89] See Honegger, *Introducing the Medieval Dragon*, 94.

[90] Citing the Second Book of Kings 4:34–35, Marjorossy connects this hawk and its powers to a biblical tradition; see Majorossy, "Aventures en deux directions," 468–69.

[91] Loomis, *Arthurian Tradition*, 86 and 99–100.

[92] Loomis, *Arthurian Tradition*, 95.

[93] Andreas Capellanus, *De amore*, 270–71.

releasing Brianda from her spell. The hawk in Andreas Capellanus has an additional function, because fastened to its perch are the rules written by the King of Love.[94] Since it is obvious from the encounter of Blandin with the *donzella d'otra mar* that the author of *Blandin* was well acquainted with *De amore*, it is significant that in rescuing the hawk and freeing Brianda, Blandin also receives her love.[95]

Once the quest is achieved and Brianda is freed, they all have a feast in a beautiful orchard where the birds sing love songs (lines 1741–42). Earlier on, when Blandin had entered the orchard (lines 1299–300), the singing of the birds had made him extremely sleepy.[96] Birds that sing sleep-inducing music are acknowledged as coming from Celtic tradition; there is the account in the *Serglige Conculaind* where two birds linked together by a chain of gold visited a lake in Ulster and by their singing put the host to sleep.[97] In this same work, says Brown,

> [T]he landscape of the Other World is rather fully described. It is marked by splendid trees full of singing birds. These trees bear fruit, and three hundred men are nourished by the fruit of each tree. One notable tree stands at the door of the Other-World palace, and the harmonious song of the birds upon it is particularly dwelt on.[98]

The birds in the orchard, then, are yet another indication that Blandin's adventure takes place in a Celtic or fairy Otherworld.

A final note concerns Blandin's desire to have nothing but Brianda's love as his reward (lines 1666–70). This is very similar to the passage in *Jaufre* where the hero tells Brunissen that he wants not her land nor her silver, but simply her love (lines 7964–77). The two passages are strikingly similar and add evidence to the hypothesis of direct borrowing by the *Blandin* author from *Jaufre*.

94 Andreas Capellanus, *De amore*, 280–81.

95 Cf. Adler, "Sovereignty as the Principle of Unity in Chrétien's *Erec*," 922: "A contemporary audience of the *Erec* may well have seen in their mind, fastened to the Sparrow-hawk's perch, the parchment on which (as André was going to tell them later on in the century) were written the rules of love as the King of Love himself had pronounced them."

96 See Pfeffer, "The Birds and the Bees and *Blandin de Cornoalha*."

97 Brown, *Iwain*, 34; cf. Lewis, *Classical Mythology*, 78–86.

98 Brown, *Iwain*, 84.

Resolution (lines 1865–2405)

The resolution serves as a recapitulation of Guilhot's exploits as Blandin looks for him, and the only two new adventures do not provide any new evidence for the sources used by the author. The combat with the lord of the castle in order to set Guilhot free is such a commonplace of literature—combat by sworn friends on each other's behalf—that it is impossible to trace it to any particular source.

The marriage of two sworn comrades to sisters would seem to be unique to *Blandin*. It is a neat and convenient way to tidy up loose ends or persons, and it enables the two heroes to settle down to conjugal bliss in the same spot at the same time. Marie-Geneviève Grossel suggests that the wedding of hero and heroine at the end of *Jaufre* can be read as the union of the troubadour themes of *Joven* and *Amor*, youth and love.[99] The weddings that conclude *Blandin* may have their roots in the ending of *Jaufre*, though we cannot say that *Blandin* concludes with a similar celebration of poetic virtues.

Conclusions

Arthur C. L. Brown, in his study of *Iwain*, made the following observation,

> Everybody knows that the most complicated story can be taken apart into simple elements, and these simple elements can then be found separately almost anywhere. It is not the finding of a single element that proves a source. The combination of elements alone is significant. The more elements already in combination a supposed source can show, the stronger, other things being equal, is the probability of its being the true one.[100]

In a work like *Blandin*, a late production with elements from different traditions, it is difficult to posit a specific source. There are significant correspondences with *Jaufre*, the well-known Occitan Arthurian romance; it may be assumed that the author of *Blandin* knew *Jaufre*. But the problem of the ultimate source of *Blandin* is one which is more difficult to resolve, as it seems unlikely that a single source exists. Nevertheless, there are many elements in *Blandin* that could ultimately come from a single source.

[99] Grossel, "Conclure le roman en terre d'oc," 133.

[100] Brown, *Iwain*, 7.

There have been frequent references to the custom motif found in *Blandin*, and it is possible to see most of the major episodes referring in some way to a form of the custom. To see this as a source, we must first take into account the medieval device of duplication of material and persons. Lewis has shown that this device may be noted particularly in Chrétien's *Yvain*.

> We are familiar now with this process of duplication which Chrestien so often practised in order to embellish or spin out his story, and we have already drawn attention to it in the case of the Vavassor and the Lord of the Castle [p. 149], in the case of the Monster Herdsman and the two Netuns [p. 157 and p. 180], and in the case of the Vavassor's daughter and Lunete [p. 155 f.] .... On the strength of these considerations it might be argued that Chrestien duplicated in the same way the rôle of the hero in his story and out of one made two, namely Calogrenant and Yvain. On the other hand, it may well have been that Chrestien's source, if it was, as we think, the legend of Theseus and the Minotaur, told of one or more heroes who at certain recurring intervals came to try conclusions with the Minotaur. In that case Chrestien, by merely following his source, would have been led to repeat a large portion of his narrative with but little change, and that would account for the repetition there is in the rôles of Calogrenant and Yvain.[101]

Following Lewis's conclusions about *Yvain*, it is possible to argue that Guilhot and Blandin were one and the same person in the source of *Blandin*. If this were the case, many of the incidents could be explained as coming from just one source, that of the custom group of stories.

In agreement with this hypothesis is the fact that Guilhot is involved in a combat with a knight who is the guardian of a fishpond and who is also *gardant lo bosch et lo vergier* (line 815). This description would seem to correspond with the episode of the magic fountain in *Yvain*, and it is significant to note that Guilhot is associated with lions, killing two at the castle in the first adventure. Moreover, the poet mentions that Guilhot *se portet come un leon* (line 941). The connection with Chrétien's *Yvain* is seen again in the earlier part of Blandin's adventure, for he frees two damsels from the clutches of a giant, similar to the Pesme Avanture episode in *Yvain*, and which Lewis has seen as a form of the custom.[102]

[101] Lewis, *Classical Mythology*, 197–98.

[102] Lewis, *Classical Mythology*, 2–3.

The romantic form of the custom involved the marriage of the hero with the woman he rescued from the hands of the giant or other personage who was the defender of the spring or sacred spot. In Blandin's main adventure, he rescues a woman, not from a giant, but from an enchantment; to do this, he has to negotiate three fierce creatures, one of which is an enchanted and possibly gigantic Saracen. Lewis has pointed out that Chrétien uses duplication of characters, and it is possible that the author of *Blandin* used this same device, that out of one fierce foe he made several. It is interesting to note that the two damsels rescued by Blandin offer themselves to him, as the prize for his defeat of the giant. Later, Peytavin tells him that whoever can defeat the ten knights who guard Brianda can have her. The woman as the prize of victory is a most consistent element in the accounts of the custom. In discussing duplication in *Yvain*, Lewis remarks of the main adventure and the Pesme Avanture episode:

> In both the combat takes place early the next morning, and in each case the host seems to know beforehand exactly what is before his guest. Lastly, the issue of the adventure is almost the same in both passages. Yvain, the conqueror of Esclados, marries the widow of his dead adversary and becomes lord of his castle and lands. In the episode of Pesme Avanture the Lord of the Castle tells Yvain in unequivocal terms that the conqueror of the two Netuns is to have his daughter to wife and to succeed to his castle and lands.[103]

It would then seem that Guilhot starts one major part of the adventure by killing the Black Knight, and Blandin completes it by marrying Brianda, succeeding to all her lands and treasure. (Guilhot tidily marries her sister, but not much is said about that.)

The fact that Brianda seems to be surrounded by so many fairy elements—the provision of a horse for the hero, the singing birds in the marvelous garden, and the whole atmosphere of magic and enchantment—is not incompatible with the theory that *Blandin* ultimately comes from the custom defense story. Many scholars have seen Laudine as a fairy mistress figure,[104] and Brown, in particular, advances the idea that Laudine displays

[103] Lewis, *Classical Mythology*, 93.

[104] Philipot, "Un épisode d'*Erec et Enide*," 279 and Review of *Studies on the Libeaus Desconus*, 303, where he does admit: "Il a fallu tous les efforts de la critique philologique pur démontrer qu'Esclados le Roux était un géant, Laudine une fée ...."

the traits common to Celtic fairies. His comment is interesting in view of Brianda's behavior in *Blandin*.

> Everyone, it will be observed, who has advocated what may be called the fairy mistress explanation of the romance of *Ivain*, has looked for a source in Celtic tradition. This is evidently the natural view. Chrétien practically tells us that he is following a *conte*, which he evidently expects us to regard as based on Celtic tradition; nearly all the names of the *dramatis personae* are Celtic; and the scene is laid in Wales or Armorica. There is, moreover, a special reason why this antecedent probability that the story of *Ivain* comes from Celtic sources is very great. The Celtic fées are distinctly superior beings, never surprised and taken captive by the hero, as Germanic fairies regularly are, but dwelling like Laudine in a magic land, which must be visited by the hero, who thus puts himself in their power before his courtship even begins. They retain their superiority and, like Iwain's mistress, insist on being obeyed even in the verbal details of a promise or else they punish and forsake their lover, who is always thought of as in their power. Evidently it is from creatures like these, as distinguished from German and other fairies, that such a character as Laudine must be derived.[105]

The evidence to connect Laudine with the fairy mistress tradition is textually very slight, but the traditional behavior of a Celtic fairy mistress matches the behavior of Brianda fairly closely. She is the one who has sent the *donzella d'otra mar* in search of a suitable knight to deliver her from her enchantment, and in spite of the enchantment laid on her by her father, she still seems in control of her situation. She dwells in a magic land, and Blandin is obliged to go in search of her. In most of the traits enumerated by Brown, Brianda would appear to fall into the fairy mistress category, and hence she can be considered part of the custom motif of the defense of a sacred spot and the marriage of the hero to the fairy mistress of the defender.

From this it would seem that if an ultimate source for the material used in the composition of *Blandin* can be posited, it could be found in the custom of the defense of a sacred spot and the marriage of the hero to a fairy mistress whose castle is usually near the spot. As Lacy noted, "Customs in medieval romance are an extraordinary phenomenon, and we cannot fail to be impressed by the extent to which romance texture

[105] Brown, *Iwain*, 25–26.

is woven from customal threads. ... They are also a crucial element in the generation and elaboration of narrative material."[106] The tale of *Blandin* is constructed of variations on the theme of custom, with the additional trick of splitting the original hero in two, such that half of the adventure is accomplished by Guilhot and the final half by Blandin. This division of the hero would also support the argument for a bipartite form for the whole *dictat*.

More immediate sources of *Blandin* include Occitan romances, with one or two minor references to *Flamenca* and the majority from *Jaufre*. Echoes of Chrétien's romances as well as *Le Bel Inconnu* have been found throughout, but these may well be simply part of the store of Arthurian commonplaces which the author could draw upon. The conclusion is that the author used the romantic version of the custom motif and borrowed heavily from *Jaufre* for some of the details.

[106] Lacy, "On Customs in Medieval French Romance," 985.

Travels of the Narrative

As *BLANDIN DE CORNOALHA* ends in a double wedding, it would be plausible to associate the *dictat* with some important wedding in Occitania, in the second half of the fourteenth century. One of the most politically significant Occitan weddings of that period was that arranged by Gaston Febus (1331–1391), Count of Foix and Viscount of Béarn, for his only legitimate son, also named Gaston. Gaston Febus, the father, had been battling with the Armagnac family for years, most famously fighting the Armagnac's at the battle of Launac in 1362.[1] Though the Armagnac side was thoroughly defeated, the two houses continued diplomatic skirmishes for years afterwards, a feud that has been called "the other Hundred Years' War."

In an effort to make peace between the two households, a wedding was arranged between Gaston Febus's son, Gaston (1362–1380), and Beatritz d'Armagnac (ca. 1365–post 1410), the daughter of the head of the Armagnac clan at this time, John II d'Armagnac (1333–1384); the wedding occurred in April 1379.[2] A wedding was usually celebrated with various entertainments, and a clever author might have jumped at the opportunity to compose a text for this event, in hopes of recompense or the opportunity to perform. It is possible that an anonymous author composed *Blandin de Cornoalha* in exactly these circumstances. However, this marriage was not celebrated with great pomp, even though it marked the end of decades of fighting between two houses each seeking to control large swaths of southwestern France. It was the opportunity to unite two different courts—that of Foix-Béarn and that of Armagnac—and establish

[1] Ransoms acquired as a result of this battle made Gaston a very rich man—he is reported to have received 600,000 florins in ransom money (Vernier, *Lord of the Pyrenees: Gaston Fébus*, 59).

[2] Pailhès, *Gaston Fébus*, 224.

peace once and for all. However, the wedding was a very quiet affair;[3] neither the Armagnac nor Foix-Béarn extended families were in attendance. We know that Gaston Febus did not attend the religious ceremony, a nuptial mass performed in Manciet (in today's department of the Gers).[4] The civil ceremony held a few days earlier also had few in attendance.

We know very little regarding the honeymoon (at the time of the ceremonies, the groom was 17; the bride perhaps 14 years old). It appears the couple may never have cohabited; Gaston the younger probably returned to his father's court, and it is possible that Beatritz, fairly young, returned to her home territory, perhaps to Rodez, a seat for the Armagnac family.[5] If the *Blandin* story had been composed for her wedding, we can imagine that she or a family member brought a copy of the text back to Rodez.

Unfortunately, perhaps unwittingly, in 1380 Gaston, the son, was involved in a plot to kill his father and was imprisoned by his father, in the tower of Moncade in Orthez. After a conversation between father and son, Gaston *fils*, the only legitimate heir, was inadvertently killed by Febus (the details are sketchy; it has been suggested that Febus accidently slit his son's throat).[6] This unfortunate family tale was thoroughly concealed by Gaston Febus. Contemporary historian Jean Froissart attempted unsuccessfully to investigate, but the details of the death remain the mystery of Febus's life.

In 1382, roughly two years after the death of young Gaston, Beatritz remarried, taking as husband Carlo Visconti (1359–1403), who moved his bride and her possessions to his home in Milan, Italy; if we assume she kept a hard copy of *Blandin*, it moved with her. She and Carlo had four children, a son Marco (1383–?), a daughter Verde (stillborn, 1384), a daughter Bonne (1385–1433), and a son, Giancarlo (?–1418). Given the birth dates of three of these children, we can presume that Beatritz and Carlo were a good couple, successfully bringing new Visconti's into the world.

[3] Vernier calls it "a rather low-key ceremony," *Lord of the Pyrenees*, 81.

[4] Pailhès, *Gaston Fébus*, 224.

[5] Pailhès notes that Beatritz was not present at the court of Gaston Febus in 1380 (*Gaston Fébus*, 250).

[6] By August 1381, Beatritz's family was trying to recover her dower, see Cabié, "Notes et documents sur les différends des comtes de Foix et d'Armagnac," 504 and passim.

The Visconti family was very important politically in the late fourteenth century, particularly as its members fought each other for pre-eminence in the northern Italian peninsula. Gian Galeazzo Visconti (1351–1402) was the winner of this fight, success achieved, in part, by imprisoning and poisoning his uncle, Bernabò, who was Carlo's father and Beatritz's father-in-law.

After the capture and death of Bernabò Visconti in 1385, Carlo and his family fled Milan, seeking refuge where they could. Beatritz, pregnant, went to Ripaille, near Lac Léman (today's Haute Savoie), where she gave birth to her daughter Bonne. Ripaille was chosen because her cousin Bonne de Berry lived there with her, that is Bonne's, husband Amadeus VII, Count of Savoy; Carlo went initially to Parma and then to Bavaria, where two of his sisters had married.[7] Beatritz never returned to Italy. It is possible that Beatritz took her library with her when she fled to Savoy. Alternatively, books she owned may have remained in Milan after Gian Galeazzo Visconti took control of the city.

The presence of Beatritz at the court of Savoy complicated negotiations by that court with Gian Galeazzo Visconti. In fact, the Count of Savoy signed a new treaty of alliance with Gian Galeazzo at the end of 1385.[8] It is most probable that Beatritz did not stay long with her cousin Bonne. Beatritz's daughter, young Bonne, called Bonne d'Armagnac, was born at the Savoy court[9] and would spend her early childhood there before moving to Paris in 1392, to the household of her cousin, French queen Isabeau of Bavaria. Bonne "grew up under the queen's care."[10] Bonne would marry Guillaume III de Rohan, seigneur de Montauban in Brittany.[11]

[7] José, *La maison de Savoie*, 1:303; Chamberlin, *The Count of Virtue*, 79.

[8] Camus, "La maison de Savoie et le mariage de Valentine Visconti," 122, 124–26.

[9] Cordey cites a document that would place Bonne d'Armagnac's birth in October 1386 (*Les comtes de Savoie*, 251n). If his understanding is correct, one can assume that Carlo and Beatritz did see each other after being chased from Milan. However, Cordey sets the death of Bernabò in 1384, so it is possible that his dates are wrong.

[10] See Bruchet, *Le chateau de Ripaille*, 30; Tracy Adams, *The Life and Afterlife of Isabeau of Bavaria*, 241–42.

[11] Autrand suggests that young Bonne, known as Bonne d'Armagnac or the Mademoiselle d'Armagnac, was raised by Bonne de Berry, which suggests the young girl spent her youth in the Armagnac region (*Jean de Berry*, 290). Bruchet says that young Bonne was at the Savoy court from 1387 to 1392 (*Le chateau de Ripaille*, 30n)—i.e., until the

Amadeus VII of Savoy died in 1391, leaving his widow and his mother, both named Bonne, to dispute the regency.[12] Ultimately, the widow, Bonne de Berry, left Savoy to marry her cousin Bernard VII d'Armagnac in 1393.[13] Let us remember that Bernard was Beatritz's brother. Given the probability that Beatritz had left the Savoy court well before the date of this marriage,[14] it is unlikely she had any influence on the marriage negotiations of Bonne de Berry and Bernard d'Armagnac.[15]

We know that Beatritz d'Armagnac ultimately found refuge in lands held by her brother Bernard, who supported her until she died sometime after 1410.[16] She is thought to have ended her days near Albi, at Castelnau-de-Montmiral (Tarn).[17] Paul Durrieu reports that the account books of Bernard record frequent expenses for Beatritz, such as gifts in kind and in cash and purchases of clothing for her.[18]

As for Carlo, his efforts to regain power in Italy were unsuccessful. He tried to find supporters in his fight against Gian Galeazzo, but to no avail. His travels are documented through Bavaria and Italy; there is a suggestion that he also visited Gascony, where he might have seen his

age of six or seven. Thanks to the Duke de Berry, young Bonne would serve as one of Queen Isabeau's ladies in waiting (Grandeau, "De quelques dames qui ont servi la reine Isabeau de Bavière," 237–38; Tracy Adams, *The Life and Afterlife of Isabeau*, 241–42). King Charles VI arranged her marriage to Guillaume de Montauban in 1414; the king provided her dowry (Autrand, *Jean de Berry*, 260, 290); the queen also provided her with furnishings (meubles, vaisselle d'or) (Grandeau, "De quelques dames," 238–39; BnF nouv. acq. fr. 5087, f. 161v).

12 Demotz, *Le Comté de Savoie du XIe au XVe siècle*, 50, 166–68.

13 Demotz, *Le Comté de Savoie du XIe au XVe siècle*, 167.

14 Creton suggests that Beatritz returned to Armagnac with Bonne de Berry when Bonne married Beatritz's brother (*Bonne de Bourbon*, 237); Creton is not, however, a reliable source.

15 This marriage was arranged without Bonne's agreement by the men in her family, particularly her father and her uncles (see Jarry, *La vie politique de Louis de France*, 146; Cognasso, "L'influsso francese nello Stato sabaudo," 291).

16 Durrieu, "Bernard VII," points to a BnF, Doat document, 211, f. 254, dated February 2, 1410 n.s.

17 Other members of the Armagnac family would also reside at Castelnau; Bonne d'Armagnac (the daughter of Bernard d'Armagnac and Bonne de Bercy), the wife of Charles d'Orléans, would die there between 1430 and 1435.

18 Durrieu, "Bernard VII," 22; Durrieu also points to documents in the Aveyron departmental archives, notably côtes C1341 and C1237.

wife.[19] Carlo and Gian Galeazzo signed a peace agreement in September 1391 in which Carlo admitted defeat. He renounced his claims to his father's lands and was forced into exile in Bavaria; later he was allowed to move to Venice where he would die in 1403. Giancarlo, a son of Carlo and Beatritz, would attempt to rule in the region of Milan, but he was chased from the area in 1412 by another member of the Visconti clan and would die in Paris in 1418. Bonne, the surviving daughter, maintained the family's claims to lands in Italy, in 1429 sending a letter to Joan of Arc asking that Joan help Bonne recover her property, "unjustly usurped by Gian Galeazzo."[20]

Beatritz's first language was Occitan, the language used at the Armagnac court, though we suspect all there were equally comfortable in French. There exists a letter in Occitan from Beatritz to her father;[21] the tenor of the letter leads us to think that she could probably read Occitan, even if she had dictated the letter to a scribe and could not, herself, write.[22] We have not been able to find any books directly tied to her, and the Armagnac family may not have invested heavily in literary patronage. Nonetheless, there are small signs of literary interest at this court: at least one manuscript, BnF, latin 6489, is tied to the Armagnac family.[23] The volume contains a copy of Gervais of Tilbury's *Otia imperialia*, a catalog

[19] Romano, "Gian Galeazzo Visconti e gli eredi di Bernabò," 20n.

[20] Grandeau, "De quelques dames," 239; BnF nouv. acq. fr. 5087, f. 161v.

[21] BnF coll. Doat, 202, f. 262r–v, undated but certainly before May 1384.

[22] Durrieu's transcription: "Monsieur, jou me recomande a la vostra gracia lo plus humelment que podi; et vos plassia assaber que lo maior desirier que jou aye en aquest mon, so es de saber lo vostre bon estat, loqual plassia a Nostre Seignor que sie aitals comme jou desiri; per quau jou vos pregui tant carament comma podi que lo plus souvent que poiret le me fasset assaber, quar vous m'en faret lo maiour plaser del mon. Se del estat de part nous plassia assaber; sapiat que lo senhor mossen Barnabo, madone Regine, ses enffans, Mossenhor Mossen Charles, et jou, et nostre filh estam ben, la merci de Nostre Seignour. Mossenhor Rogier Can s'en va part dela; loqual me fa tout jorn tots los plasers que pot. Per que jou vous pregui, tant carament comma podi, que per amour de mi lo vulhat aver per recomandat. Lo dit Rogier vos dira totas la nouvelles de part dessa. Monseignor, Notre Seignor vous donne bona vida et longua. Escrich a Milas, le dotsieme jor de fevrier [1384]" (*Les Gascons*, 42n).

[23] http://gallica.bnf.fr/ark:/12148/btv1b9066547z; the binding of the volume is linked to Italian Jacobus de Sancto Petro bidellus, who was alive in 1458 and is associated with Pavia (Marinis, *La legatura artistica in Italia*, 10; Pellegrin, *La bibliothèque des Visconti*, 246).

of popes, a chronicle by Bernard Gui, along with a copy of a 1383 letter in Latin from John III d'Armagnac to Carlo Visconti (f. 145v) and a short Occitan poem on avarice (f. 174v), signed by an otherwise unknown Peyrat.[24] Elisabeth Pellegrin suggests that Beatritz may have brought this book with her when she came to Milan;[25] we think the dated text in the book suggests otherwise.[26]

Beatritz's time in Italy was spent largely in Milan, the political base of Bernabò Visconti. The language of Bernabò's court was probably a dialect of Italian, though that court's fluency in French was most likely fairly strong.[27] It is unlikely that Beatritz or Carlo spent any time in Turin, to the west of Milan.

One can postulate a potential recipient for the *Blandin* manuscript by looking at its contents. The other lengthy texts included are a chronicle of the world by Jacobus de Aquis, the anonymous *Miracles of Rome*, and the *History of Jerusalem* by Jacques de Vitry, presenting one Occitan romance among historical and/or geographic texts all in Latin (see above). The volume itself has been dated to the end of the fourteenth[28] or beginning of the fifteenth century.[29] Is it possible that this volume was assembled by Beatritz for her son or sons, providing both knowledge of the world and, in *Blandin*, a model of proper behavior? The appearance of the manuscript, essentially undecorated and on paper, suggests otherwise. Given Beatritz's background and her in-law's wealth, had she commissioned a manuscript, it would have been more luxurious in presentation. What is even more likely is that the compiler of the volume thought the romance of *Blandin* was not fiction but history;[30] it is plausible that the scribe who put the pieces together was simply bringing together a series of what he considered to be historical texts. If this hypothesis is

24 Meyer, "Quatrains sur l'avarice."

25 Pellegrin, *La bibliothèque des Visconti*, 47, 246.

26 Note that Beatritz had her first child, probably in Milan, not long after the 1382 marriage. See below.

27 Certainly, in July 1384, when Bernabò wrote a letter of condolence to John III on the death of his father John II, that letter was composed in Middle French, BnF coll. Doat, 202, ff. 109r–111r; see Durrieu, *Les Gascons*, 40–41.

28 Vitale-Brovarone, personal communication with Pfeffer, March 2014; Galano, ed., *Blandin di Cornovaglia*, 35.

29 Burrell, "A Critical Edition," 3.

30 We thank Alessandro Vitale Brovarone for first giving us this idea.

correct, then Beatritz had no hand in organizing the *Blandin* manuscript, which may have been copied not too far from Alessandria, Italy. How the manuscript arrived in the Turin library is uncertain, though it has been part of the Turin collections since foundation of the library in the first third of the eighteenth century.

A different explanation for the travels of the story relates to Beatritz's birth family, the Armagnacs. When Beatritz and her second husband Carlo were chased from Milan, her family tried to come to their rescue. Her brother John III signed an alliance with the city of Florence in 1390, promising to come to the city's aid against Gian Galeazzo Visconti. John united a large army, composed largely of marauders who had been harassing much of France in the 1380s,[31] and crossed the Alps, hoping to defeat Gian Galeazzo. Given the length of time it took John to assemble this army (the alliance was signed in October 1390; the army moved into Italy in June 1391),[32] he may well have carried a small library with him, perhaps including *Blandin*. We are suggesting here that the text of *Blandin* remained in Rodez after Beatritz's departure in 1382. In July 1391, John d'Armagnac engaged in a battle near Alessandria with mercenaries hired by Gian Galeazzo; John miscalculated badly in terms of men, terrain, and conditions, most specifically, the July heat.[33] John lost the fight badly, was taken prisoner, and died almost immediately afterward, perhaps of hyperthermia, that is, heat stroke.[34] Our hypothesis is that it was he who carried *Blandin* to Italy, where the text landed close to Alessandria, near where John d'Armagnac died. Of all attempts to explain the story's travels, this one seems the most plausible; it explains how the text arrived in Italy around the time the manuscript itself was being copied. Near Alessandria, perhaps in a monastery,[35] the text could have been copied into what is today the Turin manuscript.

[31] Bueno de Mesquita, *Giangaleazzo Visconti*, 124.

[32] John had reason to support his sister's claims; the King of France, Charles VI, had his own connections to Gian Galeazzo and did not want John to move against him (see Bueno de Mesquito, *Giangaleazzo Visconti*, 124–25). The French wanted the marauders out of France, but not necessarily attacking Gian Galeazzo (see Chamberlin, *The Count of Virtue*, 142–44; Romano, "Gian Galeazzo Visconti e gli eredi di Bernabò," 34–40).

[33] Bueno de Mesquita, *Giangaleazzo Visconti*, 131–32; see the details provided by Froissart, cited by Varvaro, *La tragédie de l'histoire*, 146–47.

[34] Durrieu, *Les Gascons*, 80–89.

[35] Busby provides examples of Italian monastic interest in secular works, *Codex and Context*, 2:787.

The manuscript that has preserved *Blandin* is fairly well known to scholars of the Roland legend, because Jacobus de Aquis included elements of two *chansons de geste* in his *récit*, referring to the Roland legend and to the story of Otinel, another epic hero, in his chronicle, the *Cronice libri imaginis mundi*, the first text in the volume.[36] The one illustration in the manuscript is an amateurish color illustration of the death of Ganelon by hanging (f. 40v; see Fig. 1). Given this mix of history and fiction in the first text in the volume now in Turin, it is possible that the scribe perceived the story of *Blandin* as history, copying the text into the book as well.

[36] Busby discusses Italian interest in *chanson de geste* material, arguing that northern Italy showed a "general enthusiasm for French literature," *Codex and Context*, 2:620.

Dating the Text

BURRELL SPOKE OF a "lack of scrupulousness in choosing the literary Provençal forms of words,"[1] observing that this lack of care pointed to a later date of composition; she suggested no earlier than the mid-thirteenth century and probably nearer to early fourteenth century in origin.[2] Alart proposed after 1330;[3] van der Horst dates *Blandin* to post 1350;[4] Galano opens the dating to sometime during the fourteenth century;[5] Asperti's research on the specific term *bacinet* points to the third quarter of the fourteenth century.[6] We agree with Asperti.

All linguistic evidence points to a text based firmly in the region of Languedoc, with occasional input from Catalan, French, and Italian, this last particularly in the manuscript's orthography. We agree with Galano that the language seen in this text is not representative of a specific place in Occitania, but is yet another example of a common literary language, mutually understood in all corners of the larger region.

Blandin de Cornoalha may well have been composed at a flourishing intellectual center, where there were trading and cultural ties to the North as well as to the South. The author is familiar with a wide swath of medieval literary works and uses his knowledge to poke fun of genres, even as he creates a genre of his own. The court of Gaston Febus is one that conforms to a flourishing center with literary aspirations; the description also suits large cities in Languedoc such as Toulouse or Montpellier,

[1] Burrell, "A Critical Edition," 112.

[2] Burrell, "A Critical Edition," 112.

[3] Alart, "Observations sur la langue du roman du *Blandin*," 304.

[4] Van der Horst, ed., *Blandin de Cornouaille*, 62.

[5] Galano, "Nuove congetture," 110.

[6] Asperti, "Bacinetti e berroviere."

as suggested by Alart.[7] Van der Horst argued in favor of the Rhône Basin and/or today's department of the Alpes-de-Haute-Provence, thinking of the papal court at Avignon as a source of literary activity.[8] The Armagnac court in Rodez would also match this description and might explain how the text came to Italy.

[7] Alart, "Observations sur la langue du roman du *Blandin*," 304.

[8] Van der Horst, ed., *Blandin de Cornouaille*, 64.

First Sightings, Prior Editions, and the Argument for this Edition

BLANDIN DE CORNOALHA is a comic medieval romance that has had an intriguing post-medieval history. We know that Jehan de Nostredame was familiar with the title, though it is difficult to comprehend what he actually knew of the story. In 1575, he described *Blandin* as a fine romance, "un beau romant ...,"[1] which suggests a positive appreciation. However, we do not know how Nostredame learned of *Blandin*—all recent editors of Nostredame (Chabaneau and Anglade; Casanova) make no mention of this detail; it is highly unlikely that he read the manuscript now in Italy.

The next *Blandin* "sighting" was by the author of the catalog of the Turin library, Giuseppe Pasini, who described the text as a comic poem about lovers, a "poema ludicrum & amatorium."[2] Such a description is accurate but may imply a certain disdain for the poem. The Baron Portalis des Luckets, posted to Turin in the early nineteenth century, is properly cited as the first individual to have studied our text carefully.[3] Ludovico Savli d'Igliano may have read the tale in the Turin library before 1823; he praises its realism and mentions the elegant analysis of the tale completed by Portalis des Luckets in 1813.[4]

In 1824, Louis-François de Villeneuve published a historical romance entitled *Lyonnel ou la Provence au XIIIe siècle*, in which we find this note:

> We can add that to amuse Richard of Cornwall, brother of Henry III, Sancho sent him a lovely romance in Provençal rhyme, of the

[1] Nostredame, *Les vies des plus célèbres et anciens poëtes*, 140.

[2] Pasini, Berta, and Rivautella, *Codices manuscripti bibliothecae regii taurinensis*, 2:151.

[3] See Renier, "Una vecchia memoria sul 'Blandin de Cornoalha,'" 476.

[4] Savli d'Igliano, "Del cavaliere errante, romanzo di Tommaso III, marchesse di Salvazzo," 6n.

> loves of *Blondin de Cornouailles and of Guilhem de Mireinas* [*sic*], and the great feats of arms they accomplished for the lovely Brianda and for Erlande [sic], ladies of incomparable beauty.[5]

This summary of *Blandin* points to familiarity with more than simply the title of the courtly romance; it is most likely, however, that de Villeneuve learned of the tale from Nostredame, whom he cites on more than one occasion, though not at this point.

Early in the nineteenth century, François-Just-Marie Raynouard had a copy of the Turin text made for his use by Constance Gazzera, at the time a librarian in the Biblioteca de Torino; the French scholar included sixty-one lines cited from *Blandin* in his *Lexique roman*. He introduced *Blandin* with these words, "This little poem contains the speedy and animated retelling of the adventures of two knights whose names provide the title."[6] These words suggest that Raynouard may have liked the work, even if he described the language as "very incorrect," a fault he attributed to the copyist. In the *Lexique roman*, he published a summary of the entire tale, with selected excerpts.[7]

However, respect for the work was now declining. Contemporary with Raynouard was the German scholar Friedrich Christian Diez, who had no interest in our romance. Diez said that *Blandin* was a "a tale poor in creativity and pitiably composed."[8] By 1846, critical esteem reached a new low point: Claude Fauriel called *Blandin* "pitiful in all regards."[9]

The first publication of the entire text, as a semi-critical edition, was done by Paul Meyer in 1873.[10] Meyer's edition was based on a copy of a copy: the transcription by Gazzera, copied by L. Gautier on behalf

[5] "On ajoute que pour le réjouir [Richard de Cornouailles, frère de Henri III], Sanche lui envoya un très beau roman en rimes provençales, des amours de *Blondin de Cornouailles et de Guilhem de Mireinas* [sic], et des beaux faits d'armes qu'ils achevèrent pour la belle Briande et pour Erlande [sic], dames d'une incomparable beauté," Villeneuve, *Lyonnel ou la Provence au XIIIe siècle*, 2:210n. We thank Jacques de Caluwé for supplying this reference.

[6] "Ce petit poème contient le récit rapide et animé des aventures de deux chevaliers dont les noms lui servent de titre," Raynouard, *Lexique roman*, 1:315.

[7] Raynouard, *Lexique roman*, 1:315–20.

[8] "Un récit aussi pauvre d'invention que pitoyablement conduit," Diez cited by Nelli and Lavaud, eds., *Blandin de Cornouailles*, 450.

[9] Fauriel, *Histoire de la poésie provençale*, 3:94.

[10] Meyer, ed., "Le roman de *Blandin de Cornouailles*."

of Guessard, who traveled to Italy to compare the Gautier copy with the manuscript[11] and to prepare the text for publication, which never occurred. In the 1870s Guessard passed the transcription to Meyer, who published it in a major scholarly journal, *Romania*. Meyer gets credit for publishing a version of the entire text, but he dismissed the *dictat* as Catalan, practically tossing the text over the Pyrenees. Sample comments from his article include lines such as "a careless copyist" and "irregularities we impute to the author"; he concludes his introduction with: "I do not want to disgust the reader and silence myself."[12] One has the impression that Meyer could not wait to throw *Blandin* away.

Those French scholars who responded to Meyer's edition failed to find material to praise. In 1874, Alart wrote that *Blandin* "does not shine great light on romance literature";[13] Chabaneau wrote of "this insipid rhapsody."[14]

English-language scholars who considered the work as part of French literary history appear to have been influenced by the French critical evaluation of *Blandin*. George Saintsbury describes *Blandin* as less interesting than *Flamenca*,[15] a statement true enough, but that does not give *Blandin* its due. At the very end of the nineteenth century, Frederick John Snell wrote that our tale is "of no great mark or likelihood."[16] There is the suggestion that Snell does not know the work first hand, but is accepting the judgments of the French critical establishment.

Giulio Bertoni called for a new edition of what he called a "mediocre poem" in 1921;[17] an Italian edition of the text was completed by Lorenzino Delorenzi as a thesis in Romance Philology at the University of Turin in 1926. Delorenzi never formally published the thesis, which

[11] Bertoni, "Correzioni al testo di *Blandin de Cornouailles*," 408.

[12] "Un copiste ... peu soucieux," "d'irregularités imputés à l'auteur," "Je ne veux pas en dégoûter le lecteur, et je m'en tais," Meyer, ed., "Le roman de *Blandin de Cornouailles*," 173.

[13] "N'est pas à jeter un grand lustre sur la littérature romane," Alart, "Observations sur la langue du roman du *Blandin de Cornouailles*," 10.

[14] Chabaneau, "Notes critiques," 31.

[15] Saintsbury, *A Short History of French Literature*, 26.

[16] Snell, *Periods of European Literature*, 3:24.

[17] Bertoni, "Correzioni al testo di *Blandin de Cornouailles*," 408.

has been generally ignored by scholars[18] and which we have been unable to consult.

Negative evaluations remained in place for a good while longer. In 1945 Alfred Jeanroy wrote of *Blandin*, "the creativity is weak ... the style flat and colorless."[19] René Nelli and René Lavaud, who undertook to translate large excerpts of *Blandin*, alerted their readers to its "really poor and monotonous style and clumsy versification."[20] Charles Camproux described the work as "of lesser value," repeating the thoughts of earlier scholars.[21] Robert Lafont and Christian Anatole, who sought to valorize as much of the Occitan literary tradition as they could in their massive *Nouvelle histoire de la littérature occitane*, used the term "monotonous" to describe *Blandin*.[22]

Catalan and Spanish scholars were happy to adopt *Blandin* as their own. Criticism of the work was slightly more nuanced, as can be seen in Jaume Massó Torrents's phrase, "this strange work."[23] There has been significant Iberian peninsular interest in *Blandin*, as can be seen in the 1983 translation by Arseni Pacheco, even though he says of *Blandin*, that it is "not a text with great literary pretentions"[24] and that it is "a unique and curious example of medieval romance."[25] Another Iberian translator, Jordi Tiñena, described the work and its perceived faults, stating that these problems "place the narration at a notably inferior level."[26] There exist at least

[18] The thesis is not cited by van der Horst, ed., *Blandin de Cornouaille*, nor by Galano, ed., *Blandin di Cornovaglia*.

[19] "L'invention est faible ... le style plat et incolore," Jeanroy, *Histoire sommaire de la poésie occitane*, cited by van der Horst, ed., *Blandin de Cornouaille*, 66.

[20] "Style vraiment pauvre et monotone et sa versification malhabile," Nelli and Lavaud, eds., *Blandin de Cornouailles*, 450.

[21] Camproux, *Histoire de la littérature occitane*, cited by van der Horst, ed., *Blandin de Cornouaille*, 66.

[22] Lafont and Anatole, *Nouvelle histoire de la littérature occitane*, 1:241–42.

[23] "Aquesta obra estranya," Massó Torrents, *Repertori de l'antiga literatura catalana*, 512.

[24] Pacheco, "El Blandin de Cornualha," 150: "no és un text de grans pretensions literàries."

[25] Pacheco, ed., *Blandín de Cornualla i altres narracions*, 12: "un exemple curios i singular de *roman* medieval."

[26] Tiñena, ed., *Blandín de Cornualla*, 20: "situen la nostra narració en un nivell literari notablement inferior."

two other translations of *Blandin* into Catalan, one by Maite Guisado, who did not provide editorial comment to her translation, and a second by Vicent Vidal Lloret, completed as a master's thesis at the University of Alicante.

Historians of Catalan literature have regularly included the work in discussions of medieval literature of the region, though they may not have considered it as a Catalan work. Most recently, Miriam Cabré and Anton Espadaler included *Blandin* in their treatment of verse narratives appreciated in medieval Catalonia, describing the romance as "enigmatic."[27] Cabré and Espadaler do not think highly of *Blandin*, which they say "seems to respond to a lower, formulaic register";[28] in fact, the two Catalan scholars have a hard time including *Blandin* in their discussion of narratives, except that the story of Sleeping Beauty, a feature in *Blandin*, relates closely to the more truly Catalan tale, *Fraire de Joi e Sor de Plaser*.[29]

In the early 1970s two young scholars returned to the manuscript. Margaret Burrell completed her doctoral dissertation, a critical edition of the text, at the University of Toronto;[30] Cornelius van der Horst completed a diplomatic edition of the text as his doctoral work at the University of Utrecht, an edition published not long after.[31] The publication of van der Horst's work led Burrell to set her own edition aside until the 2010s. The Dutch scholar's work is meticulous, but he does not take into account lines added in the margins or missing rhyme lines—serious lacunae, in our opinion; we also disagree with a certain number of his readings. His presentation of the text also makes it difficult for the nonspecialist to read.

At roughly the same time, French-language translations of the text, in whole by Jean-Charles Huchet[32] or in part by Nelli and Lavaud, appeared. While these translations have their merit, they also have issues. Nelli and Lavaud worked from the Meyer edition, with all its "improvements" to the text; Huchet used van der Horst's diplomatic edition, which

[27] Cabré and Espadaler, "La narrativa en vers," 1:322.

[28] "Sembla respondre a un registre estilístic més baix i formulari," Cabré and Espadaler, "La narrativa en vers," 1:323.

[29] Cabré and Espadaler, "La narrativa en vers," 1:323.

[30] Burrell, "A Critical Edition."

[31] Van der Horst, ed., *Blandin de Cornouaille*.

[32] Huchet, tr., *Blandin de Cornouaille*.

omitted lines. Nelli and Lavaud abbreviated the story;[33] Huchet's translation is fluid and reads well, but is based on an edition that does not present the full text in its best light.

Subsequently, Galano offered a critical edition of the text for an Italian audience, perhaps following on Lazzerini's suggestion that *Blandin* was worthy of more study.[34] Galano's edition has merit, but she follows Meyer sometimes slavishly. As did Meyer, Galano sought to re-establish an octosyllabic rhythm for a now-lost original text; unlike the French scholar, Galano tried to base her emendations by referencing similar lines in the work itself. She too fails to include some lines we believe belong in the text. Furthermore, her print edition did not include the linguistic analysis one normally expects of a critical edition, though she published some linguistic studies in other venues.[35]

Insofar as the English-speaking audience is concerned, the only attempt to offer the text to English readers was completed by Ross Arthur, who worked with Burrell's 1974 edition to create a translation of *Blandin*. Arthur's self-published translation can be difficult to access.[36]

[33] Nelli and Lavaud published and translated lines equivalent to our lines 985–1106, 1381–442, 1613–80, 1749–988, and 2319–76 in their edition, *Blandin de Cornouailles*, 450–73.

[34] Galano, ed., *Blandin de Cornovaglia*; Lazzerini, *Letteratura medievale in lingua d'oc*, 226.

[35] See Galano, "Il *Blandin de Cornalha*" and "Nuove congetture."

[36] Arthur, tr., *Blandin de Cornoalha e Guilhot de Miramar*. The translation appears available online at http://oliverakhtar.me/download/qnufXwAACAAJ-blandin-de-cornoalha-e-guilhot-de-miramar-a-generic-medieval-adventure-romance, a site whose trustworthiness is uncertain.

A Table of Concordance

Each line number below occurs after a line which has been added in that edition. The last number of each edition is also indicated.

Van der Horst edition	Meyer edition	Galano edition	This edition
221	222	222	221
222	223	223	223
261	262	262	264
588	591	591	593
695	699	699	701
800	805	805	807
1313	1321	1321	1325
1413	1421	1421	1428
1419	1427	1427	1435
1877	1885	1885	1895
2386	2394	2394	2405

The Comedy of *Blandin*

ANY NUMBER OF elements in the *Blandin* story suggest it was intended as a parody, especially as a parody of other romances. This observation has been made by a number of scholars, including Jacques de Caluwé, Norris Lacy, and Juan Miguel Ribera Llopis; we agree.[1] Furthermore, as Suzanne Fleischman suggested with regard to *Jaufre*, it may be that a modern inability to perceive the parody has led to a devaluation of the skill of the anonymous author.[2] As she observed, "Parody is a very powerful naturalizing device in that it frees us from the demands of poetic seriousness and the strict observation of conventions, and rends the curious features of the text intelligible."[3]

Scholars have struggled to fit *Blandin* into a generic box—is it part of the matter of Britain, a story tied somehow to King Arthur, an Arthurian romance? The only way this story connects to Britain is that Blandin says he is from Cornwall; the only logic for calling *Blandin* an Arthurian romance is because the story speaks of the adventures of two knights. But if the anonymous author sought to poke fun at Arthurian romance, then such a weak linkage makes sense. As de Caluwé continues, "We might ask if, in this work which 'dialogues' with Arthurian material, the essential originality is parodic intent."[4]

The very name of Guilhot Ardit de Miramar invites such reflections. The second name, Ardit, "bold," specifically, is consistently undermined by the author, as the character is often anything but bold and brave.

[1] Several historical targets of parody are considered in Pfeffer, "*Blandin de Cornoalha*, Yet Another Look."

[2] See Fleischman, "'Jaufre' or Chivalry Askew."

[3] Fleischman, "'Jaufre' or Chivalry Askew," 103.

[4] "On peut se demander si dans cette oeuvre qui 'dialogue' avec la matière arthurienne, l'intention parodique ne consitute pas l'originalité essentielle," Caluwé, "Le roman de *Blandin*," 63.

De Caluwé goes so far as to describe the knight as an early example of the lazy Southerner or "capitaine gascon."[5] If Guilhot kills a giant, it is "a juvenile giant," the son of a giant (line 336). After each one of his adventures, Guilhot needs help—he is either wounded or taken prisoner. Given the choice of which road to take, Guilhot opts for the wide road, symbolic of the easy choice, "unworthy of any knight worthy of the title."[6] To the end, Guilhot is somewhat second-rate, unable to find his own wife and dependent on Blandin to make the match.

The valiance expressed in Guilhot Ardit's name is undermined by his behavior in ways that can only be ironic or parodic. It is unlikely that any fourteenth-century knight would have climbed a tree to get a better view of his surroundings, as Guilhot does (lines 229–36); the thought of a knight in armor climbing a tree can only have made a medieval audience laugh. Moments before the fight with the Black Knight, rather than inspecting his mount and armor or thinking of his mission, the narrator tells us that Guilhot flares his nostrils and grinds his teeth, "enfla las narres / et cruys las dens entre las beres" (lines 703–4)—surely a comic vision. Keith Busby's comment on the end of this scene merits repeating: "There is something irresistibly comic about [Guilhot's] realizing this goal by flinging the body unceremoniously into a pond and decamping without further ado."[7] As Pacheco observed, Guilhot is impetuous and lacks respect for any of his adversaries.[8] Though the premise of the story would have him as a perfect knight, he is hardly a paragon. In truth, the very nature of the presentation of the two knights, constantly reminded to behave "as good knights do," pushes the reader to see that their behavior consistently falls short and is certainly not on a par with romance expectations.

The hero's name also lends itself to examination. De Caluwé related Blandin's name to the Catalan word *bland*, meaning "soft, without energy,"[9] though his behavior is not in parallel with this interpretation. Both Blandin and Guilhot have the dubious habit of taking a nap when danger nears, as after Blandin picnics with the *donzella d'otra mar*.

[5] Van der Horst, ed., *Blandin de Cornouaille*, 71; Caluwé, "Le roman de *Blandin*," 63.

[6] Caluwé, "Le roman de *Blandin*," 64.

[7] Busby, "*Blandin de Cornoalha*," 9.

[8] Pacheco, "El Blandin de Cornualha," 157.

[9] Caluwé, "Le roman de *Blandin*," 64.

More significant is the frequent use of a diminutive for the hero, repeatedly called Blandinet. We can attribute the occasional use of the diminutive as a crutch to achieve a longer line, but the repeated use of this crutch is unlikely. More plausible is that the author was diminishing his hero, offering the irony of the diminutive to poke fun at the character.[10] Just as Guilhot flared his nostrils at the sight of danger, Blandin, too, thinks "through his nose." As he prepares to capture the white hawk, he announces, "Jou n'ay ja enflat lo nas" (line 1446), he has already flared his nostrils and is ready for the challenge.[11]

In the description of the Saracen, the nose again is a key element in the portrait. This guardian of Brianda is described in monstrous terms (Espadaler calls it "naive tremendism" and sees the description as stemming from popular traditions[12]):

> El ha de golla un palm o mais
> e a las dens grans comme verre,
> fort e duras come ferre.
> E a las narras ben fendudas,
> e a las aurelhas ben ponchudas,
> e es ben negre, veramen,
> e ferejos a tota gent.
>
> His mouth is as big as a hand, or bigger,
> and his teeth are as long as a boar's tusks,
> hard and strong as iron.
> He has nostrils split in half
> and pierced ears.
> He is completely black
> and ferocious towards everyone. (1418–24)

Striking in this description is the emphasis on facial features—teeth as hard and sharp as a boar's, implying their deadliness, and, again, a reference to the nostrils, split, which might suggest prior battles or facial jewelry as might befit the character. Readers of medieval romance expect villainous characters to be described in negative terms, but this description exceeds

[10] Martínez makes a similar observation in "'Blandin de Cornualla,'" 446. See Ribera Llopis, "*Blandín de Cornualla*," 358, for more on this angle.

[11] Martin de Riquer also saw these descriptions as ironic, *Història de la literatura catalana*, 2:25.

[12] Espadaler, "El meravellós," 147.

those expectations significantly, to the point of comedy. If the "split nose" means the Saracen's nose is flattened, then this element is fully in keeping with descriptive conventions established by Chrétien de Troyes.[13]

At a more general level, de Caluwé observes that knights in medieval romance are usually in service of some ideal or cause, not clearly the case here. If Blandin and Guilhot have a mission, it would seem to be getting in and out of trouble and, almost by luck, finding themselves wives. The episode of the Black Knight serves as a typical example: Guilhot kills the knight before he learns of the Black Knight's cruelty, punishment before the crime has been made known.

Norris Lacy, the scholar who most pointedly makes the case for a parodic reading of *Blandin*, sees the comedic elements from the very start of the story, when the two knights ride for six months without encountering any adventure at all,[14] hardly the expected frame for a medieval romance. Lacy suggests that the formulaic "behave as good knights do" should be read not as an admonition or simple advice. As he states, the heroes are "predicating their actions on their assumptions about proper chivalric comportment. They are thus playing the role of valiant knights as they understand it: they are doing their best to *be* 'like good knights.'"[15]

Related to the refrain of "behaving as good knights do" are the words spoken by the damsel sent by Brianda to seek help, that she is "a maiden from afar, / seeking adventure" (lines 1013–14), words we rarely hear spoken by women in medieval tales and strikingly reminiscent of the lines of Blandin and Guilhot, "We are knights from afar, / in search of adventure" (lines 517–18).[16] This *donzella d'otra mar*, albeit a horse thief, is as manly as the heroes of our story.

The role of meals and dining in *Blandin* is another potential source of comedy. Guilhot regularly worries about his stomach. When the two knights should be preparing for a battle, Guilhot's first concern relates to food:

[13] See Colby, *The Portrait*, 78–79.

[14] Lacy, "Halfway to Quixote," 175.

[15] Lacy, "Halfway to Quixote," 176, Lacy's italics.

[16] The Occitan lines are almost as parallel as our translation: "Nos sem cavalliers d'Orien, / sercans avantura veramen" (517–18); "Jou suy donzella d'otra mar / che avantura vaoc sercar" (1013–14). We thank the anonymous reader who called this comedic element to our attention.

> ... let's dismount here
> and we will fight in the morning."
> They dismounted
> and moved to the middle of the meadow.
> Guilhot said, "What shall we eat,
> because we have very little food." (283–88)

The passage that bridges the adventure with the Black Knight and the family of giants serves as a lunch break, to use Busby's description:[17]

> Guilhot saw that he lay dead.
> He took his lance and went on his way.
> He rode quickly
> until it was dinner time.
> He dined by a spring
> that he found in a beautiful meadow.
> As soon as he had finished,
> he mounted his horse, ... (903–10)

Fleischman thought Jaufre's avoidance of food, drink, and rest as a parody of the knight unwilling to be distracted from his quest (Jaufre ultimately collapses from exhaustion).[18] Blandin and Guilhot's interest in food and drink parody both the *Jaufre* story, but also the convention of the knight devoted to his quest above all.

Lacy's fourth comedic theme is that of rest and sleep. "For two knights so intent on finding adventure, these two are among the most somnolent of all romance heroes."[19] Rather than converse with a young lady, Blandin takes a nap (lines 1059–64); his siesta allows her to steal his horse. When he comes into the beautiful garden, Blandin's first impulse is to fall asleep (lines 1299–301). As Lacy observes, "Gardens are associated, naturally enough, with love, and we twice learn of his love (for a total of three women) when he is in such a place; but they are no less associated with sleep."[20] Guilhot is even more interested in sleep, dozing when Blandin returns from rescuing the two damsels (line 192).

17 Busby, "*Blandin de Cornoalha*," 9.

18 Fleischman, "'Jaufre' or Chivalry Askew," 113.

19 Lacy, "Halfway to Quixote," 177.

20 Lacy, "Halfway to Quixote," 178.

The end of the story carries its own comic elements. After defeating two monsters and a fearsome Saracen, Blandin retrieves the hawk and asks Brianda's brother, "Is this the bird?" (line 1608) as if there were any other to be found—a rather funny statement in context. We might expect the reunion of Blandin and Guilhot to be "an emotionally supercharged narrative climax."[21] The author, however, says nothing of their meeting; Blandin's words are as nonchalant as can be:

> Then he took Guilhot Ardit
> and said to him,
> "Guilhot, let's get ready to leave
> quickly, without delay!
> We have nothing more to do here!" (2201–5)

Multiple scholars have read the romance as a promotion of bourgeois values, a comic reaction to those of the nobility. Pacheco has argued that the two marriages at the end represent a comic twist, as the knights become models for bourgeois husbands,[22] abandoning adventures to stay with their brides (lines 2395–96). Ribera Llopis sees *Blandin* as part of a trend to make noble knights more middle class, an ironic modification leveling the distance between reality and fiction.[23] Lacy suggests that the abandonment of the quest for adventure represents something of a contradiction, as the knights give up behavior that had been their model up to this point.[24]

> Once they are married, they (and their narrator) apparently see no reason for them to pursue adventure further. And that may well be because a good many other romances of chivalry recount no additional adventures once the knight has won and married a woman. That is a further indication that these protagonists, like Quixote, have been reading books, or at least hearing stories, and are seeking to act them out.[25]

[21] Busby, "*Blandin de Cornoalha*," 14.

[22] Pacheco, "El Blandín de Cornualla," 153.

[23] Ribera Llopis, "Ese creciente destino burgués de los antiguos héroes documenta esa modificación irónica establecida mediante la nivelación de la realidad y la ficción," "*Blandin de Cornualla*," 359.

[24] Lacy, "Halfway to Quixote," 180.

[25] Lacy, "Halfway to Quixote,"180.

Keith Busby describes Blandin as a "staid, 'middle-class' hero, who never lets his heart rule his head, and who sets great store by material comfort,"[26] hardly the individual who should be the hero of a medieval romance. And Carolyn Jewers notes that medieval knights in Occitania were "a more urban, mercantile class of knight,"[27] another rationale for the bourgeois ending.

As Busby noted, "*Blandin* treats in an ironic and comic manner ... features of the received romance tradition."[28] He adds that the *Blandin* author regularly implements generic conventions to disappointing and therefore comic effect.[29] Espadaler argues that *Blandin de Cornoalha* reflects a literary tradition with strong southern roots, willing to poke fun at the northern French romance corpus, a conclusion similar to Busby's. The Catalan scholar sees the Occitan tale of *Jaufre* as being a first instance of this different approach to storytelling: *Jaufre* opens with King Arthur being thrown in the air by a magician-knight—not the normal respect shown the king.[30]

While the comedy does not rise to the level of burlesque as in *Jaufre*,[31] the author of *Blandin* was certainly willing to parody romance conventions, albeit in slightly more subtle fashion than with the physical comedy found in *Jaufre*. For years, *Blandin de Cornoalha* has suffered from the negative reactions of critics. Perhaps reading the text from different vantage points allows us to give *Blandin* the credit it is due.

26 Busby, "*Blandin de Cornoalha*," 14.

27 Jewers, "The Name of the Ruse," 197.

28 Busby, "*Blandin de Cornoalha*," 3.

29 Busby, "*Blandin de Cornoalha*," 19.

30 Espadaler, "El meravellós," 147. See also Eckhardt, "Reading *Jaufre*."

31 See Fraser, "Humour and Satire in the Romance of *Jaufre*."

Conclusion, Presentation of the Edition and Translation

BLANDIN DE CORNOALHA has real qualities. It was written by an author who found the tradition of courtly narrative amusing and who was happy to use its motifs and commonplaces to create a new story. The narrative moves briskly and is full of pleasant surprises. Hiccups in the plot and the occasional errors in versification, allowed to remain in this edition rather than being uniformly corrected, suggest what an anonymous reviewer has called "a kind of aristocratic nonchalance."

Scholars have long denigrated the author of *Blandin de Cornoalha*, from the mid-nineteenth century to the late twentieth. We hope to have demonstrated that the *Blandin* author was more clever than the world has thought. Jacques de Caluwé made the solid point that the author knew how to construct a story, such that every episode was needed to tell the whole tale, even when that necessity was not immediately obvious. The example he offered relates to the encounter with the *donzella d'otra mar*, which begins at line 993. We might think that once Blandin leaves her company, that she is forgotten, except that Brianda will explain her purpose later in the *récit* (lines 1776–77). By the same token, at the end of the story, in order to find Guilhot, Blandin will retrace his friend's steps and have many similar encounters.[1] Martínez Pérez made the case for a well-structured narrative, recounted with vivacity.[2] The author was familiar with Occitan and French literature of his period; he used that knowledge to invent a new narrative genre, the *dictat*, which is what he called his tale.

Pfeffer and Burrell decided that this Occitan story deserved a good, fluid English translation, that it was time to review the text in manuscript and bring to English-reading audiences a new edition and translation of

[1] See Caluwé, "Le roman de *Blandin*," 61–62.

[2] Martínez Pérez, "Consideracions sobre la estructuración narrativo-literaria del *Blandin*."

Blandin de Cornoalha. To this end, we have used material from Burrell's unpublished doctoral dissertation and consulted the manuscript in Turin anew to create a completely new edition of the poem, notably incorporating lines that were omitted or ignored by prior editors. In what follows, the critical edition is by Pfeffer with assistance from Burrell; the editions of Meyer, van der Horst, and Galano were all considered as variant readings; the translations of Nelli and Lavaud and Huchet were also consulted. It is our hope that with this volume, the story of *Blandin de Cornoalha* will receive the respect it merits, as a romance from the late Middle Ages, poking fun at the literature of the time, perhaps composed in honor of a prince's wedding, carried across the Alps to find a home in an Italian manuscript.

In this edition, we have emended the spelling and grammar of the text as little as possible, following principles that may be described as Bédierist or "best-manuscript."[3] Our thinking is that the language of this text is noteworthy in many respects and that to insert editorial corrections would obscure the linguistic interest of the *dictat*; our only changes to the text occur at lines 415, 758, 1313, 1608, and 1691. Notes to this edition allow the reader to compare our edition to those of Paul Meyer, Cornelius van der Horst, and Sabrina Galano. In general and unlike Meyer and Galano, we have retained all manuscript spellings. The letter *i* has been replaced with a *j* when a consonantal sound was clearly intended, using twenty-first-century Occitan spelling as a guide.

The scribe used a good number of abbreviations, though nothing exceptional for the period. As a rule, we have expanded abbreviations according to the forms used by the scribe when he spelled a word in all letters. The most consistent example of a much abbreviated word is the name of Blandin's friend, Guilhot, frequently abbreviated to *G*. The most frequent form, in all letters, was *Guilhot*, which is how we have expanded the abbreviation throughout. Though the text uses *Blandin* and the diminutive *Blandinet* somewhat interchangeably, the translation always refers to the hero as Blandin.

The scribe shows some knowledge of punctuation, using a form of the colon and of the period. We have considered his punctuation, but our general rule has been to punctuate the Occitan text so that it made grammatical sense and told the story. Given the way the author linked lines

[3] See Foulet and Speer, *On Editing Old French Texts*, 38.

with conjunctions such as *e* or *et*, "and," we have tended to ignore this conjunction as we considered how to insert punctuation. Furthermore, *e* or *et* is not always translated.

We have considered this text as if it had been delivered orally, before an audience of appreciative listeners. We think markers such as *ve vos* (lines 126 and 2399) point to such a presentation mode.[4] Our interpretation of the final lines, only slightly reworked from the text in the manuscript, is in keeping with this understanding of performance. We have also suggested breaks in the narrative, parallel to chapter divisions.

Our translation is intended to give a good sense of the text, line by line. In some cases, we have used the story to drive the translation, particularly when referring to the heroine's anonymous sibling, always referred to as the *donzel* and never identified as Brianda's brother, though they share a father (line 1329) and he consistently calls her his sister (for example, line 1326). The Occitan text can be repetitive, and we have sought to make our translation less so, insofar as possible. Therefore, we have not necessarily repeated verbs, particularly when the author uses three different verbs to express a single activity. Also, we have purposefully chosen not to translate every instance of *verayament* or *apertament*, in order to let the story flow.

[4] Galano makes a similar case in "Indizi di oralità nel *Blandin de Cornoalha*."

Occitan Text[1]

[E]n non de Dieu commenzeray[2]
un bel dictat et retrayrai
d'amors et de cavalaria
e d'una francha compagnia[3]
che van far dos cavaliers[4]
de Cornoalha, bons guerriers
che volgron per lo mond annar
e lur [a]vantura cerchar;[5]
e la un, se Dieu me valha,[6]
ac non Blandin de Cornoalha;
e l'aotre si fa appellar
Giot Ardit de Miramar.[7]
E diray vos premierament
consi elos feron verament:[8]
la fe del cors elos sy doneron
et sobre sans, els jureron
che els si tenrrien fialtat[9]
la un a l'autre sans barat.
E quant ayso agron promes,
cascun va penre son arnes[10]
e montan sobre bon destrier,[11]
cascun comme bon cavalier;
E parten se de leur hostals[12]
come valens, se Dieus my sal.
Van s'en e tenon lor chamin.[13]
Aysso fu un diluncx ben matin,
E intren s'en per los desertz
come bons cavaliers e apertz;[14]
tot jorn lur avanturas sercan[15]
et de lur novellas parlan. locuti[16]
E ben miech an es cavalcheron[17]
che avantura non troberon.
E puis, quant ven un jorn [matin],[18]
els van tenir lo lur camin
e intren s'en per un boscage,
com bons cavaliers de parage.[19]
E quant agron grant temps annat[20]
per lo boscage e calvacat,[21]

Notes to the Occitan text begin on p. 228.

English Translation

In the name of God I shall begin
a fine *dictat*[a] and tell
of love, of chivalry
and of the close companionship
between two knights,
good warriors of Cornwall,
who wanted to go around the world
in search of their adventures.
One of them, God help me,
was named Blandin of Cornwall
and the other was called
Guilhot the bold of Miramar.
First I shall tell you
what they did:
they swore fealty each to the other:
on relics they swore
that they would uphold fealty
one to the other without fail.
When they had promised this,
each took his equipment
and mounted upon his good warhorse,
just as a good knight does.
They left their lodgings
as valiant knights, may God save me.
They set out on the road.
Early on a Monday morning
they went through a wilderness
as good knights do;
searching all day long for adventure
and having a good chat. speaking
They rode through a good half of a year
without finding adventure;
then came one day when
they were on their road,
they entered into a wood
as brave knights do.
When they had spent a lot of time
riding through the wood,

[a] See Versification and Genre for discussion of *dictat*.

els viron venir un brachet
che s'en venc a elos tot drech;
e met se tresto primier[22]
e va amb els per lo sendier.
Adonc els se merevilheron
quant lo brachet achi troberon
e disseron la un a l'autre,
"Aysso es avantura, sen fauta."[23]
Adonchas Blandinet a dich,[24]
"Segan lo entro a la nuech[25]
e veyrem cal chamin tenrra[26]
ni cal avantura mostera."[27]
Adonc lo brachet tot corren
s'en va entra per un torrent,[28]
e aqui trobet una cava in fovea
(che dedins terra s'en intrava).
E met se dins lo cap primier
che depuys hom no·l poc vezer.[29]
Aysso vi Guilhot Ardit[30]
de que fu fort esbaït,[31]
e Blandin non fu avissat[32]
dal can, on s'en fu intrat,[33]
e dis a son companh G[uilhot],[34]
"Vesses lo can achi en loch?"
Respont G[uilhot] et ha parlat,
"Per esta cava es intrat." cava castellana
E adonches Blandinet a dich,[35]
"Esperas my, Guilhot Ardit,
car jou, per sert, volle intrar,[36]
dedins l'avantura sercar.[37]
Tres jours my attendes ayssi,
pueys non fasses conte de my."[38]
Respont G[uilhot] et a ly dich,
"So che playra a vos, ami,[39]
penssas de anar quant vos volres,[40]
car vos ayssi me trobares."
Aqui presseron cumiat,[41]
e Blandinet s'en es intrat,
tot armat d'armes vermelhas
e aotras a gran merevelhas,[42]
tot jort avant per la escura,
com bon cavallier d'avantura.[43]
E quant ac un gran tems anat,

they saw a hunting dog
which came straight up to them,
took the lead,
and came with them on the path.
They were amazed at
finding the dog there
and said to each other,
"This is undoubtedly an adventure."
Blandin said,
"Let's follow it until nightfall
and we will see which path it will take
and what adventure it will show us."
The hunting dog at a run
took off through a waterfall
and found there a cave   in a cave
(which went into the earth).
The dog went in headfirst
and was lost to sight.
Guilhot Ardit saw this
and was greatly amazed;
Blandin did not know
where the dog had gone
and said to his companion, Guilhot,
"Do you see the dog anywhere?"
Guilhot said in reply,
"It went into that cave."   the cave of the chastelaine
Blandin then said,
"Wait for me, Guilhot Ardit,
for I'm definitely going
inside to look for adventure.
Wait for me here for three days,
after that, don't bother."
Guilhot said in reply,
"Whatever you like, my friend,
go whenever you want,
and you'll still find me here."
They took leave of each other,
and Blandin went inside,
armed all in red
and with other amazing weapons.
He traveled constantly through the gloom,
as befits an adventurous knight.
When he had journeyed for a long time,

el vi una gran claredat,
e aylla luench ac un hostal
en che ac trop bel portal.
A sel portal el s'en anet
e achi un porter trobet
chi li ubri tantost la porta
e dis, "Intras en sella orta,
car vos aqui trobares
aventura, si la volles."
Adonc Brandin s'en van entrar;[44]
en sela orta s'en va annar.[45]
Aqui trobet dins aquel ort,
verayament, mot bel desport:
desot un bel pomer florit
achi a l'ombra s'es dormit.
En mentre che el si dormia[46]
e reysidar non si podia,[47]
aneron venir doas donsellas,
mot bellas a gran merveilhas.[48]
Dis l'una a l'autra, "Bel cavallier[49]
dorm lay desot aquel pomier.
Prego te che l'anen reysidar,[50]
car si nos podie conquistar
d'ayssel jayan che aysi nos ten,
nos l'amarian de ben tallen."[51]
Adonch elas s'en van annar **94r/col b**
vers Blandin e van li sonar,
"Sus, cavaller, annas avant
davant che venga lo jayant,
car certas el vos ausirie
se consegre vos hi podie;
car mot d'aotres n'y a mort[52]
e fach morir a mala mort
che nos volien conquistar
per fach d'armes recobrar."[53]
Adonc Blandin che las aosit
tantost d'amors el fu f[e]rit[54]
de ellas doas (che eran bellas),
e dis lur, "Franchas damaissellas,[55]
volres vos en am my annar
si jou vos pode conquistar?"[56]
Respondon elas, "Hoc verament,
e faren vostra comandament."[57]

in the distance he saw a bright light,
and there was a residence
with a very beautiful portal.
He set off towards that portal
and there found a doorkeeper
who immediately opened the gate for him
and said, "Come into this garden,
for you will find here
adventure, if that is your wish."
At that, Blandin entered
and went into the garden.
There he found within that garden
a chance for amusement:
beneath an apple tree in flower
he fell asleep in the shade.
While he was asleep
and unable to wake up,
there came two damsels
who were amazingly beautiful.
One said to the other, "A handsome knight
is sleeping beneath that apple tree.
I think we should wake him up,
for if he can overcome for us
that giant who keeps us here,
we would love him most sincerely."
Then they went **94r/col b**
towards Blandin and called to him,
"Get up, Sir, get away
before the giant comes,
for he will certainly kill you
if he catches up with you;
he has killed many others
and has inflicted terrible deaths
on those wishing to rescue us
and set us free by feat of arms."
As Blandin listened to them
he was smitten with love for them both
(for they were gorgeous)
and said to them, "Lovely ladies,
would you be willing to come with me
if I can set you free?"
They replied, "Indeed, we would,
and we would do your bidding."

En mentre che aysi estan parlan,[58]
ve vos venir lo gran jayan
che dis, "Qual sies tu, desustrat,[59]
che tant avant t'en sies intrat?" presenter
Adonc e[l] li respondet,[60]
"Per sert, jou ay non Blandinet,[61]
chi suy vengut per conquistar[62]
aquestas, e ellas en vuelh mennar."
Adonc lo jayan fu fort irat,[63]
car Blandin li ac ayssi parlat, largement
e levet una gran massa[64]
e dis che li fara far plassa.
Adonc Blandin fu fort irat;
un sault a travers a sautat[65]
e secodet ly d'una lanssa,[66]
che portava de gran fissanza,
e a luy tan gran colp donat
per miech del cors che l'a tombat.
Adonch lo jayan nafrat se senti,[67]
e gita un gran crit e leva ssi;[68]
devers Blandin s'en va anar[69]
e tan gran colp ly va donar
che tot l'escut li a romput[70]
e Blandin per terra es cassut.[71]
Adonc lo jayan chi lo sanc perdia[72]
e restanchar no se podia,
trestot lo cor li va fallir
e achi s'anet esmortir.
Ares som dos tombat[73]
per los grans colps che son donatz.[74]
Adonch, las donsellas che aqui estavan[75]
de jounelhons a Dieu pregavon.[76]
Vessen lo jayan amortir,[77]
e van ss'en vers lur a mich,[78]
a Blandinet de Cornoalha,
che·n as facha la bataglia,[79]
e dison li, "Franch cavalier,
anas sus per lo vergier,

While they were standing there talking,
imagine,[b] the large giant arrived
and said, "What sort of wretch are you,
that you have come so far in here?" presently
He then replied to the giant,
"Actually, my name is Blandin,[c]
I have come here to free these ladies
and I want to take them with me."
At this, the giant was greatly annoyed
that Blandin had spoken to him like that broadly
and he picked up a huge club
and said that he would smash him.
Blandin was furious;
he made a leap to one side
and shook his trustworthy lance
which he was holding confidently
and gave him such a blow in the middle
of his body that he knocked him down.
The giant felt himself to be wounded,
gave a loud cry and got up;
he lunged towards Blandin
and gave him such a heavy blow
that he broke his shield entirely,
and Blandin fell to the ground.
As for the giant who was losing blood
and could not staunch it,
his heart came to a stop
and he died on the spot.
Now they are both on the ground
because of the savage blows received.
At this point, the two damsels there
prayed to God on their knees;
they see the dead giant
and go towards their friend,
Blandin of Cornwall
who has fought the battle there,
and they say to him, "Dear Sir,
go up through the garden,

[b] With "*ve vos*" the author speaks to the audience; we use "imagine" to accomplish the same effect.

[c] The Occitan text has a diminutive for reasons of meter.

car vos lo jayan aves mort
e faich morir a mala mort.
Recorda vos de vostra amya
e de nobla cavallaria."
E quant B[landin] aus las noellas
d'aquestas franchas damoysselas
levet si e pres corage,
com bon cavallier de parage.
E vi lo jayant estandut;
vaye ss'en ver el, l'escut romput,[80]
e senti lo an pauch polsar;[81]
tantost la testa li va levar.[82]
E las donsellas gran gauch agron[83]
quant lo jayan achi mort viron,[84]
e disson li, "Cavaller ardit,[85]
fach de nos a vostre delit
car tos temps mais vos serviren
e lialat nos vos tenren;
e prec vos che·ns volhas gitar[86]
d'ayssi, senhor, et an vos mennar."
Respon Blandin apertamen,
"Doncas anen nos veramen;
la fora ha un cavallier
chi m'aspera per lo sandier;[87]
e serie mot esbaït[88]
si non vessie venir amich."[89] vel anogie, de nocte
Adonques Blandinet la[s] pren[90]
per las mans blanches et va ss'en
e va ss'en ver Giot Ardit.[91]
Et atroban lo, che s'es adormit.[92]
Adons Blandin li va sonar,
"Levas, companch, pansen d'anar,
car l'avantura ay atrobada[93]
che nos avion demandada.
Ve vos ayssi, doas donsellas,
franchas, bellas a merevilhas,
che ay conquistadas d'un jayan
che era plen de mar tallen."[94]
Adonc Gioth, che las vis venir,[95]

for you have killed the giant
and moreover made him die a terrible death.
Thank you for your friendship[d]
and valiant chivalry."
When Blandin heard the words
from these lovely ladies,
he got up and took heart,
as good knights do.
He saw the giant stretched out
and went towards him with his broken shield;
he felt him barely breathing;
and promptly cut off his head.
The damsels were overjoyed
when they saw the giant dead there,
and they said to Blandin, "Bold knight,
do whatever you like with us,
for from now on, we will serve you
and will be ever loyal to you.
I beg you to remove us from here,
my lord, and take us with you."
Blandin immediately replied,
"Right, let's go;
out there is a knight
who is waiting for me on the path.
He will be very dismayed
if he does not see his friend coming."   or at night, at night
Then Blandin took them
by their white hands, and they went
on and on towards Guilhot Ardit.
They found him asleep.
Blandin then called to him,
"Get up, my friend, let's go,
for I have found the adventure
which we were asking for.
Look, here are two damsels,
high-born and stunningly gorgeous,
whom I rescued from a giant
who was full of wickedness."
Then Guilhot, who saw them coming,

[d] The Occitan term *amia* or *amya* is difficult to translate as it represents many stages of friendship, up to and including the status of lover (see Paden, *An Introduction*, 360, s.v. amiga). A somewhat literal translation of the line would be "Now remember your lady."

apert si leva de dormir
e dis lo, "Tresche ben vengut[96]
sias vos, companch, si Dieu m'ajut,[97]
car sertas gran paor avia
de vos, quant venir non vos vessia, anno MCCC ...
e era en corage de intrar[98]
dins la cava vos sercar.[99]
Repaussas vos e parlerem
en qual partida nos tenrren."
Respon Blandin, "Pansen d'annar,[100] **94v/col a**
car jou non vuelh repausar.[101]
Portas la una vos devant[102]
e jou l'aotra. Anem avant."[103]
E Giot pris una donsella[104]
e mes la si davant la sella,[105]
e Blandinet feis aytrestal
de l'autra, car ben ho val.[106]
Ares s'en van per lo boschage,[107]
los dos cavallers de parage
e las donsellas van anb els.[108]
..................................[109]
che calvacan a myeia via.[110]

[New chapter in story]

Achi fallit lo dia.[111]
Adonc Blandinet a dich,[112] videbimus
"Che faren nos, G[uilhot] Ardit?[113]
Car lo jorn ven che·ns vol falhir[114]
per la nuich che va ss'en venir."[115]
Respont Gioth, "Jou monteray[116]
sus un arbre e regarderay
si veyrie qualche masage[117]
ont tengesson nostre hostage."
Adonques el s'en va annar
et en un arbre va montar;
e regardet d'amon, d'aval;
si vigra calche ostal.[118]
Ayla [a]val vi un castel[119]
che a son semblant erat[120] mot bel
e dis a son compagn Blandin,[121]
"Pensen d'anar nostre camin
car jou ay vist la un castel[122]
che jamais no lo vi plus bel.
Pensen de calvacar apert[123]

immediately arose from his sleep
and said to him, "You are truly most welcome,
my friend, so help me God;
I was certainly very afraid for you
when I didn't see you coming back, the year 13 ...
and I was of a mind to go
into the cave to look for you.
Have a rest and let us talk
about the direction we should take."
Blandin replied, "Let's go on; **94v/col a**
I don't want to rest.
Take one in front of you
and I'll take the other. Let's go."
Guilhot took one of the damsels
and put her in front of the saddle,
and Blandin did likewise
with the other, as was right to do.
Then they went through the wood,
those two valiant knights,
and the damsels went with them.
....
who were riding in the middle of the road.

[New chapter in story]

Dusk fell.
Then Blandin said, we will see
"What are we to do, Guilhot Ardit?
The daylight is fading,
and night is coming."
Guilhot replied, "I shall climb
a tree and look around
to find some hamlet
where we can take our rest."
Thereupon he went
and climbed up a tree;
he looked all around
if he could spot some dwelling.
Down the valley he saw a castle
which looked very fine to him,
and he said to his companion Blandin,
"Let's take to the road
for I have seen a castle
more beautiful than I've seen before.
Let's ride quickly

che de jours iscan del desert."
Apertamen es cavalcheron[124]
tant che·l desert detrays laseron[125] in al ... a trays lo bosch
e intren s'en per una prada
d'erba frecha che lur agrada;[126]
e al miech luoch fo lo castel
che era gratios e mout bel.[127]
E las donzellas, quant viron[128]
lo castel, elas ploreron[129]
e planhon si mout aygramen[130]
la una e l'autra verayament.[131]
E Blandinet, chi ben amava
las donzellas che menava,[132]
demandet lur de que ploravan[133]
ni per que aytal dolor menavan.
Adonques respondet la major,[134]
"Comme non menerian nos dolor?[135]
Car sel castel sol estre nostre[136]
....
....
e an lo nos tot per lor gran forza;[137]
e tenon pres tot mon lignage,
e de bons cavaliers e de grant parage."[138] el bon vel co
Respon Blandin, "Ne vos plores,[139]
car lo castel ben cobrarez.[140] recuperabitis
Respausan nos donques ayssi[141]
e combateron lo bo matin."[142]
Disseron elas, "Per Dieu non sia![143]
Pensen de tenir nostra via,
car sel chi lo ten non a pavor[144]
de vos, senhor, ni de major."[145]
Adonc Blandinet lur demanda,
"Chi es aquel [che] ten en garda?"[146]
Respondon elas, "Un jayan mout fort,[147]
frayre d'aquel che aves mort."
Respon Blandin, "Jou non partirai[148]
d'ayssi, per sert, che jou vist auray[149]
si sel jayan es aytant fort
comme l'aotre frayre che ye ay mort.[150]
Per so descalvachen ayssi
e combaterem le matin."
Ares son es descalvachas[151]
e passeron si per miech lo prat.[152]

to get out of the wilderness while daylight lasts."
Then they rode
until they left the wilderness behind after the woods
and went into a meadow
of fresh grass which pleased them;
in the middle of this place was the castle
which was gracious and very beautiful.
When the damsels saw
the castle, they burst into tears
and wept bitterly,
both of them.
Blandin, who was fond
of the damsels he was escorting,
asked them why they were weeping
and why they were grieving.
The elder then replied,
"How could we not be sad?
This castle used to be ours
....
....
and [they] took it from us with great force;
and they're holding all my family prisoner
as well as good and brave knights." as good or co-
Blandin replied, "Don't cry,
for you will get the castle back. you will recover
For now, let's rest here
and we will fight them early in the morning."
They said, "By God, no!
Let's think of moving on,
for he who holds the castle is not afraid
of you, my lord, or of anyone else."
Then Blandin asked them,
"Who is in charge of it?"
They replied, "A very strong giant,
the brother of the one you killed."
Blandin replied, "I'm not leaving here
until I have seen
if this giant is as strong
as the other brother I killed.
So, let's dismount here
and we will fight in the morning."
They dismounted
and moved to the middle of the meadow.

So dis Guilhot, "Che mangeren,
Car pauca vianda nos tenen?"
Respon Blandin, "Passeron nos
alegramen, parleren nos d'amors,[153]
e deman nos ens trobaren;[154]
per grat o per forza n'auren."[155]
Tota la nuich si repausseren[156]
tro lo matin che li leveren.[157]
E tantost quant foron levatz[158]
apertamen si son armat,[159]
e van si ben apparelhar
per lo castell a batalhar.[160]
Dis Guilloth, "De bon tallen[161]
volgra combatre an sel jayan,[162]
si vos plages a vos, senhor,
che fesseses tanta d'onor."[163]
Respon Blandin e a ly dich
apertamen, "Guillot Ardit,
si bon corage vos santes,[164]
la batagla vos prenes."[165]
Adonch Guillot apertament[166]
s'en va al castell verament[167]
e trobet lo portal ubert,[168]
e intra ss'en ben apert;[169]
e quant el fu dedins intrat,
tantost lo portal fu serat.
E vi la molher del jayan
ben plora de mal talhan,[170]
che destacava dous leons la staca
che erun malvais e fellons;
e los leons van venir[171]
vers Guilloth e van l'asallir.
E Guilloth, come valen,[172]
defendet se apertament,
e va a l'un tal cop donar[173]
che la testa li va talhar.
Devers l'autre el s'en annet[174] **94v/col b**
e un gran temps combatet,[175]
che no lo podia conquistar[176]
per ren del mont che poghes far.
E a la fin s'es avissat
e a li tan gran colp donat
che tot un bras li a rumput,[177]

Guilhot said, "What shall we eat,
because we have very little food."
Blandin said, "Let's spend our time
delightfully speaking of love
and tomorrow we'll find food;
we will take it either freely or by force."
They rested all night
until they arose in the morning.
As soon as they had got up
they put on their armor
and prepared themselves well
to do battle for the castle.
Guilhot said, "With all my heart
I want to fight with this giant;
if you don't mind, my lord,
allow me this honor."
Blandin replied and said to him,
"Guilhot Ardit,
if you feel so positive,
you take on the battle."
Then Guilhot without delay
went on his way to the castle;
he found the portal open
and entered there quickly;
the very moment he came inside,
the portal shut fast.
He saw the wife of the giant
weeping copiously and vengefully.
She unleashed two lions release her
which were cruel and vicious;
the lions advanced
towards Guilhot and sprang to attack.
Guilhot, valiant as ever,
defended himself with alacrity,
and gave one such a blow
that he cut off its head.
He went towards the other **94v/col b**
and fought with it a long time,
but he could not defeat it,
no matter what in the world he might do;
finally he rallied
and gave it such a powerful blow
that he tore off one of its limbs,

e lo leon per terra es cassut.[178]
E adonc lo jayant che aqui estava,[179]
e la batalha riguardava,[180]
vi los leons per terra estar
e commanset fort a cridar.
Adonc dos jayans vengheron—[181]
payre e filh crese che eron—[182]
devers Guilhot s'en van venir
e aqui lo van asalhir;
E Guilhot, come valent,[183]
defandet se apertament.[184]
Devers la un el s'en anet
e tan gran colp el ly donet[185]
che tot l'escut li va trenchar
e mout greumen l'anet nafrar.[186]
Adonc aquel aotre jayan,
che era plen de mal talen,[187]
devers Guilhot s'en va annar
e tan gran colp li va donar
d'una massa per lo costat
che per terra el l'a tombat.
Adonc Guilhot non pot levar
per res dou monde che poges far,[188]
car tan gran colp el avie pres
che anc no ac poder che si leves.[189]
Adonc los jayans lo presseron[190]
e en fort presson lo meseron.[191]
Dis un jayant, "Tu pagaras
lo da[m]pnage che donat m'as."[192]
Aras es, es Guilot presoner;[193]
Dieu li ajut, che ben li fa mestier.
E Blandinet, que esperava
Guilhot Ardit che non tornava,[194]
a las donzellas el a dich,
"Vauc m'en devers Guillot Ardit,[195]
car pavor ay che no l'ayan mort—[196]
aquel jayan che es plus fort.
Gardas me aysi los cavals;
far o podes car non son mals."
Adonc las doncellas ploreron[197]
e aqui gran dol menoron[198]
e cascunna lo va baysar,[199] in cortessia
e Blandinet s'en va annar.

and the lion fell to the ground.
Thereupon the giant who was there,
watching the battle,
saw the lions lying on the ground
and began to roar loudly.
Two giants then arrived—
father and son I think they were—
they went directly towards Guilhot
and attacked him right there.
Guilhot, valiant as ever,
defended himself with skill.
He launched himself at one
and gave him such a great blow
that he sliced through the giant's shield
and wounded him most grievously.
Thereupon the other giant,
who was intent on destruction,
went towards Guilhot
and gave him such a massive blow
to his side with a club
that he knocked him to the ground.
Then Guilhot could not get up,
no matter what he did,
for he had taken such a great blow
that he simply couldn't get up.
Then the giants took him away
and put him in prison.
One of the giants said, "You will pay
for the damage you've caused me."
So, Guilhot was now a prisoner;
may God help him, for he surely needed it.
Meanwhile Blandin, who was waiting for
Guilhot Ardit, who did not return,
said to the damsels,
"I'm going after Guilhot Ardit,
because I'm afraid that they have killed him—
especially that huge giant.
Look after the horses for me;
you can do that, for they're gentle."
Then the damsels wept
and sobbed;
each one kissed him out of courtesy
and Blandin took off.

Blandin s'en va trestot corren,
e an sa lanssa ben broden[200]
vers lo castel. S'en es anat
e tantost dedins s'en es intrat.[201]
En mentre che el s'en intrava
un jayan aysso regoardava[202]
e adonques son filh sonet,
che avia non Lionet,[203]
e dis ly, "Vai t'en as aquel
che s'en monta per lo castel
e defent li aqui lo pas;
tant che·l fasas tornar atrays."[204]
Adonc lo fils del jayan s'en anet[205]
apertamen vers Blandinet
e ges non ac tantost anat[206]
che Blandinet s'en es intrat,[207]
e aqui andous s'encontreron.
.................................[208] deficit hic
Lo jayan una massa portava,[209]
un quintals ho plus pessava;[210]
a Blandinet el ha donat
tant gran colp che l'a tombat.[211]
Adonc B[landin], come vayllent,[212]
se leve apertament,[213]
e fo mout fort corrozat;[214]
e devers el s'en anat;[215]
an la spassa ben brondet[216]
levet li un pe verament.
Lo jayan ac lo pe perdut[217]
e per terra el es cazut.
Adonc Blandin s'en va venir
devers el e va l'aussir.[218]
L'autre jayan vi son filh venzut[219]
e per terra estandut;[220]
vers Blandin s'en va venir,[221]
mout corrozat, e va li dir,[222]
"Mal y es nat; ars moras[223]
per lo dampnage che dat m'ais."[224]
Aqui commensse bella batalha[225]
e·l Blandin de Cornevalha,[226]
e tant grans colps els si doneron[227]
entr'andous, che per terra si tomberon;[228]

Blandin went at a brisk pace,
with his lance prepared for joust,
towards the castle. He set out
and was soon inside.
From the moment he entered,
a giant was watching his progress
and soon summoned his son,
whose name was Lionet,
and said to him, "Go find that knight
who has entered the castle
and stop him coming further;
make him turn back."
Then the giant's son went
directly towards Blandin
and had not advanced far
before Blandin entered
and they both came face-to-face.
.... something is missing here
The giant carried a club
which weighed a hundred pounds or more;
he delivered such a heavy blow
to Blandin that he knocked him down.
Then Blandin, brave as ever,
got up with alacrity
and was furious with rage;
he launched himself at the giant
with his sword brandished high
and promptly cut off his foot.
The giant, at the loss of his foot,
fell to the ground.
Thereupon Blandin went up to him
and killed him.
The other giant saw his son vanquished
and stretched out on the ground:
he rushed towards Blandin,
raging with fury, and said to him,
"You bastard, you're going to die
for the loss you've caused me."
He then begins a strong attack
on Blandin of Cornwall,
and they struck such great blows
to each other that they both fell to the ground;

e levan ss'en apertamen,[229]
la un e l'autre verayemen.[230]
L'un vers l'autre s'en van venir:
aqui vigras armes cruzir!
Ares batalhon aspramen
amtr'andous veramen;[231]
e Guiloth, che la batalha aussie[232]
de la presson, "Las," el dissie,
"Ares fusse jou an tu, Blandin,[233]
che jou t'ajudes et tu a my."[234]
Entretant el s'avisset[235]
com pogra anar vers Blandinet;[236]
e va ss'en come fellon[237]
vers la porta de la presson;
e en los brasses tan fort tiret[238]
che per terra tot ho tombet.
Adonx hy issi apertament[239]
de la presson verayment.[240]
Dins una salla s'en intret
e achi pro d'armes trobet;
Apertamen s'en va armar
e vers Blandin s'en va annar.
E dis li, "Cavalier, amic, **95r/col a**
ve vos ayssi Guilot Ardit.
Recorda vos de vostra amia[241]
e de nobla cavallaria."
Adon Blandin ac trop gran gauch[242] vel saltum melius
quant vi G[uilhot] e fi un saut;[243]
vers lo jayan s'en es anat
e tan gran colp li a donat
che tot l'escut li va trenchar,[244]
e per terra lo fes tombar.
Adonc lo jayan veramen
se levet apertamen,[245]
e volgh annar ver Blandinet;[246]
en son camin Guilot trobet

getting up quickly,[e]
one and the other.
They threw themselves at each other:
now you saw[f] the clashing of armor![g]
They both battled on
tenaciously;
and Guilhot, who heard the battle
from the prison, said, "Alas,
would that I were with you now, Blandin,
for I would help you and you me."
At that he considered
how he could go to Blandin.
He went stealthily
towards the door of the prison;
he pulled at it so strongly with his arms
that he threw it to the ground.
With great speed
he fled the prison.
He went into a room
and there found a pile of armor:
he quickly armed himself
and went towards Blandin.
He said to him, "Blandin, it's me, **95r/col a**
look, it's Guilhot Ardit.
Remember your girlfriend[h]
and the rules of chivalry!"[i]
Blandin then was overjoyed or jumped, better
when he saw Guilhot, and he jumped up;
he went towards the giant
and hit him so hard
that he sliced completely through his shield
and knocked him to the ground.
At that, the giant
got up fast,
intent upon going at Blandin;
in his path he found Guilhot

[e] It is clear both knights are engaged in the fight.

[f] The Occitan uses a future tense, but English usage prefers maintaining a past tense.

[g] A clear authorial intervention.

[h] We understand this as referring to one of the damsels met earlier in the story.

[i] A formulaic expression, seen before.

che li donet un colp de lanssa
e pasa lo per miech la panssa.
Adonc lo jayan se santi nafrat[247]
e per terra el es tombat,
e ges tantost non poc surgir[248]
che Blandin sus li va venir,
e levet li un beroyer
che portava, de fin acier;
e Guilhot li va ayudar[249]
e antr'amdos lo van matar.[250]
Ares son mors los dos jayans
che eran plens de mals talens.[251]
Apres s'en intren per lo castel,[252]
che era gratios et bel;[253]
e puyesses las donzellas soneron[254]
e ellas tantost vengheron.[255]
Gran gauch agron, non gial parlar;[256]
cascunna son amic va bayssar.[257]
Adonch elas si meron per hostal[258]
e regarderon d'amon, d'aval,[259]
e en una presson atroberon[260]
tot lor lignage de que eron;
e viron aqui lor payre histar[261]
e mais lo frayre Baltassar.[262]
Adonc elas van venir[263]
vers Blandinet e van li dir,[264]
"Senhor, amic, aysi venes,
e mos amics delieurares."
Adonc Blandin, verayamen,[265]
s'en va a la presson apertamen
e va los tos d'aqui gittar
e de aquella penna desliurar.
Adonc lo senhor del castel
e tot lor linhage amb el[266]
feron aqui granda honor
als dous cavaliers de valor.
E las donsellas van bayssar[267]
tot lur linage e abrassar.[268]
Tot enssens, de gran gauch che avien,[269]
ploravan quart de presson ysion.[270]

who gave him a thrust from his lance
deep into the middle of his stomach.
The giant felt himself to be wounded
and fell to the ground
and, unable to get up again,
lay there as Blandin rushed upon him
and lifted the helmet
of fine steel which he was wearing;
Guilhot moved to help him
and between them they killed him.
Now both these giants were dead
who were filled with malevolence.
After that, they went into the castle,
which was elegant and beautiful;
then they summoned the damsels
who came at once.
They were pleased beyond words;
each kissed her beloved.
Then they searched[j] through the palace,
looking high and low,
and in a prison
found their entire family;
they saw their father there
as well as their brother, Balthasar.
After that, they came
to Blandin and said,
"Sir, love, come,
and you will release our kin."
Then Blandin
rushed to the prison
and rescued them,
releasing them from their captivity.
Thereupon the lord of the castle
and all his family with him
paid their highest respects
to the two brave knights.
The two damsels kissed
and hugged all their family.
All together, on leaving the prison,
they wept tears of joy.

[j] The Occitan uses future tenses in this section; we follow English usage which prefers past tenses.

Aqui feron mot bella festa[271]
tos ensems e ben honesta.[272]

[New chapter in story]

E quant elos agron repausat,
aysso fu ben myech jort pasat.[273]
Adonques Blandinet a dich,
"Che faren nos, Guiloth Ardit?
Voles che repaussen aysi[274]
aquesta nuch tro lo matin?"
Respon Guillot et ay li dich,[275]
"So che plara a vos, amy."
Adonques parlet tot lo linage[276]
e disseron, "Cavaliers de bel parage,[277]
volres vos en tantost annar,[278]
che non voles plus reposar?
Per amor e per cortessia,
per Dieu, senhors, aquo no sia
che nos fassas tal desonor,
car nos morïan de dolor.[279]
Repausas vos un mes o dos,
tant quant playra a vos, senhors,[280]
e dal castel las claus p[re]nes,[281]
e si vos plays, senhors en sares."[282]
Respon Blandin, "Gentils senhors,
si a vos plays, perdonas nos,
car nos non poden remanir[283]
e conven nos a despartir.[284]
Nos sem cavalliers d'Orien,[285]
sercans avantura veramen,[286]
e conven la nos a sercar
per lo desert senza tardar,[287]
car aotrament non serian presiat[288] [non] intrabunt honorem
ni per bons cavalie[r]s reputat.[289]
Per que reges vostre castel
car, per ma fe, el es mout bel.[290]
E dic vos que·l podes gardar[291]
a tot lo mont per bataglar.
E randes graties a Dieu[292]
che vos ajudat, non pas jou."[293]
Ares parlaron las donzellas[294]
gratiosamen a merveilhas,[295]
ausen che non volian remaner;[296]
en sospiran elas van dir,

They held a splendid feast
with everyone present.

[New chapter in story]

When they had finished,
at least half a day had passed,
and then Blandin said,
"What shall we do, Guilhot Ardit?
Do you want us to stay here
tonight, until the morning?"
Guilhot replied,
"Whatever you want, my friend."
Then all the family spoke up
and they said, "Worthy knights,
do you want to go away so soon?
Don't you want to rest a bit?
For the sake of love and courtesy,
by God, it must not happen
that you do us such a dishonor,
for we would die.
Stay a month or two,
as long as you please, my lords.
Take the keys of the castle,
and, if you wish, you'll be masters of it!"
Blandin replied, "Noble lords,
please forgive us,
for we can't stay,
and we must leave.
We are knights from afar,
in search of adventure.
We must go on our search
across the wilderness without delay;
otherwise we would not be esteemed   they would [not] be honored
nor considered worthy knights.
So, rule your castle yourselves,
for, in my opinion, it is very beautiful.
I assure you that you can protect it
against the whole world by fighting.
And give thanks to God
who helped you, not I."
Now the young women spoke up
graciously,
on hearing that the knights didn't want to stay.
With sighs, they said to them,

"Gentils cavaliers de parage,
che nos amen de fin corage,[297]
che vos en vulhas tantost annar?[298]
Per ren dal mont non se pot far![299]
Nos vos pregon, gentils senhors,
che remangas per nostra amor
aquesta nuch tro lo matin,
e puis tenres vostre camin."[300]
Las donzellas tant los pregeron[301]
che aquella nuch remangeron;[302]
E puis quant vench lo dia clar,[303] **95r/col b**
els panseron de cavalcar.
Lur camin tengron vers Orient[304]
antr'andos veramen;[305]
e van parlan de l'avantura
che entr'andos era venguda.
E quant furon lunch del castel,[306]
els van ausir un can d'aossel[307] unum cantum
chi dissia en son cant,[308]
"Gentils senhors, annas avant
e atrobares un gran desert.[309]
Intras vos ben apert,[310]
e quant seres jus un bel pin[311]
che trobares en lo camin,
la un tenga a la part drecha[312]
per una cariera estrechia,[313]
e l'autre tenga a l'autre man.[314]
Aventura trobares mout gran."[315]
Adonc si van mereviglar[316]
quant ausiron l'aussel parlar[317]
So dis Guilhot, "Aves aussit[318]
d'ayssel ausel, che vos a dich?"[319]
Respon B[landin], "Hoc veramen,
de que fo merveillat fortmen;[320]
mas per tot sert nos sercaren
l'avantura, si trobar la porrien.[321]
Per so pensen de calvacar;[322]
veyrem si la poyrem trobar."
Els cavalcheron tot apert
tant che atroberon lo desert.
Apertamen es calvacheron[323]
tro che lo pin trobat agheron.
Adonc dis lo bon Blandin,[324]

"Kind knights of high rank,
whom we love with all our hearts,
why do you want to go so soon?
For all the world, this can't happen!
We beg you, noble lords,
to remain here for love of us
this evening until the morning,
and then resume your journey."
The young women begged them so much
that they remained that night.
When daybreak came **95r/col b**
they prepared to ride on.
They headed towards the east,
both of them together,
and spoke of the adventure
which they had experienced.
And when they were far from the castle
they heard the song of a bird a song
which said in its song,
"Good sirs, travel further
and you will find a vast wilderness.
Go straight in
and when you are beneath a handsome pine
which you will find on your way,
let one of you go to the right
on a straight path,
and the other to the left.
You will discover an exciting experience."
They then began to marvel
when they heard the bird speak.
Guilhot said thus, "Did you hear
that bird and what it told you?"
Blandin replied, "Yes, I did,
and I am most surprised;
above all, let us go in search
of this adventure, if we can find it.
So, let's ride on
and we'll see if we can find it."
They rode straight on
until they found the wilderness.
They continued riding
until they found the pine tree.
Then said Blandin,

"Guihot Ardit, ve vos lo pin![325] In illis partibus aves locuntur
Ayssi coven ayan conselh
de so che nos a dich l'ausel.[326]
Ayam lo bon, si nos poden,[327]
consy gouvernar nos poyrem."[328]
Desot lo pin descalvaqueron
e aqui lor conselh tengeron.
So dis Blandin, "Che cogitas,
Guilhot Ardit? Ni vos penssas
de dos camins? La un prenes,
aquel che mais vos amares,[329]
car forza es che anen sercar[330]
l'avantura si la poyren trobar."
Respon Guilhot e va li dir,[331]
"Mout irat sui dal departir,[332]
totas las ves che nos voliem,
..................................[333]
Mas plus che avantura vol ayssin[334]
jou vol tenir lo gran camin.[335]
E diray vos che nos faren:
si a vos plais, nos enpenren[336] nos adiscemus
en qual loch nos poyren trobar,
che non nos qualha fort sercar."
Respon Blandin, "Per Sen Tomas,
Guilot Ardit, aysso me plas.[337]
Troben nos jus aquest pin[338]
lo jort apres de Sent Martin."
Adonch elos si van abrassar[339]
e en la bocha estrech bayssar.
Ploran, planhen, se despartiron
lo cada un de dol che agron.[340]
La via estrecha teng Blandin,
Guiloth Ardit, lo gran camin.[341]

[New chapter in story]

Guilloth pensa de calvacar[342]
apertamen senza tardar
e intra s'en per lo desert
cum bon cavalier e apertz.
El primier hom che el trobet[343]
so fu un pastre, aqui dinet,
e Guiloth li va demandar,[344]

"Guilhot Ardit, there is the pine tree! In this place, birds speak
Here we must consider
what the bird told us.
Let us think, if we can,
about how to proceed."
They dismounted under the pine
and held their council.
Blandin said, "What do you think,
Guilhot Ardit? What's your thinking about
the two roads? You take one,
whichever you prefer,
for it is important that we look for
adventure, if we can find it."
Guilhot said in reply,
"I get cross
every time we decide to part,
....
But we need adventure more.
I want to take the broad path,
and I'll tell you what we'll do:
if you like, let's think about let's discuss
where to find each other
so that we don't have to look too far."
Blandin replied, "By St Thomas,
Guilhot Ardit, what a good idea! I like that!
Let's meet under this pine
the day after St Martin's day."[k]
At that they hugged each other
and kissed each other on the mouth.
Weeping and lamenting, they parted,
each overcome with grief.
Blandin took the narrow route,
Guilhot Ardit, the broad road.

[New chapter in story]

Guilhot thought to ride on
straightaway without delay,
and trotted into the barren lands
like a brave, bold knight.
The first man he met
was a shepherd, eating a meal,
and Guilhot asked him,

[k] St. Martin's day is November 11, so the reunion will take place on November 12.

"Digas, pastre, as che mangar?"
Respon lo pastre, "Se dieu my don,[345]
hoc; jou un cartier de moton[346]
che un mien frayre m'a trames,[347]
bel e rostit. Si en volles,[348]
e mangias en, si a vos plays,
car, per ma fe, gran gauch n'array."
Adonques Guilhot descalvachet[349]
e an lo pastre se dinet.
e mentre che els se dinavam[350]
e lur novas aqui contavam,
viron venir un mesagier[351]
mot fort coren per lo sandier;
e davant els aqui passet,[352]
che anc mot el non bur sonet.[353]
Adonc Guillot si va levar[354]
e al mesagier va cridar[355]
e dis, "Amic, tornas atrays,[356]
e si ty plais, am mi parleras."[357]
Adonc lo mesagier va cridar,[358]
"Gentil senhor, laysas m'anar[359]
car tant grant es la coch che ay,[360]
che per ren dire non la say."
Respon Guiloth, "Si choia as,[361]
tol la; penras ben a de pro das.[362]
Digas me ta mesageria,
si non dire la ti faria."[363]
Adonch respon lo mesagier,[364] **95v/col a**
"Jou suy dal Negre Cavaller,[365]
che es mot san et apert[366]
e esta en garda d'un desert.
E deman deu aver batalha
an dos cavaliers de Cornialha.
Per so, sengor, el my tramet[367]
a un syen fraire Leonet[368]
chi li trameta son caval,
car lo sien, senhor, tan non val."
So dis Guilloth, "Encara mais[369]
me diras, se a tu plais.[370]
Digas, lo Negre Cavalier,
che tu me fas tan bon guerrier,[371]
en cal loch lo porray trobar?
Car, per ma fe, la vuelh annar."

"Tell me, shepherd, do you have anything to eat?"
The shepherd replied, "Thanks to God,
yes; I have a haunch of mutton
which my brother sent me,
roasted and tasty. If you'd like some,
then eat it, please,
for, indeed, I'd be most happy."
Guilhot dismounted
and had dinner with the shepherd.
While they were eating
and telling each other stories,
they saw a messenger approach,
running hard down the path;
he passed in front of them
without saying a word or making a noise.
Then Guilhot got up
and shouted to the messenger,
saying, "Hey, friend, turn back,
and speak to me, please."
The messenger shouted back,
"Dear sir, let me go on
for my business is more urgent
than I can possibly say."
Guilhot replied, "If you're in a hurry,
you should slow down.
Tell me your message
or I'll force you to."
Then the messenger said, **95v/col a**
"I come from the Black Knight,
who is very cunning and swift,
and who is on guard in the wilderness.
Tomorrow, he must do battle
with two knights from Cornwall.
For this reason, my lord, he is sending me
to his brother, Lionet,
who will send him his horse
for his own, my lord, is unworthy."
Then said Guilhot, "One more thing,
tell me, please.
This Black Knight
who you tell me is such a good warrior,
where can I find him?
Because, I really want to go there."

Adonc respont lo mesagier,[372]
"Vos, senhor, noble cavaller,
lo trobares en un desert[373]
che hon appella Claus Cubert.
Mais volgra vos aconselhar
che per ren no·i vogeses annar,[374]
car totz aquelos che passon lay[375]
per lo desert ont el istay,
tos, senhor, i los fa langir
e a mala mort morir."[376]
Respont Guilhot, "No t'a que far
si fa langir o·m fa pennar.[377]
Aras t'en va, en non de Dieu,[378]
car, se Dieu plais, taul faray jou."[379]
Adonch Guillot pren son arnes,
e cumiat dal pastre pres,
e cavalchet trestout apertz
tant che atrobet aquel desert.
E intren s'en am bon corage[380]
come bon çavalier de parage.[381]
E quant el ac gran temps anat
per lo desert e cavalcat,
el va trobar un gran vergier
ont avia trop bel pesquier.
Cubert era d'un bel pavaglon[382]
trestot entorn la l'aviron.[383]
Adonques fort se meravilhet[384]
quant tal pesquier aqui trobet;
en mentre ch'el istava rigardan[385]
aquel pesquier et remiran,
el vi venir lo cavalier
che li ac dich la mesagier.[386]
E venc sus un gran caval corrent,[387]
d'arnes cubert verament,[388]
e dis, "Cal sies tu, cavalier,
che sies intrat en mon vergier?
Pensa tantost descalvacar[389]
e de tot ton armes layssar,[390]
car, per ma fe, tu penras mort[391] de heremita nota ultra
plus che sies intrat en lo mien ort.[392]
Per sert, jou te trayray los feges[393]
....
e te faray mangar a cans,

The messenger replied,
"You, Sir, knight,
you will find him in a wasteland
which is called the Covered Close.
But I would advise you
that you should not go there for any reason;
all those who cross
the wasteland where he is,
all, my lord, he makes suffer
and die a terrible death."
Guilhot replied, "It's not your business
if he makes me suffer in pain.
Go on your way, in the name of God,
and, God willing, I shall do the same."
Then Guilhot took his armor,
took leave of the shepherd
and rode off straightaway
until he came to that wilderness.
He entered it fearlessly,
as good knights do.
And when he had gone for some time
riding through the wasteland,
he found a big orchard
where there was a most beautiful fishpond.
It was covered by a beautiful canopy
surrounding it on all sides.
He was much surprised
at finding such a fishpond here;
while he stood there looking
in admiration at that fishpond,
he saw a knight ride up
just as the messenger had told him.
He came up on a large swift horse,
covered completely in armor,
and said, "Who might you be, knight,
that you come into my orchard?
Dismount at once
and lay down all your armor,
for, by my faith, you will die, about the hermit, see later
since you have intruded into my garden.
Indeed, I shall disembowel you
....
and I shall feed you to the dogs,

a mos mastins et a mos alans."[394]
Adonc Guiloth enfla las narres[395]
et cruys las dens entre las beres[396]
e dis, "Cal sies tu, tant malvat,
che tant vilment m'ais parlat?[397]
Jou non te presse un boton,[398]
an ti rumpiray ton pavalhon.[399]
E si tu abre .i. voles far[400]
pensa tantost de batalhar.
Per so che as dich, jou lo rompiray,[401]
e ges per tu non estaray."
Adonc el s'en va anar;[402]
e·l pavalhon li va trinchar.[403]
Adonc lo Negre Cavalier,
che era in garda del paschier,[404]
fo mout irat et fort felon[405]
quant vi romput son pavalhon;[406]
e devers el s'en va venir
e tan gran colp lo va ferir
sobre la penna de l'escut
che ben dous pals l'en a romput.
Apres Guillot lo va ferir
de colp de lansa, sans mentir,
che tot l'escut li va trenchar[407]
e mot grevement l'anet nafrar.[408]
Aqui ben myech jorn combateron[409]
che conquistar non se pogheron.
Apres si van tals colps donar
che per terra se van tombar,
la un de sa, l'autre de la,[410]
cambas enversas, s'en vira.
Esteron tosts amortisit[411]
per miech del sol e esbaït,
e ges levar non si podian
per los grans colps que pres avian.
A cap da temps, si van levar[412]
e torneron a batalhar.
Al premier colp che si doneron[413]
adonques las espasses romperon—[414]
adons furon ben comminals. **95v/col b**
E meron mans per los ponhals,[415]
e trop greumens els se nafreron;[416]
e gran sanc andos perderon.[417]

to my mastiffs and my hounds."
At that Guilhot flared his nostrils,
took the bit between his teeth
and said, "Who the devil are you
to speak to me so rudely?
I don't give a damn for you
and I shall destroy your canopy.
If you want to make it a shelter,
be ready to fight for it.
Because of what you've said, I shall destroy it
and will not stop because of you."
Then he advanced;
he began to hack at the canopy.
Then the Black Knight,
the guardian of the fishpond,
was most angry and wrathful
when he saw his canopy broken;
he went towards Guilhot
and gave him such a stunning blow
on the flap of his shield
that he tore away a foot and a half of it.
Then Guilhot struck him
a blow with his lance,
which pierced his shield
and wounded him most grievously.
They fought for most of the day
for neither could defeat the other.
They had dealt so many blows
that they both fell to the ground,
one here, one there,
imagine, their legs in the air.
They lay there completely exhausted
and breathless on the ground,
and could hardly get up
because of the blows they'd received.
After a while, they rose to their feet
and resumed battle.
At their first blow
they broke their swords—
now they were both equal. **95v/col b**
They drew their daggers
and inflicted grievous wounds on each other;
each lost vast amounts of blood.

E Guiloth vi che mal annava[418]
car tot son sanc el escampava;
an gran corage so es pres,[419]
che tot son coltel, li a mes
per miech del cols (l'y a donat),[420]
e per terra el l'a tombat.
Adonques Guilhot sus ly montet,[421]
e hostet li son bacinet,
e dona li per miech la gorja,
che semblet manescalc en forja,
e nafra lo per miech lo col
che encar rendre non se vol.[422]
So dis Guilhot, "Tu te rendras[423]
o per tot sert aras moras."[424]
Adonc lo cavalier va dir,
"Jou sui venzut, sensa mantir,[425]
et prego te che·m dones un don:[426]
plus che tu veses che mort suy,[427]
un pauch a beure my daras,
car, per ma fes, marsi n'aras."
So dis Guiloth, "Che ty daray[428]
che vin ni ayga jou non ay?"[429]
Respon lo Negre Cavaler,
"Das my de l'aiga del paschier."[430]
Respon Guilhot che de bon talen,[431]
"Aquo farai jou veramen."[432]
Adonc Guilhot s'en va anar
e de l'ayga li va portar.[433]
En mentre d'ayga li donava
aquel cavalier s'en passava.
Achi morit el verament,
de que Guilhot fu mot dolent;
Car mais amera che visches
e a marse el l'ages pres.
Adonch dix lo bon Guillot,[434]
"Dieus ti perdon, chi faire o pot.
Ayssi non pode alre far,[435]
prec Dieus che en vulha perdonar."[436]
Adonc el pris el cavallier[437]
e gitet lo en lo peschier,

Guilhot saw that it was looking bad,
for he was bleeding heavily;
with an heroic effort
he picked up his dagger,
thrust through the neck
and threw him to the ground.
Then Guilhot straddled him,
removed his helmet,[1]
stabbed him through the throat
(with a blow worthy of a blacksmith)
and wounded him through his neck,
for he was unwilling still to give up.
Guilhot then said, "You will surrender,
or, for sure, you'll die."
Then the knight said,
"I am utterly defeated,
and I beg you to do me a favor:
since you see that I am dying,
give me something to drink,
unless, by my faith, you have no mercy."
Guilhot said, "What shall I give you?
I have neither wine nor water."
The Black Knight replied,
"Give me water from the pond."
Guilhot replied willingly,
"I shall certainly do that."
Then Guilhot went off
and brought him water.
While he was giving him water,
the knight passed away.
He was indeed dead,
for which Guilhot was most sad.
He would have preferred the knight alive
so that he could grant him mercy.
Thereupon Guilhot said,
"May God who can, forgive you.
I can do nothing else here,
but pray that God forgive you."
Then he took the knight
and threw him in the fishpond,

[1] See Asperti, "Bacinetti e berroviere," for a discussion of this specific item of military equipment.

per so che chins non lo mangesson
ho aotres besties che vengeson.[438]
D'aqui se partit lo bon Guilloth[439]
sus son caval, tot de gran trot.
Apert s'en va, tot nafrat.[440]
En son camin el a trobat[441]
un saint armita verament
che l'aculhil payssiblament.[442]
En son hostal el lo menet
e en son liech el lo coget.[443]
De so che Dieus ly a donat
lo bon prodome l'a confortat;[444]
achi e lo va desermar[445]
e sas plagas li va megar.
Adonch dis lo bon prodons,[446]
"Digas vos, noble gentil hom,
cal es aquel che vos a nafrat[447]
ni chi tant mal vos a adobat?"[448]
Respond Guilhot e va li dir,[449]
"Aysso a faich, senssa mantir,
un noble cavallier apert
....[450]
e per so car jou pa[ssa]va[451]
per lo desert ont el stava,[452]
podes vesser comme m'a adobat.[453]
mas, per sert, el non a ren goassagnat,[454]
car, per ma fe, e l'ay tot mort[455]
dins un peschier en lo sien ort."
Dis l'ermita, "Dieu n'aya grat!
Che ben set ans y a histat[456]
gardant lo bosch e lo vergier;
a mort trop nobles cavaliers
So era hom de gran corage
e atressis de gran lingnage.
Per so, senhor, avissa vos,[457]
car sos parens son grans sengnors
e poyriam vos far otrage,
o, per avantura, dar damgnage;[458]
car sapias que els ho saveran[459]
e puys tantost vos serqueram.
Per so, senhor, se m'en crezes,
de mon hostal non yssires,[460]
car els volran tan[to]st serca[r][461]

so that dogs would not eat him
or any other animals which might come.
Guilhot left there,
mounted on his horse, moving at a fast pace.
He went on, badly wounded.
On his way he found
a holy hermit
who greeted him peaceably.
He led Guilhot to his dwelling
And laid him down in his bed.
With that which God had given him,
the worthy man tended him;
he removed his armor
and tended to his wounds.
Then the good man said,
"Tell me, noble knight,
who is it who has wounded you
and caused you so much pain?"
Guilhot said in reply,
"Truth to tell, it happened thus:
There was a noble knight
....
and because I crossed through
the wilderness where he lived,
you can see how he treated me!
But, in fact, he gained nothing,
for, by my faith, I killed him
in a pond in his own garden."
The hermit said, "God be thanked!
For he has been here seven years
guarding the wood and the garden;
he has killed too many noble knights.
He was a man of great valor
and likewise of a good family.
For this reason, sir, be warned,
for his kin are great lords
and could do you harm
or perhaps do you injury;
for you know they'll find out
and hunt you down.
So, my lord, believe me,
don't leave my lodging,
for they will want to search

en loech si vos poyran trobar."
Respon Guiloth, "Si my van sercant[462]
en vostre hostal my trobaran,[463]
car, per ma fe, non fugeray;
per tot quant son, non m'en yrai.
Car jou my sente tal corage[464]
che non feran ges poinch d'autrage.
E si ho fan, nos nos bateren[465]
e sus los camps batalharen.
Mas prege vos, che vuelhas pensar[466]
e faich viandes leu comprar.[467]
Ve vous ayssi d'aur e d'argent,[468]
despandes pro apertament,
per so che sia tost garit
lo bon Guilhot Ardit.[469]
E puys vengon ardidament
tos sos parens apertament."
Aqui s'estet Guilhot Ardit **96r/col a**
tro che fu sanat e gairit,[470]
e puis un jorn pris cumiat[471]
del sante ermita ond hestaich.[472]
D'aor e d'argent el li donet
et en la bocha baysset,[473]
per so car l'avia servit
dins son hostal et acuglit.
Adons l'armita lo va sengnar,
e·l bon Guilhot s'en va annar.[474]
Guillot s'en va, sus son caval,
e va sercant d'amont, d'aval;
e tot un jorn el calvachet[475]
che anc avantura no atrobet.[476]
E puis quant vench l'autre matin,[477]
el encontret en son camin
un cavaler armat de negre,
che menava mot gran brega,[478]
cridant mout fort, "Las! Che faray?[479]
De grant dolor, per sert, moray
si no trobe lo cavallier[480]—
sel chi a mort lo bon garier!"
Adonc Guilhot lo saludet[481]
e de noves lo demandet[482]
e dis, "Cavallier d'avantura,
de que menes tan gran rancura?

the area to see if they can find you."
Guilhot replied, "If they come searching
they'll find me in your lodging,
for I promise I won't flee;
I shall not leave here for all the world.
I feel so powerful
that they will do me no harm at all.
And if they do, we will fight each other
and do battle in the fields.
But I ask that you think about
buying food quickly.
Here, have some gold and silver,
spend it wisely,
so that good old Guilhot Ardit
may be speedily healed.
Then let them come boldly,
all his family."
Guilhot Ardit stayed there **96r/col a**
until he was completely healed.
Then came the day when he took leave
of the holy hermit.
He gave him gold and silver
and kissed him on the mouth
for having helped him
and welcomed him in his lodgings.
The hermit then gave him the sign
of the cross, and Guilhot went on his way.
Guilhot, mounted on his horse,
went ranging far and wide
and rode for an entire day
without finding adventure.
Then, the next morning,
he found on his way
a knight armed in black,
who was making a lot of noise,
crying most loudly, "Alas, what shall I do?
I shall certainly die of grief
if I don't find the knight—
the one who killed the great warrior!"
At that Guilhot greeted him,
and asked him for news,
"Knight on a quest,
why are you grieving so much?

Demandas vos sel cavalier
che a mort l'autre al peschier?"
Respond l'autre, "Hoc, verament;[483]
de que suy plen de mariment,
car lo myen fraire m'a mort[484]
e faich morir a mala sort.
Per so lo vogra fort trobar[485]
e amb el volgra bataglar."[486]
Respond Guilhot apertament,[487]
"Trobat l'aves vrayament,[488]
car hieu suy sel che·l vos a mort[489]
per gran batalha dins un ort."
Adonques l'autre cavallier,
che era frayre del mort primier,
anet gitar un fort grant crit.[490]
"Sies tu aquel che l'as aosit?[491]
Pensa tantost de batalhar,
car tu non podes escampar.[492]
Sies tot sert che ares moras[493]
per lo mien fraire che mort as."
Respon Guilhot, "Jeu non ho say,[494]
se per avantura jou moray."[495]
Adoncha s'en van intrar[496]
en un bel camp per batalhar.
L'un ver l'autre s'en van venir,[497]
de colp de lansa se van ferir.
E Guilhot li va tal donar[498]
che de part en part le va passar.[499]
Adonch lo cavallier, de contrent,[500]
si tombet de son caval trestot freit,[501]
che anc mot non poch parlar[502]
per ren che Guilhot poges far.
E Guilhot vi che mort jassia,
sa lanza pren et teng sa via.[503]

[New chapter in story]

Apertament va cavalchar
tro che fo hora de dinar.
En una font che el trobet, De fonte reperto
sus un bel prat el se dinet.[504]
E tantost quant el fo dinat,
ni sus sum caval fu montat,[505]
el vi venir gran calvacada[506]
de cavaliers per miech la strada,

Are you asking about that knight
who killed the knight at the pond?"
The other replied, "Yes indeed;
that's why I'm full of sorrow,
for he has killed my brother
and made him die a terrible death.
So I really want to find him
and do battle with him."
Guilhot replied immediately,
"You have indeed found him,
for I am he who killed your man
in a fierce battle in a garden."
Then the other knight,
who was the brother of the dead first knight,
let out a long loud cry.
"Are you the one who killed him?
Get ready to fight right now,
for you cannot escape.
Be absolutely sure that you will die,
for you have killed my brother."
Guilhot replied, "I don't know about that,
unless it is my fate to die."
Then they went into
a fine field to fight.
They moved toward each other
to strike with their lances.
Guilhot struck him so hard
that he pierced him through and through.
Then the knight, for his part, fell
from his horse, completely done
and unable to say a word,
no matter what Guilhot could do.
Guilhot saw that he lay dead.
He took his lance and went on his way.

[New chapter in story]

He rode quickly
until it was dinner time.
He dined by a spring the found fountain
that he found in a beautiful meadow.
As soon as he had finished,
he mounted his horse,
and saw a large band
of knights in the middle of the road

cridant mot fort an gran rimor,[507]
"Mora, mora lo traydor!"
E Guilhot vi tanta de gent
che contra el venium corrent.
Son bon caval el brochar[508]
e a una part se va tirar.[509]
Adonch vengron dos cavaliers[510]
al bon Guilhot, che se randes.
Respos Guilhot tot corrozat,[511] Respon in gra ... in dos ... t in scachy
"No ho feray ges de bon grat,
car non es de bon cavallier
che se renda al colp primier.
Mas se aotrage me volles far,[512]
pansas tantost de batalhar."[513]
Adonc dison los cavalliers,
"Tu ho veyras tantost ades."
E torn essen apertament[514]
vers lo senhor veraymen[515]
e disson li, "Senhor corteis,[516]
non se vol rendre per nulla res."
Adonc lo senhor va comandar[517]
che tos l'anesson batalhar.
D'aqui partiron .xxiii.
che·l bon Guilhot menasson pres.[518]
E Guilhot, chi los vi venir,[519]
brocha caval et va ferir.[520]
Per miech de tos el va passar
e dos per terra en fa tombar.
Aqui se portet come un leon,[521]
Guilhot Ardit, lo bon baron,
mais contra tos el non podia,
car de grans colps el rezevia.
Adonc el, la lansa al punch, †[522]
tiret s'atrays un paoch lunch,[523]
e va cridar aytam com pot, zaza[524]
"Un per un, venes a Guilhot,
e non vengas totz avissas,[525] **96r/col b**
car semblant es paor ayait."[526]
Adonc respont un cavallier,[527]
cossin german del mort primier,
"Tu sabes ben, per veritat,
che gran dampnage tu n'as donat.[528]
Per so seras ho mort, ho preis,[529]

making a great noise and shouting
"Death! Death to the traitor!"
Guilhot saw a great many people
charging toward him.
He spurred his good horse
and withdrew off to one side.
Then two knights came
to Guilhot to demand his surrender.
Guilhot replied angrily, He responded ...
"I'll not do that willingly,
for it is not the practice of a good knight
to surrender at the first blow.
But if you want to do me harm,
prepare for a battle at once!"
Then the knights said,
"You'll see it soon enough!"
While turning quickly
towards their lord,
they said to him, "Sir,
he is unwilling to surrender at any cost!"
Then the lord commanded
them to go and fight.
Twenty-three of them left,
and came menacingly toward him.
Guilhot, who saw them coming,
spurred his horse and attacked.
He went right through their midst,
and knocked two of them to the ground.
He fought like a lion,
Guilhot Ardit, the good baron,
but he could not prevail against all of them,
because of the strong blows he received.
So, with his lance in his hand, †
he withdrew a short distance,
and shouted as loudly as he could, hey!
"Come to Guilhot one at a time,
and don't be so hesitant! **96r/col b**
It looks as if you're afraid!"
Then one knight replied,
a cousin of the first dead man,
"You know well,
that you have done us great harm,
and so, you'll be killed or captured,

si nos poden per nulla res."
Et Guilhot vi ch'elos venion[530]
encontra luy tan com podian;[531]
Una autra ves el va ferir
per miech de totz, senssa mantir;
e lo primier che el encontret,
de colp de lanza a mort lo met.
Adonques totz lo cavaliers[532]
li van venir, davant, darieres,[533]
e disson ly, "Ren ti, ren ti![534]
Si non, per sert, tu non penrras fin."[535]
Respont Guilhot, "Jou dich vos ay[536]
che de bon grat non my renderay.[537]
Si per forssa penrre my podes,[538]
puyes en fasses so che volres."[539]   A-
Adonques un li vanc detras[540]
e pres lo fort a tros de bras;[541]   ennan van ze tost
e puisses un autre s'avansset[542]
e son caval el ly nafret.
Lo caval se senti nafrat[543]
e per terra el es tombat.
Adonch Guilhot fon esperdut[544]
e rendet se coma vensut.[545]   Pero sena o.
Adonch els lo van liar[546]   sit una sac ... in nostro vulgari ab illo. R.
e en lor castel lo van menar;
e en fort preson lo messeron,[547]
che nulla merssi non agheron.[548]
Ares es Guilot pressoner,
Dieus li ajut, che ben li fa mester.[549]

[New chapter in story]

D'aqui se part lo bon Blandin[550]
e va ss'en per l'estrech camin,
e intra s'en per lo boscage
come bon cavallier de parage.[551]
Apertamen el va sercar[552]
avantura, si la porria trobar.[553]
E quant el ac un temps anat
per lo boscage ont era intrat,
el va vezer una donzella,
mout gratiosa a meravilhas,[554]
che goardava en un prat[555]
un caval blanc, tot ensellat.[556]
E cantava joliamen[557]

if we can do anything at all!"
Guilhot saw them coming
at him as well they could.
Once more he struck
through the middle of them;
the first man that he met
he killed with a blow from his lance.
Then all the knights
came at him from the back and the front
and said to him, "Give up, give up!
If not, you won't be worthy!"
Guilhot replied, "I have told you
that I won't give up willingly.
If you can take me by force,
you can do what you want!" A-
Then one came up behind him
and seized him by the arms; they went quickly
then another came forward
and wounded his horse.
The horse realized it was wounded
and fell to the ground.
Then Guilhot lost hope
and surrendered. but without o.
They tied him up in a sack ... in our language with him. R.
and took him to their castle;
they put him in an inescapable prison
and would grant him no mercy.
Now Guilhot is a captive,
God help him, for that's what He does!

[New chapter in story]

[Meanwhile,] Blandin departed
and followed the narrow road.
He went into the woods
as a good knight does.
He went quickly to find
adventure, if it were there.
When he had gone for a while
through the woods he was in,
he saw a damsel,
wondrously beautiful,
who was in a meadow, keeping her eye
on a white horse, fully saddled.
She was sweetly singing

un cant d'amors veraiament.[558]
E quant Blandin vi la donzella,
apertamen s'en va vers ella,[559]
e bellament la saludet
E d'amors li demandet.[560]
e dis, "Donzella de gran parage,[561]
com es ayssi en tal boscage?"[562]
E li, "De qui es tam bel caval?[563]
Preg Dieus che lo garde de mal,[564]
car, per ma fe, el es mout bel[565]
a cavalchar a tot donzel."[566]
Adonc la donzella respondet[567]
cortessament a Blandinet
e dis, "Senhor, per veritat,
diray vos atot de bon grat.[568]
Jou suy donzella d'otra mar[569]
che avantura vaoc sercar,[570]
e vuelh penrre ma dinada[571]
an mon chival per esta prada.
E si dinar am mi vos plaissia,[572]
per ma [fe], gran gauch n'auria,[573]
car de viandes ay abastament[574]
a mi e a vos verament."
Blandin, quant aossi la cortessia[575]
che la donzella li dissia,
respondet li corteissament
come bon cavallier verament[576]
e dix ensi, "Donzella de parage,[577]
jou penseria de far aotrage[578]
si plus avant jou cavalchava[579]
et jou am vos non my dinava.[580]
Si lo convit jou non prenia,[581] vel ria melius
per sert, faria gran vilania.
Per vostra amor jou lo penrray,[582]
e an vos jou me dineray."[583]
Adonc Blandin descalvachet[584]
e la donzella acompanhet.
La donzella mes tantost taula
dejus l'ombra de un bel sausse;[585]

a song of love.
When Blandin saw the damsel,
he approached her quickly
and greeted her politely.[m]
He asked for her love,
and said, "Damsel of high rank,
what are you doing in these woods?
And whose beautiful horse is that?
I hope to God, He looks after it!
By my faith, it is fine enough
for any young lord to ride."
Then the damsel replied
to Blandin courteously,
saying, "My lord, truly,
I'll tell you this willingly.
I am a maiden from afar,[n]
seeking adventure.
and I want to eat my dinner
in this field, with my horse.
If it would please you to eat with me,
it would please me greatly.
I have plenty of food,
both for myself and for you."
Blandin, when he heard the polite offer
which the damsel made,
he replied to her courteously,
as a good knight does,
"Worthy damsel,
I would be insulting you
if I rode on further
without dining with you.
If I didn't accept your invitation — or, better, take
it would surely be a boorish thing to do.
For love of you, I'll accept,
and I will dine with you."
Then Blandin dismounted
and kept the damsel company.
The damsel set the table
in the shade of a beautiful willow

[m] This opening is reminiscent of a pastorelle.

[n] Nelli and Lavaud understand *otra mar* as meaning Great Britain, *Blandin de Cornouailles*, 453n.

estandet blancha toagla[586]
davant Blandin de Conivalha.[587]
E commaseron a dinar[588]
e leur viandes a mangiar.[589]
Adonch Blandinet parlet[590]
e a la donzela demandet[591]
e dis li a, "Francha creatura,[592]
preg vos che me digas l'avantura[593]
che vos disses che annas cerchan.[594]
Digas m'o leu, de bon talen,[595]
car, sus ma fe, vos prometeray[596]
che de bon cor vos serviray." terrai secret[597]
Dis la donzella, "Gran merces
de so, senhor, que dich aves,
car vos non podes ajudar
a m'avantura sercar.[598]
Mais an per ho dinaren nos,[599]
et puysses diray la vos."[600]
Aqui dineron franchament
andous ensems verayament;[601]
e quant agron de tot dinat,[602] **96v/col a**
deportant se per miech lo prat.[603]
Adonc Blandin ac gran tallent
de dormir verayment,[604]
e dis, "Donzella, sans mentir,
grant tallent ay d'un pauc dormir.[605] lo fassia li gran jorn
Preghe vos che aysi nos repausen[606]
per aquest prat et dormiren."
Dis la donzella, "En nom de Dieu,[607]
car atressi gran sompn ay jou."[608]
Adonquas el s'en va annar,[609]
e sot un bel pin s'en van paussar.[610]
Aqui dormi le bon Blandin
sus lo bel prat, desot un pin.
E la donzella, quant sentit
che Blandinet fon adormit,
tot plain ella se levet[611]
e pres lo caval de Blandinet.[612]
Apertament sus va montar
e mot corrent s'en va annar.
Va s'en fugent per lo camin
an lo caval del bon Blandin,
e layssa lo sien per mich del prat,[613]

and spread a fine white cloth
before Blandin of Cornwall.
They began to dine,
eating their food.
Then Blandin spoke
and asked the damsel,
"My dear girl,
pray tell me the adventure
which you say you are seeking.
Tell me briefly and freely,
for, by my faith, I promise
that I will serve you loyally."
I will keep it secret
The damsel replied, "Thank you
for your offer, my lord,
but you cannot help
me seek my adventure.
But let us eat,
and then I will tell you about it."
There they ate in relaxation,
the two of them together;
and when they had eaten,
96v/col a
they played in the meadow.
Then Blandin had a great urge
to sleep.
He said, "Damsel, without telling a lie,
I really want to take a nap.
It's the middle of the day
I pray you, let us rest here
in this meadow and sleep."
The damsel said, "In the name of God,
yes, for I, too, am very tired."
Then they went
and lay down under a lovely pine tree.
Blandin fell asleep there,
under the pine in the beautiful meadow.
When the damsel saw
that Blandin was fast asleep,
she rose very quietly
and took Blandin's horse.
She mounted it promptly,
and rode away quickly,
fleeing down the road
with Blandin's horse,
leaving her own in mid-meadow,

desot un arbre, estachat. la staca
E torna ss'en apertament
ver sa maysson verayament.[614]
E quant Blandin ac pro dormit,[615]
apert se leva tot ardit.
Cuget trobar la companilha[616]
che el de premier avia,[617]
e non la trobet verament,
de que fu merveilhat fortment.
E regardet d'amont, d'aval;
aytan pauch vi lo sien caval,[618]
mais vis aquel de la donzella
che sus lo dos porta la ssela.
Adonquas el s'en va annar
e apertament sus va montar.[619]
E quant el fon desus montat,[620] li lassa la brilla a la pastura
en un bel camp el l'a menat,
e aqui el lo asaget,
E vi che trop ben si portet.[621]
Adonch el dis, "Se Dieu m'ajut
per un trobat, aotre perdut."[622]
Apres tantost d'aqui partit
quays tresque tot efelonit,[623]
e va jurar sobre sa testa
che nonc' aura nulla festa[624]
tro son caval aya trobat
e sella che l'en a mennat.[625]
E intre ss'en per lo boscage
come bon cavalier de parage,[626]
e van sercan de la donzella[627]
apert si en trobaria novella.[628]
E ben tres jours el cavalchet,
che anc avantura non atrobet.[629]
E puis quant venc le quart matin,[630]
el encontret en son camin
un escuder tot cavalchant[631]
che venia mot fort plorant,
credant, "Catyeu! My las! Che faray?[632]
De grant dolour per sert morray!"
(Acorava de faim [e seid][633]
deman el peria tot de freid.)[634]
Adonc Blandin lo saludet,
e de novas li demandet.

tied up under a tree. tied up
She turned swiftly
towards her house.
When Blandin had slept sufficiently,
he jumped up.
He thought he would find the companion
who was with him before,
but he didn't,
which surprised him greatly.
He looked high and low;
he couldn't see his own horse,
but he saw the damsel's,
wearing its saddle on its back.
Then he went
and mounted quickly.
Once he had mounted it, he left the bridle in the pasture
he took it to an open field
and tried it out there.
He saw how well it behaved,
and said, "God help me,
one horse lost, another one found!"
Then he galloped off,
growing more and more furious,
and swore by his head
that he would never celebrate a feast
until he had found his horse
and the woman who took it.
He went into the woods
as a good knight does,
looking for the girl
to see if he could get wind of her.
He rode for a good three days,
and had no luck.
Then, on the morning of the fourth day,
on the road he met
a squire riding along,
who was weeping profusely
and crying, "Wretch! Alas! What'll I do?
I will surely die of grief!"
(He would die of hunger [and thirst]
or perish from the cold.)
Then Blandin greeted him
and asked him for news.

E va li dire de que tant plorava,[635]
ny per che aytal dol menava.[636]
Adonc respondet lo scuder,[637]
"Diray vos o, bon cavalier,
debes saber, per veritat,
che mon maystre a batalhat[638]
per una dona encantada[639]
che en esta terra s'es trobada,
que goardon .x. bons cavaliers[640]
en un castel che es ayssi pres.
E chi podia conquistar
los cavaliers per batalhar,[641]
dis si que aurie hom la donzella,
che es mot gratiosa e bella.
E mon maystre, per amor
che gazanhes pres e honor,
volc combatre am los cavaliers;
mais, per ma fe, mal li n'es pres!
Q'assi, quant el la vol intrar[642]
dins lo castel per bataglar,[643]
los cavaliers tos se leveron
e chi, senhor, a mort lo meteron.[644]
Per zo, senhor, hyc vaoc plangent[645]
la siena mort verayament."[646]
Respont Blandin de Cornialha,
"Non vos plores, se Dieus vos valha,
car hom deu penrre bon conort
d'un homme, quant ho vey mort.[647]
Mas faich ayssi quant vos diray.[648]
An my yres, si a vos plays,[649]
e lo castel my mostrares[650]
e la donssela, si podes.
Apres sares mon servidor,
et jou seray vostre senhor,[651]
car jou feray verayament[652]
che vos entendres per content.[653]
E si aysso vos plays a far,
digas cum vos faich appellar."
Adons respondet lo scuder,
"Aquo feray mot volentiers,
e dic vos, per veritat,[654]
che Peytavin soy appellat."
Adonques els trestot corren[655] **96v/col b**

He asked why he was weeping
and lamenting so much.
The squire replied,
"I will tell you, good knight.
You should know,
that my master fought
on behalf of an enchanted lady
who lives in this country.
Ten good knights guard her
in a castle which is nearby.
Whoever can conquer
those knights in battle,
they say that he will have the damsel,
who is most beautiful and gracious.
My master, for the love
which wins prowess and honor,
wanted to fight those knights;
but, by my faith, he suffered for it!
When he tried to go
inside the castle to fight,
all the knights rose against him
and, my lord, they killed him.
That is why, my lord, I am grieving
his death sincerely."
Blandin replied,
"For God's sake, don't cry.
A man must take consolation
from another when he sees death.
Rather, do as I tell you.
Please come with me
and show me the castle
and the damsel, if you can.
Then you will be my servant,
and I will be your lord;
I will see to it
that you will be satisfied.
If you like this,
tell me your name."
The squire replied,
"I will do this willingly;
in truth,
I am called Peytavin."
Then they rode quickly **96v/col b**

se van al castel veramen;[656]
e quant foron sus al portal,
Blandin deusent de son caval.[657]
E Peytavin el l'avisset,[658]
e son caval li commandet,[659]
e va ly dir, "Esperat my[660]
apertamen tro lo matin.
E plus avant no m'esperes,[661]
car vos novellas en sabres."
Adonc Blandin s'en va anar
e al castel s'en va intrar.
E aqui trobet .x. cavaliers[662]
che apparrian bons guerriers,[663]
tos armats de fina malha,[664]
com valens gens, se Dieu mi valha.
E ayssi come el volc intrar,[665]
los cavaliers si van levar
e disson li, "Atras! Atrays![666]
Car aysi tu non interras."[667]
Respon Blandin, "Si Dieu m'ajut,[668]
non vol, ma lanssa ni mon escut,
che jou torne atras per nulla res.[669]
An verray com vos defandares.[670]
Pert tot sert, jou interrai[671]
e per tot quant s'es non isteray."[672] vel non osteray
Adonques un gran chivaler
avanset se trestot premier,[673]
e vers Blandin s'en va venir.
E tan gran colp lo va ferir
d'una destral sul basinet
che fuoch e flamma en salit.[674]
Adonch Blandin s'enfelonit,
et quant aquel l'ac ayssi ferit,
devers el s'en es anat,[675]
et tam gran colp li va donar
d'una lanssa per la peytrina
che un palm l'en passa tras l'esquina,
e tombet lo, tot estandut
en terra, mort sus son escut.

to the castle;
and when they reached the gate,
Blandin dismounted from his horse.
He gave orders to Peytavin,
entrusting his horse to him,
saying, "Wait for me
here until the morning.
Don't wait for me any longer,
for by then you will have heard news."
Then Blandin went
to the castle and went inside.
There he found ten knights,
who looked like good warriors,
all armed in fine mail,
God help me, like brave men.
As he tried to enter,
the knights rose up
and said, "Back! Back!
You won't get in here!"
"With God's help," answered Blandin,
"for the sake of my lance and my shield,
I'll not turn back for anything.
First, I'll see how you defend yourselves.
I'm definitely coming in,
and not leaving no matter how many you are!" I will not exit
Then a huge knight
stepped forth first
and advanced toward Blandin.
He struck so hard a blow
to his helmet with his axe
that fire and flames leapt out.
Then Blandin grew angry,
after the knight had struck him;
he went toward him
and struck him so hard a blow
to the chest with his lance
that it came ten inches° out his back.
He felled him, stretched out
on the ground, dead on his shield.

° For the sake of comprehensibility, we translate "one palm" as ten inches. Though English speakers think of a palm as closer to four inches, the Occitan audience would have understood a larger measure (see Pansier "Lexique provençal-français," 3:125).

Adonques los aotres chivaliers
li van venir devant et derriers,[676]
e van lo tot environnar,
et de gran colp li van donar.
Adonc Blandin ac gran corage,
com bon cavalier de parage.
Brandet l'espassa et va ferir
un cavalier, sensa mentir,[677]
e det li tal sul bacinet
che entro el manton lo fendet,
e tombet lo tot estendut
en terra, mort se son escut.[678]
.... [un cavallier][679]
mot corayos et fort sobrier
devers Blandin s'en va anar,
et tan gran colp li va donar[680]
d'una jusarma sus l'escut
che ben dous palms l'en a fandut.
Adonc Blandin fu fort irat,
quant aquel l'a anesy tochat,[681]
e tan gran colp el li donet[682]
entre lo camalh e basinet,[683]
che la testa ly va talhar
et per terra lo fy tombar—
e tombet lo tot standut[684]—
en terra mort, se son escut.
Adonch lo senhor del dich castel[685]
mot corrosat s'en vench vers el
e va lli dir fellonnament,
"Aras moras verayamens,[686]
plus che m'ais mors mos cavaliers[687]
che eron tam nobles guerriers."[688]
Adonques el lo voch ferir[689]
d'un colp de lansa, sans mantir,
mas che Blandin s'avisset[690]
et en lo scut lo paret.[691]
Adon Blandin, lo bon baron,
vers el s'en va come fellon

Then the other knights
came at him front and back,
and completely surrounded him
striking him with great blows.
Blandin took heart
as good knights do.
He swung his sword down and went
to strike a knight.
He struck his helmet
so hard that he split his head down to the chin,
knocked him to the ground,
stretched out dead on his shield.
.... [The next knight],
very proud and menacing,
advanced towards Blandin
and struck so hard a blow
to his shield with his halberd,
that it cut off twenty inches.[p]
Blandin was infuriated
when this man hit him,
and he struck him so hard a blow
between the chainmail[q] and the helmet
that it cut off his head
and felled him right down—
completely stretched out—
on the ground, dead on his shield.
Then the lord of this castle
came angrily toward him
and threatened him menacingly,
"Now you'll definitely die,
since you've killed my knights
who were such brave warriors."
Then he wanted to strike him
with his lance,
but Blandin was on his guard
and parried the blow with his shield.
Then Blandin
attacked him furiously

[p] Again, we translate "one palm" as ten inches (see note o to line 1202 on p. 167).

[q] *Camalh*, "camail," is a technical term for a flexible sheet of mail attached to a helmet and covering the throat, neck, and shoulders.

et tant grant col li va donar[692]
che las jambas li va taglar.[693]
Et tombet lo, tot estandut[694]
en terra mort, se son escut.
Adonch los autres chivaliers
che vinien trestos derriers
viron aqui lor senhor mort.
E van penrre top mal conort,[695]
e commansseron a plorar
et mot gran dol aqui mennar.[696]
E quant Blandin vi che ploravam[697]
e tan fort se desconfortavam,[698]
apertamens s'en va ver els[699]
e voch combatre mais amb els.
Els cavaliers lo viron venir[700]
e commanseron a fugir,
e intren s'en trestot fugent[701]
per lo castel verayament.[702]
E Blandinet l'escut al bras
apertament los sec detrays.[703]
En mentre che els s'en intravan
Blandinet ensems cridavan[704]
"Gentil senhor, subre la nostre fey,[705]
per Dieu, nos prenes a merci,[706]
car nos faren coma bonna gens[707]
trestot vostre commandement."[708]
Respont Blandin, "Per veritat,[709] **97r/col a**
aquo feray jou de bon grat,[710]
sy sus la fey mi prometes
che lialtat vos my tenrres."[711]
Respon els, "Vrayament[712]
d'aquo faren bon sacrament
che lialtat nos vos tenrrem
e de bon cor vos serviren."[713]
Adons els se van desarmar
e sobre sans, li van jurar
che els lialtat ly terrien
e de bon cor lo servirien.
Adonc Blandin pres lo sacramens[714]
de .vi. che eran, verayamens,[715]
e trestoz els los botet[716]
en una presson che atrobet.[717]
Apres tantost s'en va anar

and struck him so hard a blow
that it cut off his legs.
He knocked him to the ground,
stretched out dead on his shield.
Then the other knights
who were coming from behind
saw their lord dead there.
They fell into despair,
began to weep
and lament grievously.
When Blandin saw them weeping
and so disconsolate,
he went towards them quickly
and wanted to fight them.
The knights saw him coming;
they began to flee
and went running
into the castle
with Blandin, his shield on his arm,
following right behind.
While they were going inside,
they called out in unison to Blandin,
"Kind lord, upon our faith,
by God, grant us mercy!
Like good people, we will
follow all your orders."
Blandin replied, **97r/col a**
"I'll certainly do that,
if you will swear to me
your loyalty to me."
"Truly," they replied,
"we will swear
our loyalty to you
and will serve you willingly."
Then they disarmed
and swore by the saints
that they would be loyal to him
and serve him willingly.
Then Blandin took the oath
from all six of them,
and put them all
in a prison that he had found.
Then he went quickly

e per lo castel s'en va intrar.
E va sercan de la doncella,[718]
apert si en trobera novella.
En mentre che el annava regardan[719]
per lo castel e remiran,
un gran vergier el atrobet in viri[d]ario
e tantost el dins s'en intret.[720]
Lo vergier era gratios
e de ramage ben fulhos.
Aqui avia tantas d'auzels[721]
mot mervilhos et bels,[722]
che cantavon mot doussament[723]
en lor langage, veramen.[724]
E quant Blandin los va ausir,
tantost el si vol adormir
per lo gran plasser che prennia
..................................[725]
Adonc el s'en va annar[726]
e sot un arbre s'en va pausar.[727]
En mentre che el estaba escoutan[728]
aquels ausels che van cantan,
e regardet tot devant el[729]
e vi un gratios donzel
che si estava jus un pomier
e al poinch tenir un esparvier.
Adonc Blandin se va levar
e devers el s'en va annar;
cortessament lo saludet[730]
et de novas li demandet.
E dis, "Donzel gratios,[731]
preg vos che digas, per amors,[732]
si sabes per esta encontrada
una donzella encantada.
Car jou, donzel, la vach sercan[733]
e vogra fort deliurar."[734]
Adonc lo donzel respondet
cortosament a Blandinet
e va li dir, "Bon cavalier,
..................................[735]
aquella che vos demandas[736]
ma sorre es, si a vos plais.[737]
E e dedins aquel pallais[738]
d'aqui no pot ysir jamais,

and entered the castle.
He was looking for the damsel,
to see if he could get news of her.
As he was looking around
the castle and admiring it,
he found a large garden in the garden
which he immediately entered.
The garden was beautiful
and filled with leafy trees.
There were so many birds there,
most marvelous and beautiful,
singing sweetly
in their own language.
When Blandin heard them,
he immediately wanted to sleep,
taking great pleasure [in it].
....
Then he went
and rested under a tree.
While he was there listening
to the singing birds
and looking all around,
he saw a handsome young man
under an apple tree
with a sparrow hawk on his wrist.
Blandin rose,
approached him,
and greeted him courteously,
asking for information.
He said, "Young man,
pray tell me
if you know of an enchanted damsel
anywhere in this land.
Because I am looking for her
and would like to release her."
The young lord answered
Blandin courteously
saying, "Good knight,
....
the one you are asking about,
if you please, is my sister.
She is inside the palace
and can never come out.

car nostre payre l'ancantet[739]
en aquels temps che el perdet
tot son contat et mais sa terra
ayso fu per la granda gherra.
E va layssar .x. cavaliers
en garda c'omme non sa intres.[740]
Per so suy fort merevilhat
com tant avant n'es si entrat,
car los senhors non vos an mort
e fach morir a mala mort."
Respon Blandin de Cornualha,
"Diray vos ho, se Dieu mi valha![741]
Deves saber, per veritat,
che jou amb els ay batalhat.[742]
E ay mort .iiii. cavaliers[743]
e .vi. qu'en tene presonnes.[744]
Car no mi layssavon intrar
per la donsella desliurar."
Adonc lo donsel a parlayt,[745]
"Gentils senhor, dices veritat?[746]
Che siem mors los cavaliers,[747]
che eran tant marvais murtriers?"
Respon Blandin, "Certanament!
Che mors, che pres son, verament."
Adonc lo donzel s'anellet[748]
davant los pes de Blandinet,[749]
e va si fort humiliar.
E tot plorant lo va pregar,[750]
"Gentil senhor, no·n vos aves[751]
tro ma ssor delieurada aures!"
Respon Blandin, "No plaissa a Dieu[752]
che tant grand fauta fessa jou,[753]
che jou parta d'esta encontrada[754]
tro che jou l'aya deslieurada![755]
Per so pensas la my demostrar,[756]
car jou la vol deslieurar."[757]
"Gentil senhor," dis lo donzel, **97r/col b**
"Intren nos ci dedins lo castel,[758]
e plus che tant vezer la vos,[759]
aqui, senhor, la vos mostray.[760]
Mais, conven vos mais batalhar
si la voles conquistar.[761]
Mais jou creze sertanament[762]

Our father put a spell on her
at the time when he lost
all his lands and territories—
that was in a great war.
He left ten knights
to guard her so that no one could enter.
For this reason I'm very surprised
that you were able to get in
and that the knights didn't kill you
and have you die a terrible death."
Blandin replied,
"I will tell you, God help me!
You must know, truly,
that I did battle with them;
I killed four knights
and took six as prisoners.
They would not let me in
to rescue the damsel."
Then the young man said,
"Dear sir, are you telling the truth?
Are those knights dead,
who were such evil murderers?"
"Absolutely!" replied Blandin,
"They're either dead or in prison."
Then the young man knelt
at Blandin's feet
in humility,
weeping and begging,
"Dear Sir, don't claim this
until you have freed my sister!"
Blandin answered, "God forbid
that I should make the mistake
of leaving this land
before I have freed her!
So show her to me,
for I want to free her."
"Sir," said the young man, **97r/col b**
"let's go into the castle,
and since you want to see her,
my lord, I will show her to you.
But, know that you will have to fight again
if you want to win her.
But I certainly believe

che vos aves tant d'ardiament
che plus che aves conquistat[763]
los .x. cavaliers malvais[764]—
che atressis conquistares
so per que la deslieureres."
Respon Blandin, "Verament[765]
....
.... jou la conquisteray[766]
e en la peynna jou morray."[767] E
Adonchas els s'en va intrar,[768]
e aqui el ly va mostrar
dins una cambra la donzella,
chi era gratiosa e bella.
De grant beutat ela resplandia;[769]
tant era bella e jollia.
Et estava se esetada[770]
sobre un liech tota encantada.
E aqui avie .vii. damaysselas,[771]
mot merveylosas et bellas,[772]
che nuich e jorn la servien
e d'ella no si partien.
E quant Blandim vi la donzella,[773]
che era mout blancha e mot bella,[774]
va s'en tam fort ennamorar[775]
che el non saup en se che far.
E va dire al dich donzel,
"Sabes vos en aquest castel
nulla causa ni nulla res
per que hom la deslieures?"
Adonques respon lo donzel,
"Gentil senhor, hoc! Un aussel ogie[776]
che on appella blanc astor
e es saïns dins una tor.
Aquel convien che conquistes
si ma sor deslieurar volles.
E si vos plais a conquistar
diray vos con aves a far.
A la tor, senhor, vos ires,
e tres grans portals trobares.[777] de tribus portis

that you are courageous enough—
since you have defeated
the ten evil knights—
and that you will be victorious
and thus free her."
Blandin replied,
"....................................
.... I will free her,
or I will die trying!" A[nd]
Then they went inside,
and the young man showed Blandin
the damsel in a chamber;
she looked charming and beautiful.
She radiated great beauty,
so gorgeous and lovely.
She was seated,[r]
all enchanted, on a bed,
and seven damsels were there,
amazingly beautiful,
serving her night and day
and never leaving her.
When Blandin saw her and
how fair and beautiful she was,
he fell so deeply in love
that he didn't know what to do.
He said to the young man,
"Do you know of anything in this castle,
anything at all,
with which she could be freed?"
The young man replied,
"Yes, my lord! There is a bird bird
which is called the White Hawk,
and it is in a tower here.
You must capture it
if you want to free my sister.
And if you want to win,
I will tell you what you have to do.
You will go to the tower, lord,
and you will find three portals. of the three doors

[r] We must imagine the woman with so many pillows under her head that she appears to be sitting, rather than lying on the bed.

A la primiera, verayamen,[778]
atrobares un gran serpen;
a la segonda, un dragon
che es malvaitz et fort fellon;
a la terzia, per veritat,
un gran Sarraxin encantat,
che es aytal comme vos diray.[779]
El ha de golla un palm o mais
e a las dens grans comme verre,[780]
fort e duras come ferre.[781]
E a las narras ben fendudas,
e a las aurelhas ben ponchudas,[782]
e es ben negre, veramen,[783]
e ferejos a tota gent.[784]
El ha de barba mieya brassa,[785]
e ten al col una gran maza.
....................................[786]
D'aquel conven sias avissat
che el morir no pot jamais,
o el pendrie un deins dal cays.[787]
E quant aura perdut un deins,[788]
qual che sia, ardidament,
tantost el pendra sa vertut.[789] perdet virtutem
....................................[790]
Per so vos dich che en avisses[791]
che un dent dals cais li arabes.[792]
E puys, intras vos en la tor
e atrobares lo blanch astor,[793]
e prenes lo apertament
car far lo podes segurament.[794]
Tot aysso vos convent a far,
si ma sorre voles deslieurar."[795]
Respon Blandin de Cornivalha,
"Donzelot amoros, se Dieus vos valha,[796]
aquellas bestias my mostras,
car jou n'ay ja enflat lo nas,[797]

At the first,
you will meet a huge serpent,
and at the second, a dragon,
which is evil and ferocious.
At the third,
a large bewitched Saracen—
I'll tell you what he is like.
His mouth is as big as a hand, or bigger,
and his teeth are as long as a boar's tusks,[s]
hard and strong as iron.
He has nostrils split in half
and pierced ears.
He is completely black
and ferocious towards everyone.
His beard is half a yard long,
and he carries a huge club on his shoulder.
....
You must know
that he can never die
until he has lost a tooth from his jaw.
When he has lost one tooth,
and it doesn't matter which one,
he will at once lose his strength. he will lose strength
....
That is why I advise you
to wrench a tooth out of his mouth.
Then you go into the tower
where you'll find the white hawk.
Take it at once,
for you can do so safely.
You must do all of this
if you want to free my sister."
Blandin replied,
"God willing, my dear young man,
you will show me those beasts.
For I'm champing at the bit,

[s] While the simile of boar's teeth is longstanding (used by Chrétien de Troyes to describe the giant Herdsman in *Yvain*, line 302), it is noteworthy that "boar's tooth" (*dente di zengiaro*) is the name of a stance in Italian martial arts master Fiore dei Liberi's *Fior di battaglia*, composed circa 1410 and one of the first documents to describe arms, armor, and fighting techniques (see Mondshein, *The Knightly Art of Battle*, 56, 61). Implied is the battle skill of the Saracen.

per so, gentil donzel, che m'aves dich[798]
d'aquel Serraxin tant ardit."[799]
Dis lo donzel, "Mot volentier,[800]
aquo feray, bon cavalier."
Adonques els s'en va annar,[801]
e lo donzel li va mostrar
de contenent la dicha tor
en que era lo blanch astor.
Aqui presseron cumiat,
e Blandinet s'en es intrat.
Blandin, come bon cavalier,
intret per lo portal premier.[802]
E quant el fu dedins intrat,
el regoardet vers un costat,[803]
e vi, per un gran paviment,
de lonc en long, lo gran serpent
che fo saïlda d'una fossa,[804]
E fu si granda e si grossa
che ac de long .viii. ou .viiii. passes[805] **97v/col a**
e ben de grueyssa dos brasses. de gratitudine[806]
Adonc Blandin, tot corajos,[807]
vers lo serpent s'en va, de cors.
E lo serpent lo vi venir,
atressi lo volc assaglir.
E venc en gran golia badada[808] baglada
coma si fossa cosa enrabiada.[809]
Mais che Blandin s'avisset[810]
e tam gran colp el ly donet
de la lansa per miech del cays,
che bien ly en mes tres palmes o mays,[811]
e tenc la frem enastada,[812]
per miech del sol tot enversada.[813]
Adonc lo serpent non se po ajudar
an la gola per mal a far,
mais tantost ela se bosset
entorn entorn de Blandinet.
Adonc Blandin, comme valent,[814]
tray la spassa ben luxent[815]
e tant de colp el li donet
che tot lo ventre li fandet.
Adonc la serp suffrir non poch,

young man, because of what you have told me
about that fiery Saracen!"
The young man said, "I will do that
willingly, good knight."
And so they went off,
and the young man showed him,
at once, the tower
where the white hawk was.
They parted there,
and Blandin went inside.
Like a good knight, Blandin
went through the first door.
When he had entered,
he looked to one side
and saw on a large flagstone
the huge serpent, stretching out
as it slithered out of a ditch
which was big and wide,
eight or nine feet long **97v/col a**
and two good yards in depth. in thickness
Then Blandin, all fired up,
advanced toward the serpent,
and as soon as the serpent saw him,
it was ready to attack him.
Its jaws were gaping as it advanced gaping
like something rabid;
but Blandin was ready,
and struck it such a blow
with his lance in the middle of its jaw
three palms[t] or more;
he skewered it firmly,
and turned it upside down on the ground.
The serpent wasn't able
to do any damage with its mouth,
but at once it started swelling up
and wound all around Blandin.
Then Blandin valiantly
drew his shining sword
and struck it so many blows
that he split open its belly.
The serpent couldn't stand

[t] See note o to line 1202 on p. 167.

veriament, aquel joc,[816]
mais tantost perdet la vida[817]
e romas morta, esmarrida.[818]
E Blandin vi che era morta
e laysset la, detrays la porta.
E puysses s'en va trestot corrant[819]
al segon portal, veramen,[820]
e vi lo dragon che dormia. vel aliud animal
Per miech del sol el si jassia,
e ges non li volc mot sonar[821]
mais tot avant, si va intrar.
Avant s'en intra lo bon Blandin[822]
tant che atrobet lo Sarraxin. vel sarrazin[823]
E ayssi quant el vole intrar,[824]
lo Sarraxin, sant mot sonar,[825]
lo vench asalhir e requerre[826]
an una gran massa de ferre.
E mot gran colp lo volc ferir,
mais che Blandin si va gandir,
e la masa donet al sol
un tan gran colp, per Saint Cristal[827]
che tot l'ostal fes tremolar[828]
per lo gran colp che va donar.
Adonc Blandin, per gran vigor,
brandet la spassa de valor,
e donet li tal per lo cors
che un palm l'en passa tras lo dos.
Adonch lo Serraxin malvatz[829]
non fes pre nent che fos nafrat,[830]
mas comme fol, la lansa prent
e rompet la felonament.
E va levar un'aotra veis[831]
aquela massa de gran peys,
e puys s'en va come fellon
vers Blandinet, lo bon baron,
e volc lo ferir de la massa.
Mais che Blandin li fes plassa,
e va consegre un pillar
che per terra l'en va mennar.
Adonc Blandin, chi no ac lansa,[832]
tras l'espasa de fisanza.[833]

that game
but gave up
and lay there mortally stunned.
Blandin saw that it was dead,
and left it behind the door;
then he ran straight up
to the second door
and saw the dragon asleep, or some other animal
just lying in the middle of the floor.
Blandin didn't make a sound,
but just went ahead inside.
He kept moving forward
until he found the Saracen. or Saracen
When he wanted to enter,
the Saracen, without saying a word,
rushed towards him to attack him
with a huge iron club.
He wanted to give a very hard blow,
but Blandin dodged it
and the club hit the ground
so hard, by St. Cristal,
that the whole building shook
at the force of the blow.
Then Blandin vigorously
brandished his trusty sword
and struck him such a blow in the body
that it went a palm's-breadth[u] through his back.
Then the evil Saracen
didn't even notice he was wounded.
Like a madman, he grabbed Blandin's lance
and broke it furiously.
Once more he raised
that heavy club
and rushed headlong
at Blandin,
wanting to strike him with the club.
But Blandin stepped aside
and moved behind a pillar
which the Saracen knocked to the ground.
Now Blandin, who had no lance,
drew his trusty sword

[u] See note o to line 1202 on p. 167.

E va si mout fort corrozar,[834]
e devers el s'en va annar,
e tant gran colp el li donet,
che·l bras senestra li rompet.[835]
Apres li donna un altre colp
che·l vezer e l'aosir li tolc.[836]
Adonc lo Sarraxin marit
tombet al sol tot [e]sbaït,[837]
e mout gran sanc aqui perdet[838]
dels colps che Blandin a li donet.[839]
Mais morir el non podia,[840]
car proprietat avia[841]
che non pogra morir jamais
o el perdera un dent del cays.
Adonc Blandin chi aquo vi,[842]
montet dousus lo Sarraxin.
E recordet li del coltel
che li ac dona lo donzel,[843]
e trays la daga soptament.
E avisset sobre la dent,
e tant grant colp el ly donet[844]
che doas caysals li arabet.
Adonc lo Sarraxin insanglent[845]
senti che ac perdut una dent.
Alre non fis mas un sospir[846]
e soptament el va morir.
Adonc Blandin pres ben conort,[847]
quant el vi che el l'avie mort.
E intret s'en dedins la tor,
e atrobet lo blanch astor.
E va lo penrre plainnament[848]
sus en son ponch, veraiament,
e commenset s'en a salhir
an gran gauch, non voso qual dir,[849]

and, fired up with anger,
rushed toward him
and struck him such a hard blow
that it broke his left arm.
Then he hit him again
and left him deaf and blind.
The injured Saracen
fell, stunned, to the ground.
He had lost a great deal of blood
from the wounds Blandin had given him.
But he could not die,
for he had the attribute
that he could never die
until he had lost a tooth from his jaw.
When Blandin saw that,
he jumped on the Saracen.
Then he remembered the knife[v]
that the young man had given him.
He drew the knife swiftly.
He remembered about the tooth,
and he struck him so hard
that he knocked out two molars.
Then the bleeding Saracen
realized that he'd lost a tooth.
All he did was sigh,
and then he died at once.
Blandin took heart
when he saw that he had killed him.
He went into the tower
and found the white hawk.
He took it without hesitation[w]
on his wrist.
He started to jump
for joy, needless to say,

[v] This knife appears out of nowhere and is important at this moment. Van der Horst suggests that *coltel* was not intended, but rather *conselh*, unless there is a lacuna earlier. We prefer to keep *coltel*, "knife," as original and assume that in a now-missing line or lines, the knife was presented.

[w] *Plainnament*'s first meaning is "clearly, exactly, certainly," followed by "softly" or, by extension, "delicately." We think the author is playing with the several meanings of this word; our translation points to the underlying meaning of "openness" in the root word *plan*, *plana*. In contrast, see line 1629, where the same Occitan adverb is used.

per tal qual avia trobat
aquel austor et conquistat. **97v/col b**
E quant el fu sus la dragon,[850]
che era malvais et fellon,
atrobet lo, per veritat,
denpes, che s'era reyssidat.
Adonc Blandin non poc passar
per ren del mont che poghes far,
car lo dragon li defendie
aquel pas tant quant podie.[851]
Dis adonc Blandin, "Dieu me don rendas,[852]
che tot jort me crexon fassendas.
Aynsi·m conven a batalhar[853]
si plus avant voles pasar."[854]
Adonc el tornet l'astor
de contenent dedins la tor.
E puisses s'en venc come fellon[855]
apertament vers lo dragon.
e an l'espassa flamey[a]n,[856]
ben lussant et ben talhant,[857]
tant gran colp el li donet[858]
che doas costas a li rompet.[859]
Adonc lo dragon, sans mentir,[860]
devers Blandin s'en va venir
e sautet li sobre lo col
e degorar aqui lo vol.
Mais che Blandin se avisset,
e sus l'eschinna li montet.
E dirai vos con si fes el:
el annet trayre son coltel,
e dona li tal per la gola
che tot sen sanc achi li colla.[861]
Adonc lo dragon, sens mantir,
tantost comanset a morir.[862]
E Blandin vi che el moria;[863]
l'austor el prent e tenc sa via.
E intren s'en en lo castel[864]
e trobet tantost lon donzel[865]
aqui prest e apparelhat

because he had found
and captured the hawk. **97v/col b**
But when he reached the dragon
which was evil and wicked,
he found it
standing, for it had awakened.[x]
Blandin couldn't get past,
no matter what in the world he did,
for the dragon was preventing him,
with all its might, from getting past.
Blandin said, "God help me,
for the tasks keep multiplying.
Now I must fight
if I want to go further!"
He took the hawk
back into the tower.
He then rushed furiously
at the dragon.
With his flaming sword,
all shining and sharp;
he struck it such a great blow
that it broke two of its ribs.
Then the dragon
came toward Blandin
and jumped on his neck
and tried to devour him.
But Blandin was ready
and jumped on its back.
I'll tell you what he did:
he drew his knife
and struck it in the neck
so that all its blood flowed out.
Then the dragon
at once started to die.
When Blandin saw it dying,
he took the hawk and went on his way.
He went into the castle
and soon found the young man,
ready and prepared,

[x] Citing the *FEW* (s.v. PES VIII 293b), van der Horst translates *denpes* as "debout," "standing up, upright."

an las donzelas, per veritat,[866]
che aqui tos l'esperaven.[867]
D'enjunenhols, a Dieu pregavan[868]
che li dones forssa e vigor
a gazanhar lo blanc astor.
Adonc Blandin dis al donzel,
"Es aquest aquel aosel[869]
che vostra sor pot deslieurar?
Car aotre non pode trobar."
Adonc dis lo donzel, "Per veritat,[870]
aquo es el, Dieu n'alha grat."[871]
Adonquas els s'en van annar[872]
e a la donzela s'en van intrar.[873]
Et quant els li foron davant,
lo donzel de bon tallant[874]
dis a Blandin, "Gentil senhor,
baylas me vos lo blanc astor,
car jou sabe, de temps passat,[875]
la siena grant proprietat.[876]
E jou garay de contenent[877]
la myene sorre, veraymen t."[878]
Dis Blandin, "Trop ben disses.[879]
ve·l ves aysi, vos lo penrres."[880]
Adonquas lo dich donzel[881]
va penrre lo blanc aosel.[882]
E dirai vos consi el feis:[883]
la man de la donzela pris
e va li metre plannamens[884]
astor desus, verayament.[885]
E la donzella, quant santi[886]
lo blanc astor desobre si,[887]
tantost ella cobret la vida
et fo sanada e goarida.
E tot denpes se va levar,
e tantost de present comanzet a sospirar.[888]
E estet fort maravelhada
car l'avia deslieuerada.[889]
Dis adonc lo donzel, "Sorre gentil,[890]
ve vos un cavallier humil,[891]
che vos es venguda desliurar
e per faich d'armes recobrar.
Per que non vos mereveilhas[892]
mais rendes li grandas merces."

with the damsels
who were all waiting there.
Kneeling, they were praying to God
to give Blandin the strength and power
to obtain the white hawk.
Then Blandin said to the young man
"Is this the bird
which can free your sister?
I couldn't find another."
Then the young man said,
"That's the one, thank God!"
Then they went
into the damsel's room.
When they were beside her,
the polite young man said
to Blandin, "Lord,
give me the white hawk,
for I have long known
its powerful attributes.
I will quickly cure
my sister."
"You speak well," said Blandin,
"Here it is, take it!"
Then the young man
took the white hawk.
I'll tell you what he did:
he took the damsel's hand
and gently put on it
the hawk.
When the damsel felt
the hawk upon her,
at once she came back to life
and was healed and cured.
She rose to her feet
and, at once, began to sigh.
She was most astonished
that she had been freed.
The young man said, "Dear sister,
here is a humble knight
who has come to set you free
and win you by feats of arms.
Don't be astonished,
but thank him heartily!"

Ares vos diray de la donzella,[893]
las contenansas che fes ella.[894]
Ela adonc s'en va vers Blandinet[895]
e a sos pes s'anjounelhet,[896]
e dis li, "Noble cavaller,
come la flor de bon gherrier,
vos rendde grandes merses[897]
del servixi che faig m'aves.
E preg vos, lo mien senhor,[898] **98r/col a**
aytant cum pode, per amor,
que vos prengas aquest castel
e tota la signoria d'el,
e tot mon aor et mon argent,
tot a vostre comandament.
E tot quant ay, si a vos plays,[899]
preg vos che trestot ho prenas.
E per so che jou puesca recontar[900]
chi m'es venguda desliurar,
jou, Brianda, vos requer[901] [Br]ianda
che vostre non me vuelhas dir."[902]
Respon Blandin de Cornivalha,[903]
"Brianda, se Dieus mi valha,[904]
de vos non volle, per present,[905]
castel, ni terra, ni argent,
ni ren alre che vos ayas[906]
mais vostra amor, si a vos plais.[907]
Car sapias, per veritat,
che suy tant ennamorat[908]
de vos, Brianda, sans mentir,[909]
che d'amors jou cuge morir.[910]
Per che non volc point d'argent,[911] [...] voron
mas vostra amor soletament.[912] von
E plus che a vos ven a plaser,[913]
che vos mon non vulhas saber
hom m'apella, si Dieu mi valha,
Blandinet de Conivalha."[914]
Adonc respondet la donzella[915]
cortessament a meravilha[916]
e dis li, "Cavalier my plassent,[917]
la myena amor sertanament
es tot jort vostra, sens faillir,[918]
Davant tos ses che n'an dessir.[919]
Per sert, al mont non ha senhor, e sait

Now I'll tell you
what she did.
She went toward Blandin,
1648 knelt at his feet,
and said to him, "Noble knight,
paragon of warriors,
I give great thanks
1652 for the service you have done for me.
I beg you, my lord, **98r/col a**
as much as I can,
to take this castle
1656 and all it controls.
All my gold and silver
is at your command.
All that I have, if it pleases you,
1660 I beg you to take it all.
And so that I can say
who came to free me,
I, Brianda, ask you, Brianda
1664 to tell me your name."
Blandin of Cornwall replied,
"God help me, Brianda,
right now I don't want
1668 your castle, land, silver,
or anything that you possess,
but only your love.
Know that
1672 I have fallen so deeply in love
with you, Brianda,
that I thought I would die.
So I don't want any of your money, they will want
1676 rather, just your love. they go
And since it pleases you
to know my name,
I am called, by God,
1680 Blandin of Cornwall."
Then the damsel replied
most courteously
and said, "My charming knight,
1684 my love is certainly
yours for ever, without fail,
above all others who want it.
Surely, in all the world there is no lord, he knows

duc, ny rey, ni emperador,[920] ... et res
che jou ame tant sertanament,[921] ... da
et faray vos ho aparvent."[922]
Adonc ela se va levar,[923]
e vers Blandin s'en va anar,
e hostet li son basinet,
et de bon cor lo avisset.
E vi lo blanch e gratios,[924]
joly, corteys, e amoros,
e comanset lo a bayssar
de bon'amor, non qual parlar.
E Blandin fes aytrestal[925]
de Brianda, si Dieu mi sal.
Aqui esteron un gran tems,[926]
abrassas andous ensems.[927]
E puys s'aneron despartir
an gran gauch, non vos o qual dir.[928]
E la donzella saludet
lo donzel e lo baysset[929]
e atressi las donzellas[930]
d'una en una, totas ellas.
Ar vos ay dich de la doncella,[931]
las contenenssas che fes ella.
Adonc parlet lo donzellon
a Blandinet, lo bon baron,
e dis, "Vos ses tot trebalhat,
car vos aves trop batalhat.
Per che, si vos plays, anen dinar[932]
car jou n'ai fach aparelhar."[933]
Respon Blandin, "Aquo mi plais,[934]
car, per ma fe, jou sui tot las.[935]
Mas preg vos che premier annes[936]
fora al portal ont atrobares[937]
Peytavin, mon escuder,
che achi garda mon destrier.
E preg vos que·l fassas intrar[938]
e venrra si an nos dinar."[939]
Dis lo donzel, "Mot volentier
aquo feray, bon cavalier."
Adonch lo donzel tot corrent[940]
s'en va al portal verament,
e dis ly, "Compahn Petavin,[941]
aysi mi tramet mosen Blandin,[942]

no duke or king or emperor and thing
whom I will love so surely, give
and I will give you a sign."
Then she got up
and approached Blandin.
She removed his helmet
and looked at him frankly.
She saw that he was fair-skinned and charming,
handsome, courteous, and loving,
and began to kiss him
lovingly, needless to say.
Blandin did the same
to Brianda, by God.
They stayed there a long time,
locked in each other's arms.
Then they left
in great joy, I need say no more.
The damsel greeted
her brother and kissed him
and also the damsels,
one by one, all of them.
Now I've told you about the damsel
and what she did.
Then the young man said
to Blandin,
"You must be very weary
after all your battles.
If you like, let's go and eat,
for I have had a meal prepared."
"That would be great," said Blandin,
"for I'm exhausted.
But first, please go
out to the gate where you'll find
Peytavin my squire,
who is guarding my horse.
Would you please invite him in
to dine with us?"
The young man said, "Most willingly
will I do that, good knight."
Then the young man ran
to the gate
and said, "Peytavin, friend,
Lord Blandin has sent me

e manda vos que·us en intres[943]
apertament, e non tardes."
adonch Peytavin s'en entret[944]
an lo donzel et non tardet,
e los cavals van establar,
e lur sivades lur van donar.[945]
Adonc s'en tornam a Blandin,[946]
e lo donzel e Peytevin.
E quant els foron aribas,[947]
trestot ensems s'en son annas[948]
en lo vergier mout gratios,[949]
ont cantavan ausel d'amors.[950]
Aqui foron taules drissades
e bonne viandes aparelhades,[951]
e van si trestotz assetar.
Et commanseron si a dinar,[952]
tot jort parlant de lor novellas,
Blandin an las damoyselas.[953]
En mentre che els si dinavan[954]
e lur novellas achi contavan,[955]
a Blandin va recordar[956]
de la donçella d'otra mar,[957]
d'aquella che l'en avia menat[958] **98r/col b**
lo caval quant era al prat.
E dis, "Brianda, una novella
vos diray d'una damoyssela[959]
che m'a faich grant vilania[960]
mentre che en un prat me jasia.[961]
Deves saber, per veritat,[962] Hic nota de equo furato per dem[oyssela]
che mon caval m'en a menat!
Totas veis, jou no vuelh mentir,[963]
mas la vertat vos vulh dire,[964]
che un aotre m'en va layssar
che jou porghes cavalcar.[965]
Si che, compenssant vilania,[966]
un pauch m'a fach de cortessia.
Mas jou ay jurat sobre ma testa[967]
che jou non colray dengunna festa[968]
tro mon caval aya trobat
e sella che l'en n'a menat."[969]
Adonc Brianda, veraiament,[970]
dis a Blandin tot en rissent,
"Blandin, non vos en corrosses,

to ask you to come inside
at once, without delay."
Then Peytavin came inside
with the young man, without any delay.
They stabled the horses
and gave them their oats.
They returned to Blandin,
both the young man and Peytavin.
After they had arrived,
all together they went
into the beautiful garden
where the birds were singing of love.
There were tables spread there,
covered with good food,
and they all sat down.
They began to eat,
talking all day long about their news,
Blandin and the damsels.
While they were dining
and sharing stories,
Blandin remembered
the damsel from afar,
the one who had led away **98r/col b**
his horse when he was in the meadow.
He said, "Brianda, I'll tell you
a story about a damsel
who treated me very poorly
while I was sleeping in a meadow.
You should know, Here, note the horse stolen by the lady
that she actually took my horse!
In any case, without a lie,
to tell you the truth,
she left me another one
to ride.
So, to make up for her villainy,
she was quite nice to me.
But I swore by my head
that I wouldn't take part in a feast
until I found my horse
and the woman who took it."
Then Brianda
said with a giggle,
"Don't be angry, Blandin,

car vostre caval trobares.
Car sapias, per veritat,
che sella che l'en a menat,
jou, senhor, l'avie tramessa[971]
per lo mont e che serchessa
qualche noble cavallier,[972]
vallent e pros e bon gherier,
che mi poghessa deslieurar
e per faich d'armes recobrar.[973]
Per so ella vos enganet.
E Dieu o volc che vos trobet
per tal che l'anessas sercar
e che·n venghesses deslieurar.[974]
Per che non vos meravilhes,
mas preg vos che li perdones."[975]
Adonc Blandin fu fort gaussent
e mot alegre, verament,
car Brianda li dis novella
d'aquella aotra damoysella.
Dis Blandinet, "Per v[e]ritat,[976]
jou li perdonne de bon grat.[977]
E dic vos che mot mi plais[978]
plus che an vos trobada l'ay.[979]
Car jou l'agra tot jort sercada[980]
tro che jou l'agessa trobada."[981]
E quant aysso agron dich,[982]
trestot lur dinar fu complit.
Adonc de taula si leveron
e per lo vergier s'en intreron,[983]
deportant se alegrament.
Pensar vos o podes verament.[984]
Adonc Blandin va parlar[985]
e dis, "Donzella, che porrien far
de questos malastrucz cavaliers[986]
che jou tene per personiers?[987]
Playra vos che los deslieuren?[988]
O my digas che en feren."[989]
Respont Brianda ardidament,
"Deslieuras los apertament,
e anon s'en en mal gassan,

for you will find your horse.
Know that
she who took your horse,
I, sir, sent her[y]
to search through the world
for some noble knight,
a valiant hardy warrior,
who could free me
and win me by deeds of arms.
That is why she tricked you.
God wanted her to find you
so that you would go searching
and would come and free me.
So don't wonder about it,
and please forgive her."
So Blandin was happy
and delighted
that Brianda had told him
about the other damsel.
Blandin said, "Of course,
I forgive her willingly.
And I tell you, I am just so glad
to have found it!
I would have searched for it forever,
until I'd found it."
When they had said this,
the dinner was finished.
Then they rose from the table
and went into the garden,
relaxing pleasantly.
I'm sure you can imagine the scene.
Then Blandin spoke,
"Lady, what can we do
with those wretched knights
that I hold prisoner?
Do you want us to free them?
Tell me what we should do."
Brianda replied,
"Set them free quickly,
and let them depart destitute

[y] Brianda's statement suggests that the duration of her enchantment was not very long, unless she could send one of her ladies on a mission while she slept.

car, per ma fe, ayssi lur tanh."
Adonc lo bon Blandin,[990]
e lo donzel, e Peytavin ses a° … ar …[991]
s'en van annar als cavaliers[992]
che tenien per pressoniers,[993]
e van los trestotz deslieurar.
E Blandin lur va comandar[994]
che los .iiii. mors enportessan
de foras e los soteressan.[995]
Respondon els, "Per veritat,[996]
aquo farem nos de bon grat."
Adonc los jetan de l'ostal
e van lur sarar lo portal.
E puysses lo bon Blandin,
e lo donzel, e Peytavin[997]
s'en van tornar a las donzellas,
en lo vergier jugar amb ellas.[998]
Aqui feron mot bel desport
tro fon mich jort dins aquel ort.
E puysses, quant venc miech jort passat[999]
Brianda dis e a parlat,
"Blandinet, lo myen senhor,[1000]
jou vos prege, per amor,[1001]
che nos intren dins lo castel[1002]
vos, e jou, et lo donzel,[1003]
car jou, senhor, vos vulh mostrar[1004]
tot mon tesaur et mon afar."
Respon Blandin, "Aquo my play;
ardidament anen no·n lay."[1005]
Adonques totz tres s'en aneron.
En una cambra s'en intreron,
e Brianda, senssa mantir,[1006]
trestotz sos cofres va hubrir.
E puis apelet Blandinet,
e aqui ela li mostret
tot son tessaur e sos joels,
che eran mot nobles e bels.
e dis li, "Cavallier gentil,[1007] **98v/col a**
preg vos che sias tant humil,
che prengas d'aor e d'argent[1008]
tant quant vos venrra a talent.
Car, per ma fes, si en prenes,[1009]
per sert, gran plasser my fares."

for, by my faith, that's appropriate!"
Then Blandin,
the young man, and Peytavin without a ...
went to the knights
whom they held prisoner
and set them all free.
Blandin ordered them
to take the four dead knights
outside and bury them.
They replied,
"We'll do that willingly."
Then they threw them out
and closed the gate behind them.
Then Blandin,
the young man, and Peytavin
returned to the damsels
to play with them in the garden.
They had a lot of fun
in the garden until midday.
Then, when it was afternoon,
Brianda said,
"My lord Blandin,
I pray you,
let's all go inside the castle,
you, me, and my brother,
for, my lord, I want to show you
all my treasure and possessions."
"That pleases me," said Blandin,
"let's go there now."
Then the three of them went off.
They entered a chamber
where Brianda
opened all her coffers.
Then she called Blandin
and showed him
all her treasure and her jewels,
which were fine and beautiful.
"Kind sir," she said, **98v/col a**
"Please take
as much gold and silver
as you want.
If you take it,
you'll make me very happy!"

Respon Blandin de Cornoalgla[1010]
cortessament, "Si Dieus mi valha,
Brianda, jou vos dich, vos ay,[1011]
che aor ny argent non my play,
ny ren alre che vos agias,[1012]
mas vostra amor, si a vos plays.[1013]
Car jou aquella vulh servir[1014]
tant quant viuray, senza mentir."[1015]

[New chapter in story]

Ar vos ay dich de Blandinet,
consy Brianda lo conquistet.[1016]
E tot apres jou vos diray[1017]
consy el fes encara mais..
El va estar en lo castel
an Brianda et an lo donzel.
Ben un bon mes trestot complit,
che de aqui non se partit.
E puys, quant venc lo mes passat,
Blandin va penrre cumiat[1018]
de Brianda e del donzel,
e volc se partir del castel,
car de Guillot li recordet, De Guilloto recordatus fuit
e lo terme se aproppet.[1019]
Adonc Brianda se mes plorar[1020]
e mout gran dol aqui mennar,[1021]
e va li dir, tot en plorant,
"Franc cavallier, lo myen amant,
ben vesse, lo myen car senhor,
che vos non m'amas per amor.[1022]
Car se my volgesses amar,
de mi non vos volgras lunhar."
Respon Blandin e a parlat,
"Brianda, ... per veritat,[1023]
la veritat vos volle dir
per che me convient despartir.
Deves saber che en nostra terra
per seguir la bonna gherra,
....................................[1024]
....
e ben mich an, nos cavalquen

Blandin of Cornwall replied
most courteously, "God help me,
Brianda, I've told you and tell you again,[z]
that I do not want your gold and silver
or anything else you possess.
All I want is your love, please,
and I want to serve that love
as long as I live!"

[New chapter in story]

Now I have told you about Blandin
and how he won Brianda.
Next I will tell you
what else he did.
He stayed in the castle
with Brianda and her brother;
for an entire month
he didn't leave.
But when the month was over,
Blandin took leave
of Brianda and her brother
and wanted to leave the castle.
He had remembered Guilhot; He remembered Guilhot
the date of their meeting approached.
Then Brianda began to cry
and with loud sobs,
said to him, tears streaming,
"Noble knight, my love,
my dear lord, now I know
you don't really love me.
If you intended to love me,
you would not want to leave me!"
Blandin replied,
"Brianda, truly,
I'll tell you
why I must leave.
You need to know that in our land
to search for challenging battles,
....
....
We rode for at least half a year

[z] The word order in Occitan suggests emphasis, which we have provided by repeating the verb.

che anc avantura non troben.
E puis, quant venc un jort matin,
anen tenir nostre camin,
e intren nos en tot apert repplicatio
dins en un bosch per lo desert.[1025]
E aqui trobares avantura
mot aspra e mout dura[1026]
de que non vos volle contar,[1027]
mas tot avant volc parlar.[1028]
Nos intren trestot avant,[1029]
per lo boschage calvaquant.[1030]
E quant forem pres d'un castel,[1031]
anen aossir un cant d'ausel
che dissia en son cant,[1032]
'Gentils senhors, anas avant,
e trobares un grant desert.
Intras laïns ben e apert,[1033]
e quant sares jus un bel pin
che atrobares en lo camin,
la un tengha a la part drecha
per una cariera estregia,
e l'autre tencha a l'aotra man,
e avantura trobares gran.'[1034]
Adonch, quant nos agem aossit[1035]
d'aquel ausel che nos a dich,
nos cavalchen trestot apert[1036]
tant che atroben aquel desert.
E apertament nos entren[1037]
tro che lo pin trobat agem.
E aqui nos tenghem conselh[1038]
de so che nos a dich l'aussel.[1039]
E aqui no[s] nos departem,[1040] sub pino
che anc depuys non nos vim.[1041]
E preghem nos en convenent[1042]
che nos trobassen certanament[1043]
en aquel luoch, desot lo pin,[1044]
lo jort apres de Sennt Martin.[1045]
Per que a mi conven tenir
aquel terme, senssa mantir."[1046]
Adonc Brianda respondet,
mot fort plorant, a Blandinet
e dis ly, "Senhor mi, si vos plays,[1047]
un don al mens me aotrias,[1048]

1896 and found none.
Then one morning,
as we went riding along,
we quickly entered a reiteration
1900 into a wood in the wilderness.
And there we found an adventure
most harsh and difficult.
I won't tell you about all that,
1904 but instead move on with the tale.
We went forward quickly,
riding through the woods.
When we were near a castle,
1908 we heard the song of a bird
which said in its song,
'Good sirs, travel further,
and you will find a vast wilderness.
1912 Go straight in,
and when you're beneath a handsome pine
which you will find on your way,
let one of you go to the right
1916 along a straight path,
and the other to the left,
and you will discover an exciting experience.'
Then, when we had heard
1920 what that bird said to us,
we rode very quickly
until we found that wilderness.
We went in at once
1924 and kept going until we found the pine.
There we held counsel
about what bird had told us.
We separated there beneath the pine tree
1928 and haven't seen each other since.
We agreed
that we would meet without fail
there, under the pine,
1932 the day after St. Martin's Day.
So I must keep
that agreement without fail."
Brianda replied,
1936 weeping uncontrollably,
"My lord, please,
grant me at least one thing.

che quant aquel trobar aures[1049]
andos ensems, vos en verres!"[1050]
Respon Blandinet, "Jou tornerai[1051]
breument, per sert, se a Dyeu play."[1052]
Adonc el pres cumiat[1053]
de totz aqui, per veritat,
e pueis Brianda va bayssar [Blandine]t va baysar
e pensset s'en de calvachar.[1054]

[New chapter in story]

D'aqui se part lo bon Blandin[1055]
an son escudyer Peytavin.
Apert s'en van tot cavalcant,
las lor jornadas caminant.
E tant lonc temps es cavalcheron,[1056] **98v/col b**
che nuich ni jort non repauseron,[1057]
tro che foron desot lo pin
lo jort apres de Sain Martin.
E aqui van descalvacar[1058]
e·l bon Guillot van esperar.[1059]
E Blandin tres jors l'esperet expectare
che aoc Guillot gis non tornet.[1060]
E quant el l'ac ben esperat,
tro che fu lo ters jort passat,
Blandin se va meravilhar.[1061]
E dis che l'anera sercar
e che jamais non torneria
tro che novellas en sabria.
D'aqui parti lo bon Blandin
an son escudier Peytavin,
e intret s'en per lo desert
cum bon cavalier e apert.
E quant el ac grans temps anat,[1062]
per lo desert e cavalcat,
el atrobet, per tal astre,[1063]
aquel bon prodome de pastre,
an qui Guilhot se va dinar
aquel jort che i va passar..
Adonc Blandin lo saludet
et de novas li demandet,
e dis ly, "O prodome, Dieus te sal.[1064]
Digas, si Dieus ti gart de mal,
auries tu vist un cavalier
de Cornoalha, bon garrier,[1065]

When you have found him,
you'll come back here together!"
Blandin replied, "I'll certainly return
soon, God willing!"
Then he took leave
of all who were there,
kissed Brianda, Blandin will kiss
and prepared to ride.

[New chapter in story]

Blandin left there
with Peytavin his squire.
They rode along quickly,
traveling all day long.
They rode for a long time, **98v/col b**
not stopping by day or night,
until they were under the pine tree,
the day after St. Martin's Day.
They dismounted there
and waited for Guilhot.
Blandin waited for three days, to wait
but Guilhot still didn't appear.
When he had waited,
and the third day had passed,
Blandin began to wonder.
He decided to look for him
and never to return
until he had some news of him.
Blandin departed
with Peytavin, his squire,
and entered the wilderness
as a good knight does.
When he had ridden
through the wilderness for a long time,
by chance, he found
that good man, the shepherd
whom Guilhot had dined with
the day he passed that way.
Then Blandin greeted him,
and asked for news.
He said, "Good fellow, God save you,
Tell me, God preserve you,
have you seen a knight,
a good warrior from Cornwall,

che per son nom se fa appellar[1066]
Guillot Ardit de Miramar?[1067]
Jou te preghe, se tu vist l'as,[1068]
che m'o digas, se a tu plays."[1069]
Adonch lo pastre respondet[1070]
cortessament a Blandinet
e dis, "Senher, per veritat,[1071]
gran temps a che sa es passat.[1072]
E mais, che an my si dinet—
aquel jort che aysi passet—
e puys teng aquest camin.[1073]
E jou, senhor, puis non lo vi."[1074]
Adonc Blandin lo saludet
e tot avant el cavalchet,
e intren s'en per sandier[1075]
a Peytavin, son escuder.[1076]
E serca lo bon Guilhot[1077]
per lo desert aytam cum pot.
E quant el ac gran temps anat
per lo desert et ont era intrat,[1078]
el esdevenc en lo vergier
ont era aquel bel pesquier[1079]—
la ont Guillot avie mort
lo Negre Cavalier tant fort.
E aqui non va res trobar,
mas tot avant va cavalcar.
E tant lonc tems el cavalchet[1080]
tro che l'ermita atrobet,
aquel che avie garit[1081]
lo bon companh Guillot Ardit.[1082]
Adondas Blandin lo saludet[1083]
et de novas li demandet
e dis, "Bon pordome, Dieu vos sal.[1084]
Digas, si Dieu vos garde de mal,[1085]
aurias vist un cavalier[1086]
de Corn[oa]lha, bon guerrier,[1087]
che per son nom se fa appellar[1088]
Guillot Ardit de Miramar?[1089]
Jou vos preghe, se vist l'aves,[1090]
che m'o digas et non tardes."
Adonch l'ermita respondet[1091]
cortessament a Blandinet
e dis, "Senhor, per veritat,

who is called by the name
Guilhot Ardit de Miramar?
I beg you, if you've seen him,
please, tell me."
The shepherd replied
to Blandin politely,
"Indeed, my lord,
he passed this way a long time ago.
He even dined with me
on the day when he passed by.
Then he took that road
and since then, my lord, I haven't seen him."
Blandin said farewell,
rode on,
and went along the path
with Peytavin, his squire.
He searched for Guilhot
thoroughly through the wilderness.
When he had gone for a long time
through the wilderness,
he came upon the garden
and the beautiful fishpond
where Guilhot had killed
the strong Black Knight.
He found nothing there,
but rode onward.
He rode for a long time
until he found the hermit,
who had healed
his good companion Guilhot Ardit.
Then Blandin greeted him
and asked him for news,
saying, "God save you, good man.
Tell me, God preserve you,
have you seen a knight,
a good warrior from Cornwall,
who is called by the name
Guilhot Ardit of Miramar?
I beg you, if you have seen him,
tell me without delay."
The hermit replied
to Blandin politely,
"Truly, sir,

gran temps a che sa es passat
e mais, senhor, se Dieu mi sal,
estet .viii. jour en mon hostal.[1092]
E puissas teng aquest camin,[1093]
e puys, senhor, jou no lo vi."[1094]
Adonc Blandin lo saludet
e tot avant el cavalchet.
D'aqui parti lo bon Blandin
an son escuder Peytavin,[1095]
e va serchar lo bon Guillot
per lo desert aytant cum pot.
E tot aquel jort cavalchet
che aoc novellas non ha trobat.[1096]
E puys, quant venc lo jort sequent,[1097]
el cavalchet apertament.
E quant el ac ben cavalcat
tro che fon bien miech jort passat,[1098]
e vi davant si un castel[1099]
che era mout noble e bel.[1100]
E desot, ac un pauch de massage[1101] **99r/col a**
a la ribba d'on boscage.[1102]
a aqui ac, che bons che mals,
endeviron de .l. hostals.[1103]
Dins lo massage s'en intret
e aqui el descalvachet.[1104]
E quant el fon descalvachat,
vers un pordom s'en es anat[1105]
e dis li, "Prodom, Dieu vos sal,
digas, se Dieu vos garde de mal,[1106]
aurias my vist un cavallier[1107]
de Cornoalha, bon guerrier,
chi per son non se fa appellar[1108]
Guilot Ardit de Miramar?
Jou vos prege, se vist l'aves,[1109]
che m'o digas e non tardes.
Car jou, amic, lo vau sercar[1110]
e volgra lo fort atrobar."
Adonc lo pordome respondet[1111] ... atus
iradament a Blandinet ... [si]mul ... illo
e dis, "Jou vos en say novellas[1112]
che non son bonas ni belas,[1113]

he passed this way a long time ago,
and, God help me, sir,
he even stayed with me for eight days.
Then he left by that road,
and since then, sir, I haven't seen him."
Then Blandin said goodbye,
and rode on.
Blandin departed
with Peytavin, his squire,
seeking Guilhot as best they could
through the wilderness.
He rode all that day,
without hearing any news.
Then, when the next day came,
he was riding along quickly.
When he had ridden
until afternoon,
he saw a castle in front of him
that was beautiful and imposing.
Down below there was a small hamlet **99r/col a**
on the edge of a forest.
There were about fifty dwellings
there, both good and bad.[aa]
He went into the hamlet
and there he dismounted.
When he had dismounted,
he came up to a man,
and said, "God save you, good fellow!
Tell me, God preserve you,
have you seen a knight,
a good warrior from Cornwall,
who is called by the name
Guilhot Ardit de Miramar?
I beg you, if you've seen him,
tell me without delay.
I am searching for him, friend,
and I would very much like to find him."
Then the good man replied ... ly
indignantly to Blandin, at the same time ... to him
"I have news for you,
but it isn't good!

[aa] We reverse the order of lines 2045–46 in the translation.

car lo senhor d'aquest castel
e sos parens che son amb el
lo tenon fort pres et liat
ben a dos meis, per veritat.
Car el, senhor, avie mort[1114]
quatre cavaliers, mot fors,[1115]
chi eran trestotz parens[1116]
del dich senhor verament.[1117]
Per que, senhor, si m'en cresses,
d'aquest homme non demandes.
Car si vos l'anas demandant,
vos en porres far vostre dan."
Adonch Blandin li a dich,[1118]
"Jou vos preghe, cortes amich,[1119]
che vos m'emenes al castel,[1120]
car jou vuelh parlar amb el."[1121]
Respondet el, "Mot volentier,[1122]
aquo feray, bon cavalier."
Adons d'aqui els si partiron[1123]
e al castel andos annerom.[1124]
E Blandin, si Dieu mi sal,[1125]
apert va tocar al portal.
Adonc tantost venc lo portier
e dis, "Cal es tu, cavalier,
che ayssi venes tant ardit?"
Respon Blandin e a li dich,[1126]
"Jou suy Blandin de Cornualha.[1127]
E preg te, se Dieus ti valha,[1128]
che digas al senhor del castel[1129]
che jou li volho parlar amb el."[1130]
Adonc lo portier s'en intret,
e a son maystre parlet,
e dis, "Senhor, un cavallier[1131]
a defora, sobre un destrier,
e a mi dich che vos plages
che amb el parlar anessas."
Adonc lo sengnor s'en va venir[1132]
devers Blandin, senssa mantir.
E tantost el lo saludet
et de novas li demandet,
e va li dir, "Che demandas,
cavalier, ni che vos plas?"[1133]
Respon Blandin et a li dich,

The lord of that castle
and his kinsmen too
have held him bound in prison,
2068 for at least two months.
He, my lord, killed
four strong knights
who were all kinsmen
2072 of that lord.
So, my lord, believe me,
don't ask about that man!
If you go asking,
2076 you could meet disaster!"
Then Blandin said,
"I ask you, good friend,
to take me to the castle,
2080 for I want to speak with him."
"Most willingly," he said,
"will I do that, good knight!"
They left there together
2084 and both went to the castle.
Blandin, God help me,
knocked at the door promptly.
The porter came at once
2088 and said, "Who are you, knight,
who comes here so boldly?"
Blandin replied,
"I am Blandin of Cornwall.
2092 I beg you, God save you,
to tell the lord of the castle
that I want to speak with him."
The porter went inside
2096 and spoke to his master,
"My lord, there is a knight
on horseback outside.
He told me that he would like you
2100 to come and speak with him."
Then the lord came out
to meet Blandin.
He greeted him
2104 and asked him for news.
He said, "What are you asking,
knight, and what do you want?"
Blandin replied,

"Jou vene aysi car ay aosit[1134]
che vos tenes per presoner
Guilhot Ardit, lo bon guarrier.[1135]
E volgra mot fort pregar[1136]
che vos lo my volghesses bayllar[1137]
car, de bon drech, non lo tenes.
Per que vos prec che·l deslieures."[1138]
Adonc lo senhor respondet
iradament a Blandinet[1139]
e dis, "Jou tene, per veritat,[1140]
Guilhot Ardit pres et liat.[1141]
E vos, per tot vostre poder,
per ren non lo podes aver.
Sidons am my non batalhas[1142]
e per batalha my venssas.
E vos feray trop bel partit:
jou vos meteray Guilhot Ardit[1143]
a la un corn de la batalha
mout volentier, se Dieu mi valha,
e si vos venser mi podes, **99r/col b**
ardidament che l'enmenes."[1144]
Adonquas lo bon Blandinet
an gran gauch li respondet[1145]
e va ly dir, "Bon cavallier,[1146]
aquo feray mot volentier.
Et preg vos che annes armar[1147]
e che pensen de batalhar.
Car, per ma fes, vos non parles;[1148]
jamais de que tal gauchs agues."[1149]
Adonc lo sengnor s'en va intrar[1150]
e tot apert se va armar,
e puis tantost el va salhir
ambe Guillot, sensa mantir,
e intren s'en apertament
per miech del camp verayament;[1151]
E Blandin fes aytrestal.[1152]
Mot valentement, si Dieu mi sal,[1153]
adonquas els van commansar
tantost aqui a batalhar.
L'un vers l'autre s'en va venir,[1154]
de colps de lanssa se van ferir.[1155]
E tant grant colps els si doneron[1156]
che per terra andous tomberon.[1157]

"I've come here because I've heard
that you have imprisoned
the good warrior, Guilhot Ardit.
I strongly implore you
to release him to me,
for you've no right to hold him.
So I beg you, free him!"
Then the lord replied
angrily to Blandin,
"I indeed hold
Guilhot Ardit bound and imprisoned,
and no matter how strong you are,
you can't have him, not for anything,
unless you fight with me
and defeat me in battle.
I'll make a deal with you:
I will put Guilhot Ardit
on a corner of the battlefield,
most willingly, God help me.
If you can defeat me, **99r/col b**
you may definitely take him away."
Then Blandin
replied to him most happily
"Good knight,
I'll do that most willingly.
Please, put on your armor
and prepare to do battle.
By my faith, don't say that;
you'll never have that pleasure!"
The lord went inside
and armed himself quickly.
Then he returned in haste,
bringing Guilhot.
They went swiftly
into the middle of the field.
Blandin did the same.
Most valiantly, God help me,
they then began
to fight.
They rushed at each other
to strike with their lances.
They struck each other so hard
that they both fell to the ground.

E tot apert si van levar
e tan gran colps si van donar[1158]
de las spassas sus l'escut[1159]
que·ls brasses los an romputz.[1160]
Adonc lo senhor del castel
un tant grant colp li donet el[1161]—
de la spassa sul bassinet—
che fuoc e flamma en gitet.
Adonc Blandin, coma valent,
vers el s'en va apertament
e an l'espassa flameian[1162]
li va dona[r] un colp tam gran[1163]
che tot l'aubert li va passar
et mout greument l'anet nafrar.[1164]
Aqui batalheron un gran temps,[1165]
mot aspramment andous ensems,
tant che per forssa lur convench[1166]
a cobrar forssa et alench.[1167]
E quant agron alen cobrat,
la un e l'aotre s'es levat
e fieron se si asprament
an las espassas, verament,
che tomberon estaboïtz,[1168]
per miech del sol, tot esbaïtz.[1169]
A cap de temps, els si leveron[1170]
e batalhar tantost torneron.
Adonc Blandin corage pres.
E diray vos cum si el fes:[1171]
vers el s'en va apertament
et f[e]ri lo sy asprament[1172]
che per terra lo fes tombar
et mout greument l'anet nafrar.[1173]
E encaras lo cavaler
si volc levar, cum bon gerier,
mais che Blandin fo·n avissat[1174]
e tantost sus li es montat.
E hostet li apertament
l'erme del cap, veraiament,
e va li dir en alta vois,[1175]
"Cavaler, tantost rende[s] vos![1176]
Si non, per sert, ares mores,[1177]
si vos tantost non vos randes."
Adonc quant el anet aosir

Then they jumped up quickly
and struck such hard blows
on each other's shields with their swords,
that they broke the arm-pieces.
Then the lord of the castle
struck him such a hard blow—
with his sword on his helmet—
that fire and flames flew out.
Then Blandin bravely
attacked him.
With his flaming sword,
he struck such a hard blow
that it pierced his hauberk
and wounded him severely.
They fought there so long,
both of them so savagely,
that they stopped, of necessity,
to recover their strength and their breath.
Once they had caught their breath,
both of them got up
and struck each other so savagely
with their swords
that they both fell, stunned
and dizzy, in the middle of the field.
After a while, they got up
and returned to the fight.
Then Blandin took heart.
I will tell you what he did:
he rushed at him quickly
and struck him so savagely
that he made him fall to the ground,
and wounded him most grievously.
Then the knight
tried to get up, as good knights do,
but Blandin was alert to it
and jumped on him at once.
He quickly pulled
the helmet off his head.
He said to him in a loud voice,
"Surrender at once, knight!
If not, you'll certainly die,
unless you give up at once!"
When he heard

che Blandin lo volie aveir,[1178]
va sy rendre de contenent[1179]
a Blandinet verayament.
Adon Blandin levar lo fes,[1180]
e a mersy aqui lo pres,
e fes l'anar, se Dieus m'ajut,[1181]
en son castel, trop ben batut.
E puysses pres Guilhot Ardit[1182]
et enapres e[l] a ly dich,[1183]
"Guilhot, penssen nos en d'annar[1184]
apertament, senssa tardar,
car nos non fam plus ren ayssi."[1185]
Adonc tencheron lo lur camin,[1186]
e va ss'en ben apertament[1187]
tros tres emsems veraiament.[1188]
E intran s'en per lo desers,[1189]
com bon cavaliers et apertz.[1190]
E mentre che els s'en anavam
per lo desertz e calvacavam,[1191]
Blandinet anet recontar
al bon Guilhot de Miramar[1192]
l'avantura che atrobet
quant Brianda conquistet.[1193]
E atresys Guilhot Ardit[1194]
aqui a recontat e dich
consy li pres dels cavaliers **99v/col a**
che avie mors tan bons guerries.[1195]
Adonquas els, tots cavalchant,[1196]
las lur jornadas caminant,
s'en van tornar en lo castel
de Brianda et del donsel.[1197]
E quant els foron prop d'aqui,
Blandin va dir a Paytavin,
"Petavin, penssa t'en da anar[1198]
tot drech al castel sans tardar.
E dicas a Brianda novella[1199]
che ieu seray anuch amb ella."[1200]

that Blandin wanted to have him,[ab]
he surrendered with alacrity
to Blandin.
Then Blandin had him get up,
granted him mercy,
and, God help me, let him go
thoroughly defeated, into his castle.
Then he took Guilhot Ardit
and said to him,
"Guilhot, let's get ready to leave
quickly, without delay!
We have nothing more to do here!"
Then they took to the road,
and went quickly along,
all three together.[ac]
They went into the wilderness
as noble knights do.
While they were going along,
riding through the wilderness,
Blandin recounted
to Guilhot of Miramar
the adventure he found
when he won Brianda.
Likewise Guilhot Ardit
recounted to him
how his capture by the knights happened— **99v/col a**
for having killed so many good warriors.
Then they rode on,
traveling all day long,
and returned to the castle
that belonged to Brianda and her brother.
When they were near it,
Blandin said to Peytavin,
"Peytavin, go ahead,
straight to the castle at once.
Tell the news to Brianda
that I will be with her tonight."

[ab] Previous editors have suggested the scribe meant to write *aucir*, "to kill," rather than *aveir*, "to have." We have retained the manuscript's word as it makes sense in context, though obviously, "to kill" would be the stronger verb.

[ac] That is, Blandin, Guilhot Ardit, and Peytavin.

Adonc Peytavin s'ann asset[1201]
e drech al castel s'en anet.
Tantost trobet lo donzel[1202]
chi s'esbatia per lo castel.[1203]
Adonc tantost lo saludet
e dis li, "Cortes donzel,[1204]
Blandin vos manda saludar
e mays Guilhot de Miramar.[1205]
E seran tantost, senssa falha,
ayssi am vos, se Dieus my valha."[1206]
Adonch lo donzel lo va aculhir[1207]
an gran gauch, sensa mantir.[1208]
E puis s'en va trestot corrent
devers Brianda verament
e va li dir la novella[1209]
che Blandin fora anuich amb ella.
Adonch Brianda, gratiossa,[1210]
fon alegra et joyossa,[1211]
quant lo donzel et Peytavin[1212]
li disson novellas de Blandin.[1213]
E va aculhir verament
Peytavin alegrament.[1214]
Apres tantost s'en voch annar[1215]
devers Blandin, sensa tardar.
E fes adobar las donzellas
e als cavals metre la sella,[1216]
e montan sus apertament[1217]
e van ver el verayament.[1218]
E quant forem del castel ysitz,[1219]
tantost aqui els los an vistiz.[1220]
Adonc Brianda, sans mentir,
che vi los cavaliers venir,
tantost son caval va brochar l'ensperonar
e devers el s'en va annar.[1221]
E Blandinet fes aytrestal
ver Brianda, se Dieu me sal.[1222]
Aqui els s'en va aculhir[1223]
an gran gauch, non vos o cal dir!
E puys s'en tornan, verament,
vers lo castel, jugant, rissant.[1224]
E quant foron dedins intras,
tantost els son descalchas,[1225]
e tos ensens s'en van annar[1226]

Then Peytavin took off
and went straight to the castle.
He found the young man
relaxing in the castle.
He greeted him at once,
"Courteous young lord,
Blandin sends you greetings,
as does Guilhot of Miramar.
Without fail, God willing,
they will soon be with you."
The young man welcomed him
joyfully indeed.
He ran off
towards Brianda
and gave her the news
that Blandin would be with her that night.
Then Brianda, in her charming fashion,
was delighted and overjoyed
when her brother and Peytavin
told her the news of Blandin.
She welcomed
Peytavin with pleasure.
Then she wanted to go immediately
to Blandin, without delay.
She had her damsels get ready
and had saddles put on the horses;
They mounted quickly
and went to meet him.
As soon as they were out of the castle,
they saw them there.
Then Brianda,
on seeing the knights coming,
spurred her horse at once to spur it
and rushed toward him.
Blandin did the same
towards Brianda, God save me.
There they greeted each other
with great joy, needless to say!
Then they returned
to the castle, joking and laughing.
When they were inside,
they dismounted at once
and went in all together

lay ont els devion sopar. a sopar
Aqui foron taules drissades
e viandas apparalhadas.[1227]
E van si trestotz assetar,[1228]
e commansseron a sopar.
Aqui soperon, veraiament,[1229]
tos emsems alegrament.[1230]
E quant agron de tot sopatz,[1231]
Blandinet dis et a parlat,[1232]
"Tot home se pensse de cocar[1233]
e paussen nos tos entro al jort clar.[1234]
E puys domen nos parleren[1235] doman. crastina die
consy no[s] nos governarem."[1236]
Adonch Brianda et las donzellas
tantost cochar s'aneron elas.[1237]
E puissas Guilhot et Blandin[1238]
e lo donzel et Peytavin
dins una cambra van intrar
e aqui els si van colquar.
E tota la nuich li repausseron[1239]
tro lo matin che si leveron.
E tantost quant foron levatz,[1240]
Blandinet e Guilhot son annats[1241]
per la muralha del castel
e aqui tengheron lur conselh.[1242]
Adonch Blandin a dich,[1243]
"Che me conselhas, vos Guilhot Ardit?[1244]
Ayssi es Brianda, gentil,
che es francha e humil,[1245]
che jou ame de fin corage[1246]
senssa panser point d'outrage;[1247]
e ay en cor, si vos plages,
che per molher jou la presses.[1248]
E atressi conselheria
che, se a vos, Guilhot, plassia,[1249]
che l'autra sorre fremasses[1250]
e per molher la presesses.[1251]
Car mai nos val che·ns molherem[1252]
amdous emsems, plus che poden."[1253]
Adonc lo bon Guillot Ardit
li respondet e a ly dich,[1254]
"Si vos, Blandin, o conselhas
ardidament aquo my plas."

to the hall where they would eat. — to dine
The tables were set
and the food was ready;
they all sat down
and began to dine.
They all ate
in happy companionship.
When they had eaten enough,
Blandin said,
"Let everyone get ready for bed
and rest until daybreak.
Tomorrow, we will talk — tomorrow, the next day
about what we should do."
Then Brianda and her damsels
went to bed at once.
Then Guilhot, Blandin,
the young man, and Peytavin
went into a chamber
and went to bed.
They slept all night long
until the morning when they got up.
As soon as they were up,
Blandin and Guilhot took a stroll
on the wall of the castle
and there, they talked together.
Blandin said,
"What do you think, you, Guilhot?
Here's Brianda, noble,
charming, and modest,
whom I love dearly
without any thought of shame.
If you agree, my idea is
to take her as my wife.
In turn, if you agree,
Guilhot, I think that
you should take her sister
as your wife.
It's much better for us to get married
at the same time, since we can."
Then the good Guilhot
replied,
"Blandin, if you advise it,
it pleases me greatly."

Don dis Blandin, "Atras tornen[1255]
e a Brianda en parlen."
Adonquas els atras torneren[1256]
e a Brianda s'en a[ne]ron.[1257]
E Blandin la va saludar,
e a una part la va tirar,[1258]
e dis li, "Brianda, sapias[1259]
che jou volle, se a vos plas,[1260]
vostra sorre prenga per marit[1261]
mon companhs, Guilhot Ardit.[1262]
Car el es noble cavallier, **99v/col b**
valent, e pros, e bon gherrier.
Humil, cortois, et fort leal[1263]
es atresis, si Dieu me sal.
E prege vos, si a vos plais,[1264]
che vos per my aysso fayssas.
Apres vos preghe humilmen
aytant cum pode, verament,[1265]
che vos my prenghas per marit.[1266]
Car, per ma fey, tot mon delit[1267]
metray tostemps en vos servir[1268]
tant quant vi[u]ray, senssa mantir."[1269]
Adonch Brianda respondet[1270]
cortessament a Blandinet
e dis, "Senhor, per v[e]ritat,[1271]
aquo feray jou de bon grat.[1272]
Car, per ma fe, al mont vivent,
no a un altre, verament,[1273]
che jou ame tant come vos, Blandin,[1274]
lialment, an bon cor fin.[1275]
E per ma fe, plus che a vos plas,[1276]
mot volentiers jou o faray.[1277]
Mas prec vos che lo donzel[1278]
sia appellat en aquest conselh."[1279]
Adonc lo donzel fon appellat,[1280]
e d'aysso els ly an parlat.
E lo donzel, verayament,
respondet lur cortessament
e dis, "Senhor, aquo my plais[1281]
ardidament che o fassas."
Adonc van sonar Yrlanda,[1282]
che era sore de Brianda,[1283]

Then Blandin said, "Then let's go
and speak to Brianda about it."
Then they left
and went to Brianda.
Blandin greeted her,
took her aside,
and said to her, "Brianda,
please know that I would like
your sister to take as her husband
my companion Guilhot.
He is a noble knight, **99v/col b**
valiant, and bold, and a good warrior.
He is also modest, courteous, and very loyal,
I swear.
And I beg you, please,
to do the same for me.
I beg you, as humbly
as I can,
to take me as your husband.
By my faith, all my pleasure
will come from serving you forever,
as long as I live."
Then Brianda spoke
courteously to Blandin,
"Truly, my lord,
I will do that willingly.
By my faith, in all the world,
there is truly no one
whom I love as much as you, Blandin,
loyally and honorably.
By my faith, since it pleases you,
I will do it most willingly.
But I pray you, let my brother
be called to this conversation."
The young man was summoned,
and they spoke to him.
And he replied
most courteously, indeed,
"My lord, I am most pleased
that you should do this."
Then they called Yrlanda,
who was Brianda's sister,

e Guilhot la va fermar[1284]
devant trestotz e espossar.[1285]
E Blandin feis aytrestal[1286]
de Brianda, se Dieu me sal.[1287]
E quant si foren esposatz,
trestos quatre et mais juraz,[1288]
Blandinet dis a Brianda[1289]
e a sa sorre Na Yrlanda,
che convidesson lur parens.
Car els volien, verayament,
che al jort venent de Sant Anthoni[1290]
si fessa lur matrimonii.[1291]
E puis apres e el a dich[1292]
a son companh Guillot Ardit,[1293]
"Guilhot, fassen justas cridar[1294]
a tot hom che vulha justar.[1295]
Car vos et jou, verament,[1296]
tenren la taula a tous vennent."[1297]
Ayssi cum o dis, ayssi o feren:[1298]
tantost las justas cridar faren.[1299]
E puys, quant venc a la jornada[1300]
che els lur agron donada,[1301]
vengheron de nobles cavaliers[1302]
e gran ren de bons escuders[1303]
per faire honor a Brianda[1304]
e a sa sorre Na Yrlanda.
Aqui feron mot bella festa
totz ensentz, ben e honesta.[1305]
E feron justas e biorst[1306]
che dureron bens .xv. jortz.[1307]
E quant los biortz foron pasatz,[1308]
tot hom estranch s'en es anat.
E Blandin de Cornivalha[1309]
e Guilhot, se Dieu me valha,[1310]
van remanir an lors molhers
e feron cum bons cavaliers.[1311]
E d'aqui non volgron partir,

and Guilhot was engaged[ad]
and promised before all of them.
Blandin did the same
with Brianda, God help me.
And when all four of them
were engaged and, moreover, promised,
Blandin said to Brianda
and her sister Lady Yrlanda
that they should invite their family.
They wanted really,
on the next St. Anthony's Day,[ae]
to celebrate their marriage.
After that, he said
to his companion Guilhot Ardit,
"Guilhot, let's announce a tournament
to anyone who wants to joust.
You and I, truly,
will welcome all comers."
It was no sooner said than done:
a tournament was announced.
When the day came
that they had chosen for it,
many noble knights came,
and many good squires arrived
to honor Brianda
and her sister Lady Yrlanda.
All together, they threw a marvelous feast,
ample and most appropriate.
They jousted and tourneyed
for a good fifteen days.
When the tournament was over,
all the foreign knights departed.
Blandin of Cornwall
and Guilhot, as God is my witness,
stayed with their wives
as good knights do.
They didn't want to leave there,

[ad] The Occitan term is *esposar* = to espouse, to marry, though that is not what happens at this point in the story. The knights are promised to the two women—that is, engaged—with the marriage ceremony to follow.

[ae] June 13; St Anthony is considered a patron saint of marriage.

ni volgon plus gera segir,[1312]
mas che feron cum bona gent,
e Dieus lor donet pron de ben.

[Concluding words]

Aras ve vos che vos ay dich
cum Blandin et Guilhot Ardit[1313]
atroberon bonas molers,[1314]
car feron coma bons cavaliers.[1315]
E pregas Dieus che ayssi vos prenna[1316]
e che ve don la bonna strenna.
A tut et a tute, amen.

and they didn't want to go to war any more,
but they behaved like good people,
and God rewarded them well.

[Concluding words]

Now I have told you
how Blandin and Guilhot Ardit
found good wives,
because they acted like good knights.
And you should pray to God to give
you prosperity,
one and all, Amen.

Notes to the Occitan Text

1 From this point forward, unless otherwise indicated, Galano refers to the edition by Sabrina Galano, Meyer refers to the edition by Paul Meyer; Nelli and Lavaud refers to the edition by these scholars; van der Horst refers to the edition by C. H. M. van der Horst. Also included are some variant readings published by Raynouard in his *Lexique roman*.

2 Raynouard prints *nom*.

3 Raynouard prints *E una franca*.

4 Raynouard prints *bons*; Meyer prints *faire*.

5 The ms. reads *vantura*; Meyer prints *[a]ventura*; the line has seven beats. Galano notes that everywhere else in the text, the word is spelled with an *a-*, and we agree with her emendation.

6 Meyer prints *un [d'els]*.

7 Galano prints *Guilhot*.

8 The ms. reads *elos*; Galano prints *els*.

9 Galano prints *lialtat*, arguing that this word is found more frequently in the text. However, *fialtat* makes as much sense; we do not emend.

10 Ms. reads *arnees* with second *e* expunctuated.

11 Galano prints *monten*.

12 Galano prints *hostal*.

13 The scribe has abbreviated the conjunction here; based on the comparative frequency of expanded *e* and *et*, we consistently expand to *e*.

14 Meyer would correct to *Com*; Galano prints *Com*; emending spelling would bring the line into metrical conformity.

15 The line is long; Meyer would delete *lur*.

16 The first marginal notation occurs at this line, a translation of *parlan*. Henceforth, translations of the marginal notes will accompany the English translation of the text.

17 Meyer prints *bien*. The ms. reads *escavalcheron*; van der Horst prints *es cavalcheron*, arguing that *escavalcar* cannot be found in the *FEW* (94, with reference to his line 31); one can add that *escavalcar* and its variants are not found in *COM* with the exception of one example from this text; Galano prints *e[l]s cavalcheron*.

18 *matin*, first suggested by Meyer, provides needed rhyme and missing two beats.

19 Meyer prints *Con*.

20 Meyer prints *gran*.

21 Meyer corrects to *cavalcat*.

22 Meyer suggests *tresto[t lo]*; Galano prints *tresthe to[t] [lo]*; Galano observes frequency of spellings of this word in its various functions in this text (*trestot*, sixteen times; *trestotz*, five times; *trestos* and *trestoz*, twice each; *trestout*, *trestot*, and *tresto*, once each). The line is short.

23 Meyer corrects to *sen[s]*.

24 Galano prints *Bla[n]dinet*; however, there is a superscript line on the *a* and no emendation is necessary.

25 Galano prints *nuich* (see linguistic discussion §3.10).

26 Meyer prints *veyron*.

27 The ms. reads *mostera*. Meyer prints *mostrera*, Galano prints *most[r]era*. Van der Horst states "correction justifiée, bien que non conforme à la graphie du texte" (94), which has the infinitive *mostrar* (see lines 1382, 1452, and 1839) and whose scribe is more inclined to add a support vowel than to delete one. We choose not to emend.

28 Meyer prints *entra[r]*; Galano prints *intra[r]* "to enter"; we understand *entra* as a prep.; van der Horst prints *entra*.

29 Meyer prints *nol*.

30 Meyer suggests *[Tot] aysso* for meter; the line is short.

31 Galano prints *[el] fu*; the line is short.

32 Meyer corrects to *fut*.

33 Meyer suggested and Galano prints *[el] s'en fora* to bring line to eight beats.

34 Meyer and Galano expand the abbreviation to *Guillot*. We observe that *Guilhot* is the more frequent full spelling and consistently expand to that form.

35 The line is long; Galano omits initial *E*.

36 Meyer prints *iou*; Galano prints *jou*.

37 Meyer prints *la vantura cercar*.

38 Van der Horst expands to *comte*.

39 Galano prints *amy*.

40 Meyer prints *annar*.

41 The ms. reads *cumiat*; the line is short. Galano prints *cumïat*, arguing that whenever the term *cumjat* is found (her lines 672, 845, 1447, 1866, 1933), the line is short, which leads her to print *cumïat* here. We prefer not to add the tréma, though we recognize the merit of Galano's argument.

42 Meyer prints *E [d']aotras, grans*; Galano prints *gran[s]*; van der Horst prints *merevilhas*.

43 Meyer and Galano print *Con*.

44 The ms. reads *Brandin*. This is the only point in the text with this spelling of the hero's name.

45 Meyer prints *sella*.

46 The ms. reads *E nmentre*; *enmentre* is attested in *COM*, where the only examples are from *Blandin* (Galano's edition) and from the *Poème de la Guerre de Navarre*. See *FEW* III 178b s.v. MENTRE; Mistral, *Lou tresor dóu Felibrige*, s.v. *mentre*. The two words are used together several times in this text, such that one can imagine a scribe uncertain as to whether he was dealing with one word or two. Raynouard prints *ch' el*.

47 Raynouard prints *reyssidar*.

48 Raynouard prints *merveillas*; Meyer prints *gran[s] mer[a]veilhas*; Galano prints *mer[e]veilhas*; the line is an imperfect octosyllable.

49 Raynouard prints *cavalier*.

50 Raynouard prints *preg o* and *anem*; Galano prints *preg*.

51 The ms. reads *bos*; van der Horst suggests that the *n-* is written over another letter. We agree with Meyer, van der Horst, and Galano and print *nos*.

52 Meyer and Galano print *[el] n'y a* for meter.

53 Meyer prints *[e] recobrar* for meter; Galano prints *[e] per fach* for meter; the line is short.

54 Meyer prints *f[e]rit*; van der Horst and Galano accept this suggestion, otherwise the line is short; *freit* appears again at line 900, in a line that runs long.

55 Meyer prints *damoisellas*; Galano prints *damassellas*.

56 Meyer prints *iou*; Galano prints *jou*.

57 Meyer prints *vostra (com)mandament*, suggesting omission of *com-* for meter; van der Horst deciphers *vo... ...andament* and supports Meyer's reconstitution; Galano prints *vo[s] [com]mandament*; we believe the complete word is visible.

58 Galano prints *els estan*, omitting *aysi*.

59 Meyer prints *desastrat*; Galano follows Meyer.

60 The ms. has *e*; correction is possible but not required for meter; Galano prints *Adon[has] e[l]*.

61 Meyer prints *iou*; van der Horst prints *nom*; Galano prints *jou*.

62 Meyer prints *sui*.

63 Meyer would omit *fort*; the line is long.

64 Galano prints *levet [li]*.

65 The ms. reads *salut* which we correct to *sault*; Meyer prints *sa(l)ut*; Galano prints *saut*.

66 Galano prints *ly una*; she argues that *ly* is a dative pronoun and that Meyer's concerns with the verb *secodre* were unwarranted (Galano, ed., *Blandin*, 55n). As *secodre* means "to shake," we see no reason to delete *d'* which allows the sense of "struck him with a lance."

67 Meyer suggests omitting *Adonch*; Galano follows this suggestion; the line is long.

68 Meyer would delete *e* for meter; Galano omits initial *e*.

69 Meyer prints *annar*.

70 Meyer prints *lo scut*.

71 Meyer corrects to *est*.

72 Meyer emends to *jayant*. The line is long; Meyer would emend to *chi·l sanc* for meter; Galano omits *Adonc*.

73 The line is short. Meyer suggests *[ambe] dos* for meter; we have respected scribal spelling and keep *tombat*; Galano prints *so[n a]mdos tombat[z]*.

74 Meyer corrects to *che[s]*; Galano prints *che[·s]*.

75 Meyer prints *estavon*; van der Horst prints *estaven*. The line is very long; Meyer suggests emending to *Donch*; Galano omits *Adonch* and prints *estavon*.

76 Van der Horst prints *jonnelhons*; the line is long.

77 *amortir* should be past participle; Galano prints *amortit*.

78 Meyer suggests *vers [lo] lur* for meter; Galano prints *[lo] lur*.

79 Grammatically, the verb should be 3rd p. s. *a*, but the ms. is clear; Meyer prints *Che lor [a]*; van der Horst prints *Che n'as*; Galano prints *che n'a*.

80 The line is long, Meyer proposed correcting *vaye* to *vay*, which restores the octosyllable but offers a form that, as van der Horst noted, is not in the text (97, his line 172). Galano prints *vay*. We understand the scribe's spelling as use of a support vowel and suggest that he heard a single verb form: *vayessen*.

81 Van der Horst suggests the line should read *un pauch* (97, his line 173); Galano prints *un pauch*.

82 Meyer prints *la testal(i)*; Galano prints *tost la testa*; the line is long.

83 Meyer prints *donzellas*.

84 Galano prints *quan*; *quant* is the more frequent spelling of the word in the text.

85 Meyer prints *dissen*; Galano omits initial *e*.

86 The ms. reads *che ens*; Meyer prints *chens*; van der Horst prints *che e·ns*; Galano prints *che·ns*.

87 Meyer emends to *m'espera*.

88 With Galano we print *esbaït*.

89 The marginal note misunderstands *amich* as *a nuich*.

90 Meyer prints *la*; the sense suggests *las*; Galano prints *la[s]*.

91 Meyer prints *vers*; Galano prints *Guilhot*.

92 The line is long. Galano prints *atroban che·l*; we are not convinced Galano's suggestion works grammatically.

93 Meyer prints *la vantura*.

94 Meyer and Galano print *tallan*.

95 Galano prints *Guioth che·ls*.

96 Meyer and Galano punctuate *dis lo: "Tres che ...*; van der Horst choses *"Lo tres che ....* A case can be made for each side; we prefer to understand *lo* as a pronoun and connect it with the preceding words.

97 The line is long.

98 Van der Horst prints *era .n*; he says Meyer reconstructed *en*; we see *en*.

99 The line is short. Meyer suggests *[per] vos sercar* for meter; Galano prints *[de] dins* which she argues is more economical than Meyer's emendation; we do not emend.

100 Space was left for an illustrated initial letter; a large capital R is the first letter on the page; Meyer prints *anar*.

101 Meyer prints *iou non*; van der Horst prints *no*; we see *non*. The line is short; Meyer suggests *[ja] repausar* for meter.

102 Meyer prints *davant*.

103 Meyer prints *iou*.

104 Meyer prints *donzella*; Galano prints *Guilhot*.

105 Meyer prints *l'a*.

106 The line is short. Meyer suggests and Galano prints *l[a] autra* for meter.

107 Meyer prints *boscage.*

108 The ms. reads *anb*; Galano prints *amb.*

109 With Meyer and based on the rhymes, we presume a line is missing; Galano places the missing line before our line 221.

110 Meyer prints *cavalcan.*

111 The line is short; Meyer suggests and Galano prints *[lor a] fallit.*

112 The line is short. Meyer suggests *[lor] a dich*; Galano prints *adonc[has].*

113 Meyer prints *farem, Giot.*

114 The ms. reads *ven che quens*; Meyer prints *ven (che) quens* deleting *che*; van der Horst prints *ven che que·ns* and suggests that the scribe made a correction and failed to delete *che*. Given the preference of the scribe for *chi* over *qui* and *che* over *que*, it would make more sense to emend by deleting *que*, as we have done.

115 Meyer prints *nuech.*

116 Meyer prints *respon, Iou*; Galano prints *Guilhot.*

117 Meyer prints *message.*

118 Meyer prints *hostal.* The line is short. Meyer suggests reading should be *Si veyria*; Galano prints *si veyria.*

119 Meyer makes the same emendation.

120 Meyer prints *era.*

121 The ms. reads *compagn*; Meyer prints *compagn(on)*, which is curious.

122 Meyer prints *iou.*

123 Meyer and Galano emend to *cavalcar.*

124 Meyer prints *apertament - escavalcheron*; van der Horst prints *cavalcheroy*; Galano prints *e[l]s.*

125 Meyer prints *chel.*

126 Meyer prints *frescha, aggrada.*

127 Added in the margin is *mont*, a misspelling of *mout* or *mot*; Meyer omits *mout*; with *mout*, the line is long.

128 Meyer prints *donsellas.*

129 Raynouard prints *ellas.*

130 Raynouard prints *planon*; Meyer prints *mot.*

131 Meyer prints *a l'autra verayment.*

132 Meyer corrects to *che [el]*; Galano prints *che [el].*

133 The line is long.

134 The line is long; Meyer and Galano print *Adonc* for meter; Galano prints *maior.*

135 Meyer prints *Com(me)* for meter; Galano prints *Com.*

136 Meyer accepted the rhyme *nostre* : *forza*; we presume two lines are missing, based on rhymes; Chabaneau had the same idea ("Notes critiques sur quelques textes provençaux," 39).

137 The line is long.

138 The line is long. Meyer prints *gran* but would omit the first *de* and *gran* for meter; van der Horst prints *cavaliers de grant*; Galano omits the first *de* and *grant.* The marginal note is perhaps a suggested correction to the line.

139 Meyer prints *Respond.*

140 The ms. reads *ben cebrarez* with several words crossed out immediately above; Raynouard prints *cobrares*; Meyer and Galano emend to *cobrarez*; van der Horst saw the letter *o* written over the letter *e*, suggesting a scribal correction to *cobrarez*. The marginal note is a confirmation of and translation of *cobrarez*.

141 Meyer prints *donque*.

142 The line is long. Meyer prints *combat(e)ron lo lo* and suggests emending to *lo bo*; van der Horst prints *combaterom lo lo*; there is no stroke to allow a reading of *bon*; Galano prints *lo matin*.

143 Galano prints *Disson*.

144 Meyer prints *chi l(o)*; Galano prints *chi·l*.

145 Galano prints *maior*.

146 Meyer suggested *aquel [quel]*; Galano prints *aquel [que·l]*.

147 The line is long. Meyer would delete *elas*; he prints *mot*.

148 The ms. reads *partirai* though van der Horst's reading of *partriai* is not impossible; Meyer prints *Iou non part(i)rai*; Galano prints *part[i]rai*.

149 Meyer prints *iou*.

150 Meyer prints *com(e)*; Galano prints *com, je ay*.

151 Meyer prints *descalvachat*; van der Horst says that the scribe corrected *es* to *els* (100n282), but we think the added *l* is very hard to distinguish.

152 The line is long. Meyer prints *pass(er)on*, emending for meter; Galano omits *si*.

153 The line is long. Meyer prints *parlerem*; Galano omits *nos*.

154 The ms. reads *ens*; Meyer, van der Horst, and Galano print *en*.

155 Meyer prints *aren*.

156 Galano prints *repausseron*.

157 Van der Horst says there are other examples of *li* for *si* (100n291); Galano corrected *li* to *si*; Galano prints *leveron*.

158 Meyer prints *quand* and *levat(z)*.

159 Galano notes that while one might expect *armats* here, the ending given is found in several contemporary texts and cannot be considered a fault of the scribe; she suggests this rhyme is characteristic of the Provençal dialect and represents the author's pronunciation (see Galano, ed., *Blandin*, 69 [her line 294] and her "Nuove congetture," 103).

160 Meyer prints *castel*; the ms. reads *batalalh*; we follow Meyer and Galano in emending to *batalhar*; van der Horst prints *baralath*.

161 Meyer prints *[Donc], tallan*, though he recognizes the ms. reads *tallen*; Galano prints *[E] dis*.

162 Meyer prints *jayant*.

163 Meyer prints *Che[m]*; Galano prints *che·[m]*.

164 Meyer prints *sentes*.

165 The line is short; Meyer and Galano print *[per] vos* for meter.

166 Meyer prints *Adonc*.

167 Meyer prints *castel*.

168 Meyer prints *trovet.*

169 The line is short; Meyer and Galano print *[et] apert* for meter.

170 Meyer and van der Horst print *plena*; Galano prints *tota plena*; Meyer prints *maltalhan.*

171 The line is short; Galano prints *[s'en] van.*

172 The line is short. Meyer and Galano print *comme*; Chabaneau ("Notes critiques," 40), proposed *com [o]me valen*, ignoring the formulaic nature of the phrase.

173 Galano prints *l'un tal co[l]p*; there may be a slight mark between the *o* and the *p*, but we see it as more of an *o* than an *l*, the additional *o* would not offer an Occitan spelling.

174 Meyer prints *anet.*

175 The line is short. Meyer prints *[s'i] combatet* for meter; Galano prints *te[m]ps [e]* though there is a clear stroke over the *e* of *temps.*

176 Meyer prints *non*; Galano prints *no·l.*

177 Meyer prints *romput.*

178 The line is long. Meyer prints *E l(o)* for meter; Galano prints *e·l.*

179 The line is long; Galano omits initial *E.*

180 Van der Horst prints *rigoardava.*

181 Galano prints *Adonc[has]*; as is, the line is octosyllabic.

182 Meyer prints *et*; van der Horst prints *&.*

183 Meyer prints *Guilloth*, *valen*; the line is short.

184 Meyer prints *defendet.*

185 Meyer prints *donnet.*

186 Meyer prints *Et.*

187 An imperfect rhyme; Meyer prints *maltalan*; Galano prints *mal talan.*

188 The ms. reads *dou monde* (Galano reported *dou mond*); Galano prints *del mont*; see linguistic remarks §1.18 for comments on this francization.

189 The line is long; Meyer prints *Ch'anc* and *che s(i)*, for meter.

190 The use of *presseron* and *presson* in these two lines is a nice aural repetition.

191 Meyer prints *prisson.*

192 The ms. reads *dapnage.*

193 The ms. reads *es es*; Meyer and Galano print *es* once, re-establishing octosyllable. This duplicate wording may not be an error, but rather an effect at storytelling, though the repeated words make the line long. Although the scribe used the abbreviation of *per* (the letter *p* with a stroke through the stem); we expand to *presoner.*

194 Meyer prints *Guillot.*

195 Meyer prints *Guilhot.*

196 The line is long. Meyer prints *paor, (no) l'aya(n)*, for meter; Galano prints *aya* (the subject of the verb is obviously singular).

197 Meyer prints *donzellas.*

198 The ms. reads *menoron*; Meyer prints *[eis] gran dol meneron*; Galano prints *[mout] gran dol meneron*; Galano says the line is short; if *e* and *aqui* are not elided, the line is octosyllabic.

199 Meyer and Galano print *E cascuna lo*; van der Horst reported, "Il y a quelques mots illisibles en interligne qui fausseraient le vers; on peut supposer qu'ils ne font pas partie du texte" (102n368); Galano was also unable to decipher these letters. An insertion mark is clear after the word *cascunna*; we read *in cortessia* above the line. The line is long without the insertion, which we understand as a marginal comment.

200 The ms. reads *broden*, metathesis for *borden*, from *bordir*, "to joust"; van der Horst understands *bronden*; Galano prints *borden*.

201 The line is long. Meyer prints *(s'en) es*; Galano omits initial *E*.

202 Meyer prints *reguardava*.

203 Meyer prints *nom*; the line is short.

204 Meyer prints *chel* and *atra(y)s*; Galano prints *atras*.

205 The line is long; Meyer prints *(Adonc)*; Galano omits *Adonc*.

206 Van der Horst prints *tan tost*.

207 Meyer prints *Que*.

208 With the medieval reader, Meyer, and with Galano, we agree that at least one line is missing here.

209 Meyer prints *jayant*.

210 The line is short. Meyer prints *[Che] un*; Galano prints *[che] un*.

211 The line is short. Meyer emends to *che [el]* for meter; Galano prints *[un] tant*.

212 Meyer prints *vayllant*.

213 The line is short; van der Horst would emend to *leve[t]* (102n); Galano prints *[el] se leve[t]*.

214 The line is short. Meyer prints *mont fort[ment]*; Galano prints *e [el] fo*.

215 The line is short; Meyer suggests *s'en [es] anat*, a suggestion Galano follows.

216 Galano adds *[e]* at the beginning of the line. The ms. reads *brondet*; Meyer and Galano print *bronde[n]t*; van der Horst prints *brodet* and likes Meyer's suggestion; Galano prints *brondent*. We understand the Occitan verb *brandir*, "to shake, brandish, rattle."

217 Meyer prints *jayant*.

218 The line is short. Meyer suggests *et [s'en] va*; Galano prints *el [s'en] va*.

219 The line is long. Meyer prints *jayant*; Galano prints *Lo jayan*.

220 The line is short. Meyer suggests *per [la] terra*; Galano prints *[tot] estandut*.

221 The line is short. Meyer suggests *Blandin [el] s'en va*, but this suggestion seems redundant; Galano prints *[de]vers*.

222 Meyer prints *moult* and *et*.

223 Meyer and van der Horst print *yes*. The line is short; Meyer suggests *[tu] nat, ar[es] moras*; Galano prints *ar[e]s moras*.

224 Meyer prints *da[m]pnage* and *m'a(i)s*, suggesting the *-i-* should be deleted; Galano prints *m'as*.

225 The line is long. Meyer prints *commansse[t]* and *battalha*; van der Horst prints *commansse*, but admits that *commensse* is plausible (103n); Galano prints *commanse*.

226 Meyer prints *A* for *El*; van der Horst prints *E.l*. The line is short; Meyer suggests emending to *Blandin[et]*; Galano prints *el [am] Blandin*.

227 Meyer prints *tan* and *donneron*.

228 The ms. reads *li* though *si* is not impossible; Meyer would omit *li*; Galano prints *terra tomberon*; the line is very long.

229 The ms. reads *leva*; with van der Horst and Galano, we emend to *levan*.

230 The line is long. Meyer suggests emending *vera(ye)men*; Galano prints *veramen*.

231 The ms. reads *Am tran dous*; Meyer suggests *Entr'an[be]dous vera[y]amen* to re-establish octosyllabic line; Galano prints *entr[e] andous vera[ya]men*; without emendation, the line is short.

232 Meyer prints *(E) Guilloth*; Galano omits initial *e*; the line is long.

233 Galano prints *fus*; Meyer prints *iou*.

234 Meyer prints *iou*; Galano prints *ch'iou*.

235 Galano prints *[Et] entretant*; Meyer suggests *el s[i] avisset*.

236 Meyer prints *Con*.

237 Galano prints *e [puys] va*; Meyer suggests *[el] come fellon*; the line is short.

238 Meyer prints *(E) am*; Galano prints *am los brasses*.

239 Meyer suggests omitting *hy*; Galano follows suit.

240 Meyer and Galano print *veray[a]ment*.

241 We see here a mix of single and formal or plural forms; *amia* refers to one of the damsels met earlier.

242 Meyer prints *Adonc*; Galano prints *Adon[c]*. The marginal note suggests a different word.

243 Meyer prints *Quan* and *Guillot*.

244 Meyer prints *lo scut*.

245 Galano prints *[el] se levet*; the line is short.

246 Galano prints *Bla[n]dinet*; however, the *-n-* is marked with a superstroke.

247 The line is long; Meyer would omit *Adonc* and Galano follows suit; Meyer prints *senti*.

248 Meyer prints *tan tost non pot*; the ms. reads *surgar*; with Meyer and Galano, we emend to *surgir* for rhyme. The spelling *surgar*, a *hapax legomenon* at best, may not exist in Occitan (all *COM* examples are actually Latin words) and has no attestations in *FEW* XII 458a, s.v. SURGERE.

249 Meyer prints *ajudar*.

250 Van der Horst prints *andos*.

251 Meyer prints *plen* and *talans*; Galano prints *talans*.

252 Galano prints *Puys s'en intren*.

253 The line is short; Meyer prints *e*; Galano prints *[mout] bel*.

254 The line is long; Meyer would omit *E*; Galano omits initial *e*.

255 Meyer prints *[ai]tan tost*.

256 *gial* is curious; Meyer suggested *cal*; van der Horst understands *qual*; Galano prints *qual*; we understand the infinitive as *caler*, "to concern, to be necessary" (*FEW* II 84a). A related expression occurs at lines 1562, 1698, and 1704, where the orthography is *qual*.

257 Meyer prints *Cascuna* and *amis*.

258 The line is long; Meyer suggests omission of *elas*; Galano omits *Adonch*.

259 The line is long; Meyer suggests and Galano omits initial *e*.

260 The line is long; Meyer prints *(a)troveron*, suggesting omission of *a-* for meter.

261 The line is long; Meyer suggests and Galano omits initial *e*.

262 Meyer proposes *lor* for *lo*.

263 The line is short; Meyer proposes *elas [s'en] van*; Galano prints *[s'en] van*.

264 Meyer prints *et*; van der Horst prints *&*.

265 Meyer prints *veray[a]men*.

266 Meyer prints *linhnage amb'el*.

267 Meyer prints *donzellas*.

268 Meyer prints *et*; van der Horst prints *&*.

269 The line is long; Meyer prints *emssens*; Galano prints *enssems*; Meyer would omit *gran*.

270 Galano prints *ploran*; the ms. reads *qt* with a squiggle over the *q* (suggesting an -r- in the abbreviation), not a stroke (which would represent an -n-); Meyer, van der Horst, and Galano print *quant*, whereas we understand a misspelling of *quar*; Meyer and Galano print *ysien*.

271 Galano prints *mout*.

272 The line is short; Meyer prints *[Tras]tot emsems*; Galano prints *ben [e] honesta*.

273 Meyer prints *miech*, *passat*.

274 Meyer prints *repausen*.

275 Meyer and Galano print *Guilhot*; Meyer prints *a(y)*; Galano prints *a*.

276 Galano prints *Adonc*.

277 The line is long; Meyer would omit *bel*; Galano prints *disson: "Cavaliers de parage."*

278 Meyer prints *tan tost*.

279 Meyer prints *mor[r]ian*; Galano prints *[en] morian*; Galano thinks the line is short one beat; we print *morïan* to signal three syllables, making the line octosyllabic.

280 Meyer prints *plaira*.

281 Meyer prints *la[s]*; the letter *p* has no abbreviation marking; van der Horst prints *pnes*; Meyer prints *prenes*; Galano prints *p[re]nes*; the sense points to this emendation.

282 The line is long; Galano omits *en*.

283 The ms. reads *remaner* with the second *e* emended to *i*; the scribal correction restores the rhyme pair.

284 Meyer prints *ades partir*; we agree with van der Horst's explanation of *a despartir* as the preferred reading (105n512), based on the frequency of *conven a* plus infinitive and the frequency of *despartir* in our text.

285 Galano prints *[car] nos sem*; van der Horst prints *orien*.

286 Meyer and Galano print *sercan*.

287 Meyer prints *senz atardar*.

288 Meyer prints *aotrement* and *sariem pres(i)at*; Galano prints *ch'aotrament* and *preisat[s]*.

289 The ms. reads *cavalies reputat*; Meyer prints *cavaliers rep(u)tat* suggesting deletion of *-u-*, because the line is long. Van der Horst prints *cavalies reputas*; Galano omits *per*; she prints *cavalies reputa[t]s*. This is the only example in our text of this spelling of *cavallier*.

290 Meyer prints *mot*.

291 Meyer prints *quel*.

292 Meyer prints *gracies*.

293 Galano prints *vos [a] ajudat*; Galano suggests the scribe omitted an auxiliary verb to accompany the past participle; we suggest that the intended form was *ajudet*, simple past of *ajudar*; Meyer prints *iou*.

294 Meyer prints *parleron*.

295 Meyer prints *mer[a]veilhas*.

296 The ms. reads *remaner*; Meyer prints *volran remanir*; Galano prints *remanir*; this rhyme pair recalls lines 515–16. Meyer would omit *che*, because the line is long.

297 *amen* in ms.; Galano prints *amas*.

298 The line is long; Galano prints *che·us*; Meyer prints *tan tost*.

299 Meyer prints *del*.

300 Meyer prints *tenrez*.

301 The ms. reads *pregaron* and shows a scribe's effort to turn the *-a-* into an *-e-*.

302 Meyer prints *Que*.

303 The scribe left room for two octosyllabic lines at the top of column B.

304 The line is long.

305 The ms. reads *an tran dos*; Meyer emends to *Antr'an[be]dos vera[ya]men*; Galano prints *andos [ensems] vera[ya]men*. The line is short; compare to line 420.

306 Meyer prints *dal*.

307 The marginal note distinguishes between *can*, "song," and *can*, "dog."

308 The line is short; Galano prints *[lor] dissia*.

309 Raynouard and Meyer print *C'atrobares*.

310 The line is short; Meyer prints *vos [en] ben [et] apert*; Galano prints *vos [ins] ben [et] apert*.

311 Meyer prints *quan*.

312 Raynouard prints *Laun* and *par*.

313 Raynouard and Meyer print *estrecha*.

314 Raynouard prints *tengua* and *l'autra*; Galano prints *autra*.

315 Raynouard prints *mot*; Meyer prints *(mot)*.

316 Meyer prints *meraviglar*.

317 Raynouard prints *ausel*.

318 Raynouard prints *Avez*; Meyer prints *dit Guillot*.

319 Raynouard and Meyer print *nos*.

320 Galano emends to *so*.

321 Meyer prints *poyrien*.

322 The ms. reads *calvacar*, clearly metathesis; Meyer and Galano print *cavalcar*.

323 The ms. reads *escavalcheron*; Meyer and Galano print *escavalcheron*, creating the only example of this verb in *COM*; we agree with van der Horst to separate the words here.

324 The line is short; Galano prints *Adonc[has]*.

325 Meyer prints *Guilhot*; Galano prints *Gui[l]hot*.

326 A case of imperfect rhyme, assuming a vowel plus /l/.

327 Meyer prints *podem*.

328 Meyer prints *Consi*.

329 Meyer prints *que*.

330 Galano prints *anem*.

331 Meyer prints *Guillot*.

332 Meyer prints *suy*.

333 The rhymes suggest a missing line; we agree in this with Meyer and Galano.

334 Following Meyer, van der Horst thinks *plus que* should be understood as *pus que*, a hypercorrection (107n588); he points to *FEW* IX 103a and 241b, *pus* < POSTEA vs. *pus* < PLUS; Meyer prints *ayssim*. The line is long; Galano omits *mas*; she prints *pus che* and *ayssim*. See the linguistic discussion §5.8.

335 Meyer prints *iou*.

336 Meyer prints *enpenrem*.

337 Meyer prints *Guillot*.

338 The line is short; Meyer suggested *[de]jus*; Galano prints *[de] jus*.

339 Galano prints *els*; Meyer prints *abbarassar*.

340 Meyer prints *cadaun*.

341 Meyer prints *Guilhot*.

342 Meyer prints *Guilhot* and *cavalcar*; Galano prints *Guiloth* and *cavalcar*.

343 Meyer prints *El*; van der Horst and Galano print *E·l*.

344 Meyer prints *Guilhot*.

345 The line is long; Galano omits *Se*.

346 Meyer prints *iou*; there is a superscript over *moton*, which Meyer, van der Horst (his line 613), and we think was cancelled; Galano prints *monton*.

347 Meyer prints *mieu*.

348 Meyer prints *voles*.

349 Meyer prints *Adonc(ques)* and *descavalchet*; Galano prints *Adonc* and *descavalchet*.

350 *els* added above line.

351 Meyer prints *messsgier*.

352 Meyer prints *devant*.

353 The ms. clearly reads *bur*; Meyer prints *lur*; van der Horst prints *lur*, saying an *l* is written over the *b* (108n625); Galano also prints *lur*, making the same argument. We see no such emendation. Assigning a precise meaning to *bur*, not found in dictionaries, is difficult; we relate it to Guilhem IX's use of *bat* and *but* (PC 183, 12, line 26) as sounds without precise meaning.

354 Meyer prints *Guilhot*.

355 Meyer prints *messagier*.

356 Meyer prints *atra(y)s*; Galano prints *atras*.

357 The line is long. Galano omits initial *e*; van der Horst and Galano print *ti*; Meyer prints *ammi*; Meyer suggests *si t(y)* for meter.

358 The line is long; Meyer prints *(A)donc*.

359 Meyer prints *menar*.

360 The line is short; Meyer suggests *coch[a]*; Galano prints *coch[a]*.

361 Meyer prints *Guilloth* and *choja*; Galano prints *choja*.

362 The ms. reads *de prodas*. Meyer says that the *p* toward the end of the line is marked with a loop, suggesting *pro* (Meyer 181n638), but he argues that *proas* is meaningless (we understand the word as a regular 2nd p. s. present of the verb *proar*, "to prove"). Meyer prints *tolla* and *ben a de pas* and suggests correcting to *Tu la penras bona de pas*. Van der Horst prints *To lla penras ben a de pas*; he suggests that the mark on the letter *p* designates a capital letter (108n635). Galano prints *tol la penras* and *ben a de pas*. Trusting the ms., we keep *pro* (adj. or adv.), understanding *das* as "dice" (see Faure, *Diccionari d'alpin d'oc*, s.v. *dat*) and meaning "Think again, think hard of good dice." The line is long.

363 Meyer and Galano print *Sinon*.

364 Meyer prints *Adonc*.

365 Meyer prints *Iou*; Galano prints *cavalier*.

366 The line is short; Meyer would emend to *[ben] apert*; Galano prints *[tot] apert*.

367 The ms. reads *sengor*, metathesis for *segnor*, a not infrequent orthography.

368 Meyer prints *sien*.

369 Meyer prints *encora*.

370 The line is short; Meyer prints *[tu] se a ti plais*; Galano prints *[tu] me diras, se a ti plais*.

371 Meyer prints *tant*.

372 Meyer prints *respon*.

373 Meyer prints *hun*.

374 Meyer prints *non* for *no i*; Galano prints *no·i*.

375 The line is long; van der Horst suggests correction to *aquels* (108n); Galano prints *aquels*.

376 The line is short; Galano prints *[fach] morir*.

377 Meyer prints *Si[m]* and *om*.

378 We agree with van der Horst in printing *non*; we have here a poor rhyme, unless the 1st p. s. pronoun *jou* intended to rhyme with *Dieu*, as would occur in Italian (*io* : *Dio*).

379 Meyer prints *si*, *ta(u)l*, and *iou*; Galano prints *tal*.

380 Meyer suggests *E(n)*; van der Horst suggests correction to *intret*.

381 The line is long; Meyer prints *Com(e)*; Galano prints *com*.

382 The line is long; Meyer would omit *bel*; Galano omits *bel*.

383 Meyer prints *de la viron*; van der Horst prints *a l'aviron*; Galano prints *en l'aviron*.

384 Galano prints *Adonc*.

385 Meyer and van der Horst print *E mentre*.

386 Meyer prints *a* and *messager*; Galano prints *lo mesagier*.

387 Meyer prints *vent*. The line is long; Meyer would omit *gran*; Galano omits initial *e*.

388 The line is short; Meyer and Galano print *vera[ya]ment*.

389 Galano prints *descavalcar*.

390 The ms. reads *armes*; van der Horst suggests a correction to *arnes*; Galano prints *arnes*. *Armes*, "arms," is found with some frequency in *COM*; we see no need to emend.

391 The marginal note foreshadows a coming event.

392 Meyer prints *P(l)us*; Galano prints *pus*.

393 Meyer prints *iou* and *lo(s)*; the line is long and lacks a rhyme pair.

394 Meyer prints *matins*.

395 Meyer prints *Guillot*.

396 Van der Horst prints *&*; Richter suggests that *beres*, here, is the first attestation with the meaning of "jaw" ("Altprovenzalisch *barra*, 'Kiefer'?," 611).

397 The line is short; Galano prints *vil[a]ment*.

398 Meyer prints *Iou*. "Not worth a button" is an Occitan proverbial expression (Pfeffer, *Proverbs*, Appendix 2, no. 940.25).

399 The line is long; Meyer prints *An[s] ti rump(i)ray*; Galano prints *an[s], rumpray*.

400 Van der Horst prints *abre i voles* (his line 703) and suggests correction of *abre* to *abri* (109n); Galano prints *abre i voles*.

401 Meyer prints *iou lo romp(i)ray*; Galano prints *jou lo rompray*.

402 The line is short; Galano prints *Adonc[has]*.

403 Meyer prints *El*.

404 Meyer prints *peschier*.

405 Meyer prints *fellon*.

406 Meyer prints *Quan*.

407 Meyer prints *lo scut*.

408 The ms. reads *met*. The line is long; Meyer prints *greu(e)ment*; Galano prints *greument*. The scribe was clear in spelling *grevement* with a -v- which, while exceptional, is not unheard of (see DOM s. v. grevamen2).

409 Meyer prints *bien*.

410 Meyer prints *li un*.

411 The ms. reads *amortisit*; van der Horst prints *amortisis*; Galano prints *[y] tots amortitz*.

412 Meyer prints *de*.

413 Galano prints *primier*; the scribal abbreviation is clearly that for *pre-*.

414 The line is long; Galano prints *adonc*.

415 Meyer prints *les.*

416 Meyer prints *greument.*

417 Meyer suggests *an[be]dos*; the correction makes the line long; Galano says the line is short (Galano, ed., *Blandin*, 101) and prints *[mout] gran*; we consider the line to be octosyllabic.

418 Meyer prints *Guilhot.*

419 Meyer prints the text as here; he suggests correcting to *so empres.*

420 Meyer prints *col(s).*

421 The line is long; Galano prints *adonc.*

422 Meyer prints *encor.*

423 Meyer prints *Guiloth.*

424 The ms. reads *e*; Meyer proposed *O* for *e*; we agree with Meyer and van der Horst that *o* makes better sense.

425 Meyer prints *Iou suy* and *senza.*

426 Meyer prints *preg(o) te chem*; Galano prints *preg.*

427 Meyer prints *P(l)us* and *veses que*; Galano prints *pus.*

428 Meyer prints *Guillot* and *ti.*

429 Meyer prints *iou.*

430 Meyer prints *mi* and *peschier.*

431 The line is long. Meyer and Galano omit *che*; van der Horst suggests *che* is a copyist's error (111n763). The lines do not rhyme well, but they do offer a valid weak rhyme.

432 Meyer prints *ferai iou.*

433 Meyer prints *s'en va.*

434 The line is short; Meyer prints *dis [li]*; Galano prints *[li] dix* arguing that her emendation is truer to the models found in the text (Galano, ed., *Blandin*, 103).

435 Meyer prints *al re.*

436 The line is long; Meyer prints *Dieu*; Galano prints *che·n.*

437 Galano prints *le cavallier.*

438 Meyer prints *vengesson*; Galano prints *venge[s]son.*

439 The line is long. Galano prints *D'aqui·s*; Meyer prints *s(e)* and *Guillot.*

440 The line is short; Meyer suggests *[tras]tot*; Galano prints *[tres]tot.*

441 Meyer prints *trovat.*

442 Meyer prints *aculhis*; van der Horst suggests reading *aculhi*; Galano prints *aculhi.*

443 Meyer suggests and Galano prints *co[l]get.*

444 The line is long; Meyer suggests *prodom(e)*; Galano prints *prodom.*

445 Galano prints *achi e[l].*

446 Van der Horst prints *predons*; Galano prints *[li] dis.*

447 The line is long; Galano prints *che·us.*

448 The line is long; Meyer would omit *chi*; Galano does not emend.

449 Meyer prints *Respon*; van der Horst prints *Respons.*

450 The rhymes point to at least one missing line; the context suggests that more than one line has been lost.

451 Meyer prints *iou*. The ms. reads *pava*; we find no meaning for this verb and emend with Meyer and Galano. The line is short. Meyer and Galano print *[m'en] pa[ssa]va*.

452 Meyer and Galano print *[e]stava*, an emendation that makes the line long.

453 The line is long; Meyer prints *com(me)*.

454 The line is long. Meyer suggests omitting *per sert*; Galano omits *mas* and prints *no* and *gassagnat*.

455 Meyer prints *e[u] l'ay*; Galano prints *[j]e l'ay*. While Galano's emendation makes sense, it is unusual for her. In almost all of her corrections, she validates the decision by other examples in the text; there is no other example of *je*, 1st p. s. pronoun, in *Blandin*. The redundant conjunction *e* is easy to accept. With van der Horst, we do not emend.

456 The ms. reads *histich*; Meyer emends to *istat*; with Galano we emend to *histat* which satisfies the requirements of the rhyme; *histar* is found elsewhere in the text (see line 848).

457 Meyer and Galano print *avvisa[s]*.

458 The line is long. The ms. reads *damgnage*; Meyer prints *E, a(v)antura, dannage*; Galano prints *dampnage*.

459 The line is long; van der Horst prints *qu'els, sav(e)ran*.

460 Meyer prints *yssirez*.

461 Meyer says the ms. reads *tansto* (if the small *o* is present, it is lighter than any other marks on the line); he prints *tantost sercar*; van der Horst prints *tanst serca* (his line 820); Galano prints *tan[to]st serca[r]* (her line 825) crediting Meyer; we agree with Galano and follow suit.

462 The line is long; Meyer prints *Guilloth, m(y)*.

463 Meyer prints *troberan*.

464 Meyer prints *iou* and *tel*.

465 The line is long; Meyer prints *fan nos bateren*.

466 The line is long. Meyer prints *preg(e)*; Galano prints *preg*; van der Horst suggests the text should read *che·m*; Galano prints *che·[m]*.

467 Meyer prints *comp(a)rar*; Galano prints *comparar*.

468 Van der Horst prints *vos*.

469 Meyer prints *Guiloth*.

470 Meyer prints *guarit*; van der Horst and Galano print *goarit*.

471 Meyer prints *puy*; Galano prints *puys*.

472 The ms. reads *ont he staich*; Meyer prints *ont he stat*; he suggested emendation to *ont a stat*; van der Horst would correct to *hestat*; Galano prints *hestat*. The word *hestaich* is, however, similar to *histat*, line 814. We accept this as a legitimate, albeit imperfect rhyme.

473 The line is short; Meyer and Galano print *[lo] baysset*.

474 Meyer prints *El* and *Guillot*.

475 Meyer and Galano print *cavalchet*.

476 The line is long; Meyer prints *(a)trobet*.

477 Meyer prints *puys*.

478 *brega*, "noise, dispute" is fem.; Meyer prints *gran[da]*; we prefer not to emend. This is not the only example of gender confusion in our text. Galano prints *begre*. The line is short.

479 Meyer prints *Gridant*.

480 Meyer prints *trove*.

481 Meyer says the ms. reads *la* (his line 865); he was mistaken in this reading; Meyer and Galano print *lo saludet*.

482 Galano prints *li demandet*.

483 Meyer prints *Respon*.

484 Meyer prints *mien*. The line is short; Meyer suggests *[el] mort*; Galano prints *[el] m'a mort*.

485 Galano prints *vo[l]gra*.

486 The ms. reads *am bel*; with Meyer, van der Horst, and Galano, we print *amb el*; Meyer prints *batalhar*.

487 Meyer prints *Respon Guillot*.

488 The line is short; Meyer emends to *verayement*; Galano prints *v[e]rayament*.

489 Meyer prints *chel*.

490 Meyer prints *annet* and *gran cris*.

491 Meyer prints *aossit*.

492 Van der Horst prints *escapar* and states that there is an expunction mark under the *m* of the word (113n881); we see this mark but choose to ignore it. *Escampar*, "to escape," makes good sense.

493 Meyer prints *cert*.

494 Meyer prints *Ieu*.

495 The line is long; Meyer prints *(a)ventura*, suggesting omission of *a-* for meter.

496 The line is short; Meyer suggests *[el] s'en van*; Galano prints *[els] s'en van*.

497 Meyer prints *vers*.

498 Meyer prints *Guillot*.

499 The line is long; Meyer would omit *Che*; the ms. reads *le*; van der Horst prints *lo*.

500 The line is long; Meyer prints *(A)donch*; the ms. has *de cọntreṇt*, with a single dot under the *o* and under the second *n*; however, we do not think the scribe sought to delete these letters nor this word. Meyer prints *contrent (?)* with no additional comment. Van der Horst prints *Adonch lo cavallier tombet / De son caval trestot freit* (his lines 893–94); he believes the scribe sought to delete *de contrent* and *si*. We understand *de contrent* as related to French *contre*, ergo our translation; Galano prints the line as we do.

501 The line is long; Meyer prints *(Si)* and omits *son*; Galano omits *si*. The ms. reads *freit*; Galano prints *ferit*, following a suggestion of Meyer's. We understand *freit* as "fried," implying "dead."

502 The line is short; Meyer prints *auc[un]*; Galano prints *anc [un] mot*.

503 The line is long.

504 Meyer prints *Ins*.

505 Van der Horst would emend to *son*.

506 Meyer and Galano print *cavalcada*.

507 Meyer prints *a gran*.

508 Meyer proposed *[va] el brochar*; van der Horst would understand *el va brochar*; Galano prints *el [va] brochar*; the line is short one syllable and the infinitive would benefit from a modal verb, though *va* in the next line serves the purpose equally well.

509 Meyer would omit *E* for meter.

510 Meyer prints *Adonc*.

511 Meyer prints *Respon Guilot*. We can only partly read this marginal note.

512 Meyer prints *Ma se* and *voles*.

513 Meyer prints *Pensas*.

514 The ms. reads *tornessen*; Meyer prints *tornesson* and suggests emending to *tornon s'en*; Galano prints *tornen s'en*; van der Horst prints *torne ss'en*, understanding *tornen s'en* with Meyer. We understand *essen* as the present participle of *esser* and translate accordingly. A similar construction may be seen in the Occitan "Diététique": "ab estar torn caitieu fogal" (Suchier, ed., *Diététique, d'après l'Epistola Aristoteli ad Alexandrum*, line 417).

515 The ms. has pl. *los senhors*, though the context suggests that the two knights are addressing one individual. The line is short. Meyer prints *Lo senhor(s) veray[a] ment*; Galano prints *veray[a]ment*.

516 Galano prints *cortes*.

517 The line is long; Meyer prints *(A)donc*.

518 Meyer prints *Chel*.

519 Meyer prints *Guillot*.

520 Meyer proposed *brocha[l]*; van der Horst liked this suggestion; Galano prints *brocha·[l]*; addition of the article would correct the grammar of the line but is not required to understand meaning. We do not emend.

521 The line is long; Meyer prints *s(e)*; Galano prints *com*.

522 A small cross in the margin is in an ink darker than that used for the other marginal notes.

523 Meyer prints *s[e]* and *lunq*.

524 The precise meaning of this marginal note is unknown; it may be onomatopoetic.

525 Meyer prints *totz*; van der Horst and Galano print *tots*.

526 Galano prints *ayatz*.

527 Meyer prints *respon*.

528 The line is long; Galano omits *tu*.

529 Galano prints *pres*.

530 The line is long; Meyer prints *Guilloth* and *ch'elos*; Galano prints *venian*.

531 Meyer prints *con*.

532 Meyer prints *los*, Galano prints *lo[s]*, which is grammatically correct; we do not emend.

533 The line is long; Meyer prints *darier(e)s*, Galano prints *dariers*.

534 Meyer prints *li*.

535 The line is long. Meyer prints *Sinon* and proposed omitting the second *non*; van der Horst agrees; Galano omits the second *non*. We understand *penre fin* as "to have worth, merit."

536 Meyer prints *Respon Guilhos Iou*.

537 Meyer prints *mi rend(e)ray*; Galano prints *rendray*.

538 The line is long; Meyer prints *forza, m(y)*.

539 Galano prints *puys*.

540 The ms. reads *vanc* or *vauc*; van der Horst prints *vauc* which he suggests emending to *venc*; Galano prints *vauc*; we understand the verb *venir*, "to come," for which the form *vanc* is not implausible, albeit unusual.

541 The ms. reads *atros*; van der Horst proposes a correction to *atras*; Galano prints *atros*. The marginal note may serve to emend *tros*.

542 The line is long; Meyer prints *puis(ses)*; Galano prints *puis*.

543 Meyer prints *Or(a) lo caval* and *sent(i)*; van der Horst, Galano, and we see the word *Ora* expunged in the ms. Without *Ora*, the line is octosyllabic.

544 Meyer prints *Guillot*.

545 Meyer prints *venzut*.

546 The line is short; Meyer and Galano print *Adonch[as]*.

547 Meyer prints *presson*.

548 Meyer prints *merci*.

549 The line is long; Meyer prints *l(i)* and suggests omitting *ben*; Meyer prints *mestier*.

550 Nelli and Lavaud begin their excerpts here.

551 The line is long; Meyer prints *Com(e)*; Nelli and Lavaud and Galano print *Com*.

552 Meyer prints *Apertament*.

553 The line is long; Meyer prints *(A)vantura* and *(la)*; Nelli and Lavaud print *Ventura* and *porria trobar*.

554 Meyer prints *meravilha(s)*; Nelli and Lavaud print *meravelha*; van der Horst prints *maravilhas*; Galano prints *maravilha* as correction for *maravilhas*.

555 The line is short. Raynouard prints *gardava*; Meyer prints *guardava*; Meyer suggests adding *bel* before *prat*; Nelli and Lavaud print *guardava en un bel prat*; Galano prints *un [bel] prat*.

556 Raynouard prints *chaval*.

557 Meyer prints *Che* for *E*; Nelli and Lavaud print *E* and *joliamen*.

558 Meyer and Nelli and Lavaud print *verayamen*.

559 Meyer and Nelli and Lavaud print *Apertament*.

560 The line is short; Meyer suggests *[el] li*; Nelli and Lavaud print *el li demandet*; Galano prints *[el] li*.

561 The line is long. Meyer prints *(E) dis la donzella*; Meyer would omit *E* and *gran*; Nelli and Lavaud print *Dis la donzella de parage*; Galano omits *gran*.

562 Raynouard prints *aisi*.

563 Raynouard, van der Horst, and Galano print *Ai* for *E li* though the initial letter is very similar to that of line 993; Nelli and Lavaud print *qui-es*; Raynouard prints *tant*.

564 Raynouard prints *Dieu que*.

565 Meyer and Nelli and Lavaud print *mot*.

566 Raynouard prints *cavalcar*; Meyer and van der Horst print *atot*; van der Horst admits *a tot* is possible.

567 The line is long; Meyer prints *(A)donc*; Nelli and Lavaud print *Donc*.

568 Meyer emends to *o tot*; Nelli and Lavaud print *o tot*.

569 Meyer and Nelli and Lavaud print *Iou*.

570 Nelli and Lavaud print *aventura*.

571 The line may be short. Meyer prints *[ar] panr(r)e*; Nelli and Lavaud print *ar penre*; Galano prints *e [jou] vuelh penre*.

572 Nelli and Lavaud print *Si dinar, plaissía*; Galano omits initial *e*; the line may be long.

573 Raynouard prints *per ma fe* with no indication that the word *fe* is missing from the ms.; Meyer, van der Horst, Galano, and we agree this is the sense; Meyer prints *[molt] gran*; Nelli and Lavaud print *ma fe* and *n'auría*.

574 The line is long; Meyer prints *(a)bastament*; Nelli and Lavaud print *bastament*.

575 Van der Horst prints *Blandi*; Nelli and Lavaud print *Blandin* and *aossi cortessía*.

576 The line is long. Meyer prints *Com(e)*; Nelli and Lavaud and Galano print *Com*.

577 The line is long. Meyer prints *(ensi)*; with Nelli and Lavaud, van der Horst thinks *ensi* was added later, creating the extra syllables. Nelli and Lavaud and Galano omit it. While it is possible that *ensi* was added at some time after original composition of the text, the word was copied into the manuscript with no indication it was a later addition. We retain it.

578 The ms. reads *de far* with *de* expunctuated; Meyer prints *Iou* and *de far*.

579 Meyer prints *iou*.

580 Meyer prints *iou*; van der Horst prints *mi*.

581 Meyer prints *iou*. The marginal note suggests a reading of *penria* for *prenia*.

582 Meyer prints *iou*.

583 Meyer prints *iou*.

584 Nelli and Lavaud and Galano print *decavalchet*.

585 Meyer, Nelli and Lavaud, van der Horst, and Galano print *De jus* but *dejus* is also found, see *DOM* s.v. *dejos*.

586 The line is short. Meyer suggests emendation of *[E] estandet*; Nelli and Lavaud print *E estendet*; Galano prints *[e] estandet*.

587 Meyer prints *devant, Cornivalha*; Nelli and Lavaud print *Devant, Corniualha*; Galano prints *Co[r]nivalha*.

588 Meyer prints *commanseron*; Nelli and Lavaud print *commenseron*.

589 Meyer prints *viandas*; Nelli and Lavaud print *vïandas*.

590 The line is short. Meyer suggests emendation to *par[au]let*; Nelli and Lavaud print *Adonc*; *paraulet*; Galano prints *Adonch[as]*.

591 The line is long. Meyer prints *donzella*; Nelli and Lavaud print *A la donzella*; Galano omits initial *e*.

592 The ms. reads *e dis li a francha creatura* with *a* expunctuated; Meyer proposes *E dis li: "Franch[a] creatura*; Nelli and Lavaud print *dis li: "Francha*.

593 The line is long. Meyer suggests *che m(e)*—i.e. *che·m*; Nelli and Lavaud print *che-m* and *l'aventura*; Galano prints *che·m*.

594 Nelli and Lavaud print *che-annas*.

595 Nelli and Lavaud print *talan*.

596 The line is long. Meyer prints *promet(e)ray*; Nelli and Lavaud print *prometray*; Galano omits *vos*.

597 The marginal note is marked for insertion after *cor*; the addition adds little and would make the line long.

598 The line is short. Nelli and Lavaud print *mía aventura*; Galano prints *ma [a]vantura*.

599 Meyer prints *anperho*, claiming that the intended word is *empero*; Nelli and Lavaud print *enpero*.

600 The line is short; Galano prints *[jou] diray*.

601 Meyer prints *veray[a]ment*; Nelli and Lavaud print *Et iou puysses diray*.

602 Meyer prints *agront*.

603 Nelli and Lavaud print *deportan*.

604 The ms. reads *do*; Meyer, Galano, and we emend to *De*. The line is short; Meyer would emend the full line to *De [se] dormir veray[a]ment*; Nelli and Lavaud print *De se dormir verayament*; Galano prints *de [s'en] dormir, veray[a]ment*.

605 Meyer prints *gran*.

606 The line is long. Meyer prints *Pregh[e]* and *repausem*; Nelli and Lavaud print *Pregh* and *repausem*; Galano prints *preg*.

607 The ms. reads *no* with a superscript line; van der Horst, Nelli and Lavaud and Galano print *non*; we expand to *nom*, using lines 1981 and 2017, where there is no abbreviation, as our model.

608 Meyer prints *atressy* and *iou*; Nelli and Lavaud print *atressy* and *ieu*, to rhyme with *Dieu* in the line above; we maintain the scribe's spelling.

609 Meyer prints *va[n]*; Nelli and Lavaud print *van*; van der Horst suggests the subject should be corrected to *els*; Galano prints *el[s]* and *va[n]* observing that errors of this sort are found elsewhere in the text (Galano, ed., *Blandin*, 123).

610 The line is long. Meyer would omit *bel*; Nelli and Lavaud omit *bel*; Galano omits initial *e*.

611 The line is short. Meyer prints *[del] plain*; Nelli and Lavaud print *de plain*; Galano prints *[de] plain*.

612 The line is long. Meyer would omit *de* to restore octosyllable; Nelli and Lavaud and Galano omit *de*. Galano argues that Meyer's emendation represents

an older genitive form, a *lectio difficilior* (Galano, ed., *Blandin*, 125), and she makes the same emendation, though it runs counter to her principle of using other examples in the text itself for any corrections. Accepting this emendation creates the only example of this genitive form in *Blandin*; we do not emend.

613 The line is long. Meyer prints *layssa l(o) syeu*; Nelli and Lavaud print *layssa-l syeu*; Galano prints *layssa·l sien*.

614 Meyer prints *veray[a]ment*.

615 Meyer prints *quan* and *a* as do Nelli and Lavaud.

616 The ms. reads *companilha*; Meyer prints *conpani(lh)a*; Nelli and Lavaud print *companía*; Galano prints *compagnia*.

617 The ms. reads *p* with a superscript horizontal stroke; we expand to *pre-* following other examples in the manuscript; Meyer, van der Horst, and Galano print *primier*.

618 Nelli and Lavaud print *sieu*.

619 The line is long. Raynouard omits *e*; Meyer would omit *va*; Nelli and Lavaud omit *va*.

620 Raynouard prints *fo*.

621 Meyer and Nelli and Lavaud print *se*.

622 The ms. reads *per un perdut, aotre trobat*, but the rhyme can be easily restored by re-ordering the words. Meyer proposed: *Aotre trobat per un perdut* which is what Nelli and Lavaud and Galano print. The line is a proverb; compare Morawski, *Proverbes français antérieurs au XVe siècle*, #1701, "Per un perdu deus retrovez."

623 Meyer and Galano print *e[n]felonit*; Nelli and Lavaud print *tresquetot enfelonit*; van der Horst suggests the scribe forgot the stroke over the *e*; certainly there is no stroke there. However, *COM* offers multiple examples of omitted *-n-*, the spelling *efan* for *enfan*, "child," for example; we see no need to emend.

624 The line is short. The ms. reads *non caura*; Meyer prints *[ja] non aura*; Nelli and Lavaud print *ja non aura*; van der Horst prints *non caura*, which he understands as *non colra*; Galano prints *non colra*. However, *nonca*, with final *-a* elided, "never," makes perfect sense.

625 The ms. reads *l'en ammenat*; Meyer prints *a menat*; this is the last line in the first Nelli and Lavaud excerpt.

626 The line is long; Meyer prints *Com(e)*; Galano prints *com*.

627 Meyer and Galano print *va*, which is grammatically correct.

628 Galano prints *trobera*, based on examples she found elsewhere in the text. We chose not to emend.

629 The line is long. Meyer prints *(a)trobet*; Galano prints *no* in an effort to reduce syllable count.

630 Meyer prints *quan*; van der Horst prints *lo*.

631 Meyer prints *escudier*.

632 The word *meschin*, after *las*, is expunctuated. The line is long; Meyer suggests omitting *my*; Galano prints *cridant*; Galano omits *My*.

633 This line is inserted to the right of line 1117; it was not printed in Meyer, van der Horst, or Galano. The line is short and missing its rhyme word; we suggest a possible rhyme and thank Alessandro Vitale-Brovarone for the suggestion.

634 This line is inserted to right of line 1118; not printed in Meyer, van der Horst, or Galano.

635 The line is long; Meyer would omit *de*; Galano prints *dir*; Galano omits *tant*.

636 Meyer prints *Ni*.

637 Meyer prints *respondi*.

638 Meyer prints *maistre*.

639 Meyer prints *donna*.

640 Meyer prints *cavalliers*.

641 Meyer prints *cavalier[s]*.

642 Meyer and Galano print *vol[c]*.

643 Meyer prints *batalhar*.

644 The line is long; Meyer and Galano omit *a* before *mort*.

645 Meyer prints *hic*; Galano prints *yeu*.

646 Meyer and Galano print *sieua*; van der Horst prints *siena*.

647 The ms. reads *ho vey*; Meyer proposed *quant lo vey*; Galano prints *quant lo vey*; *COM* provides multiple examples of the orthography *ho* for *lo*—e.g., "le Débat de la sorcière et de son confesseur," line 34; the "*Ensenhamen* du garçon," line 65; we see no need to emend.

648 Meyer prints *Mais*.

649 Meyer prints *mi*.

650 Meyer prints *mi*.

651 Meyer prints *iou*.

652 Meyer prints *iou* and *veray[a]ment*.

653 The ms. reads *entendres*; Meyer prints *en tendres*; van der Horst and Galano print *en tenres*; we understand *entendre per content* as an idiom meaning "to be satisfied."

654 The line is short; Meyer prints *vos [iou] per*; Galano prints *e [jou] dic*.

655 Meyer prints *corrent*.

656 Meyer and Galano print *s'e[n]*; van der Horst prints *s'e van* and argues for *s'en*. The multiple examples of *s'anar* in *COM* (for example, in the *Breviari d'amor*, lines 18188, 22746, 23581, 26445, 26699, 27578 and in *Jaufre* lines 2589, 9738, 10915) suggest that the usage is not exceptional. We do not emend.

657 Meyer prints *de[u]sent*; Galano prints *des[c]ent*. Clearly the verb intended is the 3rd p. s., present indicative of *descendre*, used only once in the text; since the meaning is clear, we do not emend.

658 Meyer omits *l'*.

659 Galano prints *comandet*.

660 Van der Horst emends to *Esperas*.

661 Meyer prints *non*.

662 The line is long; Meyer prints *(E)* and *cavalliers*.

663 Meyer prints *apparian bon*.

664 Meyer prints *[Tras]tos*; Galano prints *[e] tos armats*; they thought the line was short because of the feminine rhyme.

665 Meyer and van der Horst print *Et ayssi*.

666 Meyer prints *ly* and *Atras! atra(ys)*; Galano prints *Atras! Atras!*

667 Meyer prints *intraras*.

668 Meyer prints *Respont*.

669 The line is long; Meyer prints *iou*.

670 The line is long; Meyer prints *ver[r]ay*.

671 The ms. reads *pert*; van der Horst says the *-t* must be an error. The line is short; Meyer prints *Per tot sert iou [i] interrai*; Galano prints *[car] per tot sert*.

672 Meyer prints *(s)es*; van der Horst prints *ses*; Galano prints *es*. The marginal note is a suggested interpretation of *non isteray*.

673 Meyer and van der Horst print *primier*.

674 Galano (her line 1192) replaces *salit* with *gitet*, based on her line 2148 (here 2158). Our author does repeat lines, and Galano uses that model to re-establish rhyme here. We chose to retain the manuscript reading, thinking that *basinet* : *salit* may reflect the author's pronunciation.

675 The line is short. Meyer prints *Devers [el] el*; van der Horst suggests emending to *E devers*; Galano prints *[e] devers el s'en va anar* following van der Horst. The suggested emendation does re-establish the octosyllable.

676 Meyer prints *davant* and *derriers*; van der Horst emends to *derrieres*.

677 Meyer prints *mantir*.

678 Meyer suggested correcting *se* to *sus* (his line 1212); Galano prints *sus* (also 1212).

679 A missing rhyme points to a missing line; the subject of following lines must be presented in the missing verse.

680 Meyer prints *tant*.

681 Meyer prints *ainsy*.

682 Meyer prints *tant*.

683 The ms. reads *2*, a standard abbreviation for *e* or *et*; Meyer prints *el* for *et*; van der Horst thought the ms. read *el*; he suggests *e·l*; Galano prints *e·[l]*; Meyer suggests *Entre l(o)* for meter, as the line is long.

684 The line is short; Meyer prints *[e]standut*.

685 The line is long; Meyer would omit *dich*.

686 Meyer prints *mo[r]ras verayament*.

687 Meyer prints *P(l)us*.

688 Meyer prints *tan*.

689 Use of *voch*, present subjunctive of *voler*, is curious and will recur at lines 1256 and 2253.

690 The line is short; Meyer prints *Bandin[et]*.

691 The line is short; Meyer suggests emendation to *Et en son escut*; Galano prints *[e]scut*.

692 Meyer prints *colp*.

693 The ms. reads *li va donar taglar* with *donar* clearly expunged and replaced, in a different ink, with *taglar*, which makes a better rhyme; Meyer prints *talhar*.

694 Van der Horst prints *tot standut* (his line 1235); he suggests the first *e-* of *estandut* has been wrongly expunged by the copyist (121n1235).

695 Meyer prints *penre*.

696 Meyer prints *menar*.

697 Meyer prints *ploravon*.

698 Meyer prints *tam* and *desconfortavon*.

699 The ms. reads *vers* with the *-s* expunged; Meyer prints *Apertament* and *vers*; van der Horst prints *ver*; both *ver* and *vers* are acceptable forms of the preposition, and both were used by the scribe (*ver*: seven occurrences; *vers* seventeen occurrences), meaning "towards."

700 Meyer prints *Els*; van der Horst prints *E·ls*.

701 Van der Horst prints *em*.

702 Meyer prints *veray[a]ment*; van der Horst prints *verayment*; while the scribe's orthography is exceptional, the meaning remains clear, and we do not emend.

703 Meyer prints *detra(y)s*; the rhyme is poor, but we do not think lines are missing here; Meyer's suggestion would solve the rhyme problem. Galano prints *detras*, saying that the *-y-* is expunged; we do not agree with her.

704 Meyer prints *[A] Blandinet*. The line is octosyllabic as it stands.

705 Meyer prints *[Gentil]*; *nostre* was inserted above the line, an addition that makes the line long.

706 Meyer prints *merce*.

707 Meyer prints *com(a) bona*; van der Horst notes that *gent* would be the correct form.

708 Meyer and van der Horst print *commandament*.

709 Meyer prints *Respon*.

710 Meyer prints *iou*.

711 Meyer prints *mi*.

712 The line is short; Meyer prints *Respon[don], v[e]rayament*.

713 The ms. reads *vors*, which van der Horst calls a hypercorrection (121n1266); with Meyer and Galano, we emend; Meyer and Galano print *servirem*; we think the final letter is definitely *-n*, not *-m*.

714 The line is long. Meyer prints *(A)donc* and *sacramen(s)*; van der Horst notes that *sacramens* has a final *-s* though the word is singular; he thinks the *-s* was added by the copyist (121n1271).

715 *six* (6) is written above *.vi.*; Meyer prints *verayamen(s)*; Vitale-Brovarone reads *veramen* (personal communication).

716 Meyer prints *E trestoz [.vj.] el(s) los botet*; van der Horst agrees with Meyer's *el(s)*.

717 Meyer prints *(a)trobet*.

718 Meyer prints *donçella*.

719 The line is long; Meyer prints *(En)mentre ch(e el)*.

720 Van der Horst omits *E*, which he and Galano think was expunged. Nonetheless, the word is needed for the syllable count, and we have kept it.

721 The line is long; Meyer prints *tant(as)*.

722 Meyer prints *mervilhos[es]*.

723 Illegible marginal note.

724 Meyer prints *verament*.

725 Meyer also assumed a missing line here; we assume the object of *prennia* is in the missing line(s).

726 The line is short; Meyer prints *Adonc[as]* and *anar*.

727 The line is long; Meyer prints *s'(en)*.

728 The line is long; Meyer prints *ch(e el) estava*.

729 Van der Horst suggests reading *El* for initial *E*.

730 The ms. reads *certossament*, which Van der Horst printed, arguing that the scribe intended to write *cortessament* (by metathesis; his line 1302); Meyer and Galano print *cortessament*. While one could argue that the author intended the word "certainly" and retain the manuscript's word, the logic of the story pushes us, with Meyer and Galano, to emend.

731 The line is short; Meyer suggests *dis [li]*.

732 Meyer prints *prec* and *che[m]*; Meyer's *[m]* is not necessary for the meter nor for meaning.

733 Meyer prints *iou*, *va[u]ch*. The ms. reads *sercan*; van der Horst suggests understanding *sercar*; Galano prints *sercar*; we understand *sercan* as having adjectival weight and do not emend. Unemended, these two lines demonstrate assonance rather than rhyme.

734 Meyer prints *vogra [la] fort*. The line is short; if *la* were added, we would place it before *deliurar*, so as to maintain something of the caesura, however, we prefer not to emend.

735 We agree with Meyer that the rhymes point to a missing line.

736 This is a poor rhyme, but this is hardly the first time we have seen it.

737 Meyer prints *pla(i)s*, to improve the rhyme.

738 Meyer prints *E [es]*; van der Horst suggests the same emendation; we have chosen not to emend.

739 Meyer prints *paire*.

740 The line is long; Meyer and van der Horst print *c'om(me)*.

741 The line is long; Meyer prints *[o]* for *ho*.

742 Meyer prints *iou*.

743 Admittedly poor rhyme.

744 The ms. reads *p* with a stroke through the stem, which should expand to *per-*, not *pre-*—i.e. *personnes*; Meyer prints *quen* and *presonne[r]s*; Galano prints *presonne[r]s*; van der Horst prints *qu·en*. We emend to retain meaning of "prisoner" though one can argue that Blandin is claiming to have taken six people.

745 Meyer prints *parla(y)t*.

746 The line is long. Van der Horst would emend to *Gentil*; Meyer prints *dites ver(i)tat*; Galano prints *disses*.

747 Meyer prints *morts*.

748 Meyer proposed correcting to *aginolhet*, which would make the line long. Van der Horst glossed *anellet* (his line 1341) with *anjonnelhet*, particularly as the next line suggests strongly that the action here is one of kneeling. Galano thought the *anellet* orthography (her line 1349) was the scribe's effort to maintain the meter (see Galano, ed., *Blandin*, 145n). The only example of *anellet* in *COM*, with this spelling and meaning, is this specific case.

749 Meyer prints *pas a* for *pes de*.

750 Meyer prints *ploran*.

751 Meyer, van der Horst, and Galano print *non*; Meyer and Galano print *anes*; van der Horst prints *anes*, emending from *aves*. We retain *aves*.

752 Meyer prints *(a) Dieu*.

753 Meyer prints *tan gran* and *iou*.

754 Meyer prints *iou*.

755 Meyer prints *iou*.

756 Meyer prints *demonstrar*; van der Horst prints *de monstrar*.

757 Meyer prints *iou la vol[e]*.

758 The line is long; Meyer prints *intrem, (de)dins*.

759 Meyer prints *p(l)us*; we understand *vos* as 2nd p. s. of verb *voler*, "to wish, to want." The fluctuation between informal and formal verb forms does not surprise. We do not claim that this couplet rhymes.

760 Meyer suggests emending line 1368 to *Lai senhor mostraray la vos* to re-establish rhyme. Van der Horst makes no comment. Galano thinks it is line 1367 which is faulty; she proposes *plus que tant vezer la volles*. Meyer's solution is neater, but we prefer not to emend.

761 The line is short; Meyer prints *Si [vos]*.

762 Meyer prints *iou*.

763 Meyer prints *Che p(l)us*.

764 Meyer prints *malva(i)s*.

765 If *verament* were *verayament*, the line would be octosyllabic. Mistral offers examples of *veramen* (*Lou tresor dóu Felibrige*, s.v. *veraiamen*), and we see no need to emend for spelling.

766 Meyer, van der Horst, and Galano print these as a single, long line; we think a line is missing. Our suggestion maintains the rhyming octosyllabic couplets.

767 The ms. clearly has *E*, which the marginal note reiterates, though the sense suggests *O*. Galano prints *O* (her line 1374); Meyer prints *iou*.

768 *va* should be *van*; Meyer prints *va[n]*. This is the first line in the second Nelli and Lavaud excerpt.

769 The line is long; Meyer prints *(grant)*; Nelli and Lavaud print *De beutat ela*.

770 The ms. reads *esetada*; Meyer and Galano emend to *asetada*; Nelli and Lavaud print *asetada*; van der Horst observes that we are dealing here with a past participle of the infinitive *assetar*. We see no need to emend.

771 The line is long. Meyer prints *(E)*; Nelli and Lavaud omit *E*.

772 Meyer prints *mer[a]veylosas*; Nelli and Lavaud print *meraveylosas*; an insertion is noted in the margin: *e tut hor [...]*.

773 The ms. reads *Blandim*; Raynouard and Meyer print *Blandin*; we do not emend.

774 Raynouard prints *moult*.

775 Raynouard, Meyer, and Nelli and Lavaud print *tan*; Raynouard prints *enamorar*.

776 A superscript line over *hoc* is clear, but unexplainable; we suspect that *ogie* may represent a Piedmontese pronunciation (see *FEW* s.v. AUCELLUS XXV 780a).

777 Meyer and van der Horst both see *portals* (masc.) as an error for *portas*; Lavaud and Nelli print *portas*. Note the gender agreement of *portals*, "portal, entryway," with its masc. adjective *grans*, "big, large." The author shifts to feminine *porta*, "door," in the next lines.

778 The line is long. Meyer prints *vera(ya)men*; Nelli and Lavaud print *veramen*.

779 Nelli and Lavaud print *Che-es*.

780 *verre*, "boar" (*FEW* s.v. VERRES XIV 304a). The word is a *unicum* in *COM*.

781 The line is short. Meyer prints *[E] fort[z]*; Nelli and Lavaud print *E fortz e duras*.

782 The line is long. Meyer and van der Horst would omit *a*; Nelli and Lavaud print *E las aurelhas*.

783 Meyer prints *verament*.

784 Meyer prints *fercios*; Nelli and Lavaud print *feresos*; *ferejos* would be related to the verb *ferejar*, "to scare, to frighten," see *FEW* s.v. FERUS III 478b–79a, where one also finds *fereja*, "être farouche."

785 Meyer and Nelli and Lavaud print *myeya*.

786 The couplet is incomplete; we assume a missing line.

787 The ms. clearly has *pendrie*, which must be understood as *perdrie*, 3rd p. s. conditional of *perdre*, "to lose"; Nelli and Lavaud print *un dent*.

788 Nelli and Lavaud print *perdut un dent*.

789 The ms. reads *pendra*, which must be understood as *perdra*, "will lose"; Meyer and Nelli and Lavaud print *perdra*. Though the scribe consistently uses an abbreviation to spell the various forms of *perdre*, in this case and at line 1430, he has spelled the word out in full; for this reason, we retain the spelling.

790 The couplet is incomplete; we assume a missing line.

791 Nelli and Lavaud print *che-en*.

792 Nelli and Lavaud print *Che-un*.

793 The line is long; Meyer prints *(a)trobares*.

794 The line is long; Meyer prints *po(de)s*; Nelli and Lavaud print *Car lo podes segurament*.

795 The line is long; Meyer prints *vo(le)s*. This is the last line in this Nelli and Lavaud excerpt.

796 The line is long; Meyer prints *donzel(et)*.

797 Meyer prints *iou*.

798 The line is long; Meyer would omit *gentil*.

799 Meyer prints *Seraxin*.

800 Meyer prints *volontiers*.

801 Van der Horst notes that the verb should be *van*, 3rd p. pl.

802 Van der Horst prints *primier*.

803 Meyer prints *regardet*; this and similar spellings are found elsewhere in *Blandin* (lines 378, 995, 1131), suggesting its normality for the scribe.

804 The ms. reads *sailda*; Meyer and Galano emend to *salida*.

805 Meyer prints *ou*; van der Horst prints *on*; Galano emends to *o*; we retain *ou* though it is the only example of this orthography in the text.

806 The marginal note seeks *grasitudine* to translate *de grueyssa*.

807 The ms. reads *coraios*; offering assonance, not rhyme.

808 Meyer prints *golla*; van der Horst suggests that *en* should be *an*.

809 Meyer prints *Com(a), enrabjada*; van der Horst points to *FEW* s.v. RABIES X 9b, where *enrabiar* is cited.

810 The line is short; Meyer prints *Blandin[et]*.

811 The line is long; Meyer prints *palm(e)s*.

812 The line is short; Meyer prints *tent la frem [et]*.

813 Meyer prints *tot'enversada*.

814 Meyer prints *come*.

815 The line is short; Meyer prints *[re]luxent*.

816 The line is short. Meyer prints *Vera[ya]ment aquel [mal]*; van der Horst prints *Verament*.

817 Meyer prints *Mais que*.

818 Meyer prints *remas*; the serpent is described using masc. and fem., see the linguistic discussion §5.9.

819 The line is long; Meyer prints *puys(ses)*.

820 Meyer prints *verament*.

821 Meyer prints *sonnar*; van der Horst prints *gis*.

822 The line is long; Meyer prints *l(o)*.

823 The marginal note proposes an alternative spelling.

824 The ms. reads *vole*; van der Horst prints *vol e* (his line 1485) and thinks Meyer's correction to *volc* is justified (126n1485); Galano prints *volc* (her line 1493).

825 The ms. reads *sant*; Meyer and Galano print *sans*.

826 Meyer prints *assalhir*.

827 Meyer prints *Cristol*.

828 The ms. reads *tremoral*; the rhyme requires *-ar*; this is a likely example of metathesis. Meyer was first to propose this solution, which we accept.

829 Meyer prints *Sarraxin*.

830 The ms. reads *prenent*; Meyer emends to *parvent*; van der Horst prints *pre nent* but suggests it should be *per nent*; Galano prints *per*; *COM* offers several examples of *pre* meaning *per*—e.g., Lee, ed., *Daurel e Beton*, "e pres lo pre la ma" (line 117)—so we do not emend.

831 Meyer prints *veys*.

832 Meyer prints *lanssa*.

833 The line is short; Meyer prints *[gran] fisanza*.

834 Meyer prints *mont*.

835 Meyer prints *Chel* and *senestre*; the ms. is clear, masc. *bras* should be modified by *senestre*.

836 Meyer prints *Chel*.

837 The ms. reads *sbait*; Meyer prints *[e]sbaït*; we emend.

838 Meyer prints *Mont*.

839 The line is long; Meyer prints *(a)*.

840 The line is short; Meyer prints *Mais [que]*.

841 The line is short; Meyer prints *Car [tal]*.

842 Meyer prints *Adonch*.

843 Meyer prints *lo dona[t]*.

844 Meyer prints *tan gran* and *ly*.

845 Meyer and van der Horst print *sanglent*; van der Horst understands *in* as a copyist's error (127n1535). Given the existence of the verb *ensanglantar*, "to make bloody," we do not emend.

846 Meyer prints *Al re*.

847 The ms. reads *ben*; van der Horst prints *bon*.

848 Meyer prints *plainament*.

849 The ms. reads *non vos o qual o dir*. Meyer prints *non vos qual a dir*; van der Horst prints *non vos qual dir* (his line 1546), reporting that the ms. has *non vos o qual o dir*, with both *o*'s expunged (127n1546); Galano prints *non vos o qual dir* (her line 1554) and also notes that both *o*'s were expunged (Galano, ed., *Blandin*, 158n). Usually, the scribe marks letters to delete with a dot beneath the letters; in this case, the letters appear to have been struck out. The best sense of the line may be to understand, as did van der Horst, *non vos qual dir*, though this leaves the line short. On the other hand, see lines 1704 and 2268 which offer the same phrase.

850 The ms. reads *la*; Meyer emends to *lo*.

851 The line is short; Meyer prints *[el] podie*.

852 The line is very long; Meyer prints *m(e)*.

853 Meyer prints *Aynsim*.

854 Meyer prints *vole(s)*.

855 The line is long; Meyer prints *puis(ses)*.

856 The ms. reads *flameyn*; Meyer prints *flamey[a]n*; Galano prints *flameyan*; the emendation is confirmed by the rhyme.

857 The line is short; Meyer prints *[re]lussant* and *bel talhan*.

858 The line is short; Meyer prints *[E] tan*.

859 The line is long; Meyer prints *(a)*.

860 Meyer prints *mantir*.

861 The ms. reads *sen*; Meyer emends to *son*.

862 The ms. reads *a mantir*; the scribe may have repeated the word from the line above in the exemplar; the sense requires *morir*, as Meyer, van der Horst, and Galano agree.

863 Meyer omits *E* and prints *Blandin[et]*.

864 Meyer emends to *intret*.

865 Meyer prints *lo*.

866 The line is long; Meyer prints *donzellas, ver(i)tat*.

867 Meyer prints *[tras]tos l'esperavan*.

868 The ms. reads *den junenhols*; Meyer prints *Den juvenhols* and suggests emending to *De genolhons*; van der Horst suggested metathesis from *junelhons*; Galano prints *d'en junenhols*. We understand a conjugated form of infinitive *enjunenhar*, "to kneel down," parallel to the Middle French infinitive *engenouillier* (*FEW* s.v. GENUCULUM IV 114b); *en genolhons* is found in Guillaume, ed., "Istorio de Sainct Poncz," line 3808. Compare line 1648 of our text.

869 The ms. reads *hostel*, "inn," a clear scribal error. Meyer prints *hostel* and suggests *auzel*; van der Horst prints *hostel* (his line 1592) and notes "*hostel* pour *ausel*" per Meyer (128n1592); Galano emends to *aossel*. We agree that emendation is required; the orthography *aosel* is found in our text at line 1626.

870 The line is long; Meyer prints *(A)donc, ver(i)tat*.

871 The ms. reads *alha*; Meyer prints *Dieu aia*.

872 This is the first line in the next Nelli and Lavaud excerpt.

873 The line is long; Meyer prints (E) and *donzella (s'en) va[n]*; Nelli and Lavaud omit *E*, *s'en*.

874 The line is short. Meyer prints *donzel[et]*; Nelli and Lavaud print *donzelet*.

875 Meyer prints *iou*.

876 Nelli and Lavaud print *sieua*.

877 Meyer prints *iou*.

878 Nelli and Lavaud print *myeva*.

879 The line is short. Meyer prints *ben [o] disses*; Nelli and Lavaud print *ben o disses*.

880 Meyer prints *Vel*; Nelli and Lavaud print *vos*.

881 The line is short; Nelli and Lavaud print *E adonquas*.

882 The line is short; Nelli and Lavaud print *S'en va*.

883 Meyer prints *fe(i)s*; Nelli and Lavaud print *fes*.

884 Nelli and Lavaud print *plannament*.

885 Meyer prints *[L']astor*; Nelli and Lavaud print *L'astor*.

886 Meyer and Nelli and Lavaud print *donzela* and *senti*.

887 Nelli and Lavaud print *desobre*.

888 The ms. reads *e tantost de present comanzet a sospirar*, a very long line. Meyer prints *e (tantost de present) commanzet a sospirar*; Nelli and Lavaud print *E com-*

menzet a sospirar; van der Horst prints the text as given in the ms.; Galano omits *tantost de present*.

889 The line is short. Meyer prints *Car [hom]* and *deslieu(e)rada*; Nelli and Lavaud print *Car hom* and *deslieurada*.

890 The line is long; Meyer prints *(a)donc* and *Sor(re)*.

891 Nelli and Lavaud print *Che-us*.

892 Meyer, van der Horst, and Galano say the ms. reads *merveilhas*, though we think an *-e-* has been squeezed in after the *-r-*; Meyer and Galano print *mer[a] veilhes*; Nelli and Lavaud print *meraveilhes*.

893 The ms. reads *Ares*, and the line is long. Meyer says the ms. reads *Aras vos*; he prints *Araus diray*; Nelli and Lavaud print *Ara-us*; Galano prints *Ar vos*.

894 Meyer prints *contenensas*; van der Horst suggests reading *la contenansa*.

895 The line is long. Meyer prints *(adonc)*; Nelli and Lavaud print *Ela s'en va*.

896 Meyer and van der Horst say the ms. reads *s'anjonnelhet*; our reading of *anjounelhet* is equally plausible and aligns somewhat with the orthography used at line 1604; Meyer and Nelli and Lavaud print *s'agenolhet*; Galano prints *s'anjonnelhet*.

897 The line is short. Meyer prints *[iou]* and *merces*; Nelli and Lavaud print *rendde iou grandas merces*.

898 Meyer prints *preg[e]* and *mieu*; Nelli and Lavaud print *prege* and *mieu*.

899 Meyer prints *a vos pla(y)s*; Nelli and Lavaud print *a vos plas*.

900 Meyer prints *iou* and *(re)contar*; Nelli and Lavaud print *ch'iou* and *contar*.

901 Meyer prints *Iou*; Nelli and Lavaud print *Iou, Brïanda, vos requerir*, suggesting that the phrase imitates a legal formula, though they admit, "à vrai dire sans autre ex[emple]" (465); the line is short. The marginal note calls attention to the first mention of the heroine's name.

902 The ms. reads *non*; Meyer and Nelli and Lavaud print *nom*.

903 Van der Horst prints *Corniualha*.

904 The line is an imperfect octosyllable. Meyer prints *[Na] Brianda*; Nelli and Lavaud print *Na Brianda*.

905 Nelli and Lavaud print *vole*.

906 Meyer prints *al re*; this is a poor rhyme, but it has been seen before in this text.

907 Meyer prints *vostre* and *pla(i)s*; Nelli and Lavaud print *plas*.

908 The line is short. Meyer prints *Che [iou]*; Nelli and Lavaud print *Che iou suy*.

909 Nelli and Lavaud print *sens*.

910 Meyer prints *iou*; Nelli and Lavaud print *cugei*.

911 Nelli and Lavaud print *Perche* and *vole*.

912 Meyer prints *Mais*.

913 Meyer prints *p(l)us*; Nelli and Lavaud print *pus che-a*; see note 334.

914 Meyer prints *Co[r]nivalha*; Nelli and Lavaud print *Corniualha*; this is the last line in this Nelli and Lavaud excerpt.

915 Meyer prints *donzela*.

916 Meyer prints *cortesament* and *merav[e]ilha*.

917 The ms. reads *cavalier my plassent*, with *my* inserted above the line. The line is long; Meyer and Galano print *e dis li cavalier plassent*.

918 Meyer prints *sans falhir.*

919 Meyer prints *desir.*

920 Meyer prints *ni* and *ni.*

921 Meyer prints *iou am(e).*

922 Meyer prints *ho(s)*; we do not see the use here as an example of Levy's *faire aparven* = *faire semblant* (*Petit dictionnaire provençal-français*, s.v. *aparven*); van der Horst points to *FEW* s.v. APPARERE XXV 24b "semblant." The same *FEW* article offers a French example (dated 1377) of *aparen* as "evident." Compare Combarieu du Grès and Gouiran, eds., *La chanson de Girart de Roussillon*, line 8690, where *aparvent* means "present," or "openly," rather than "seeming."

923 The ms. reads *lavar*, a scribal error. With Meyer and Galano, we emend.

924 Meyer prints *blanc.*

925 The line is short; Meyer prints *Blandin[et].*

926 Meyer prints *temps.*

927 The line is short; Meyer prints *an[be]dous.*

928 The ms. reads *o qual o dir* with the second *o* expunged; Meyer prints *o dir.* Compare with lines 1562 and 2268.

929 The line is short; Meyer prints *[si] lo baysset.*

930 The line is short; Meyer prints *atressi [fai].*

931 Meyer prints *Si* for *Ar.*

932 Meyer prints *Perche* and *pla(y)s.*

933 Meyer prints *iou.*

934 Meyer prints *pla(y)s.*

935 Meyer prints *iou.*

936 The ms. reads *pmier* with a horizontal stroke over the *p*; we consistently expand this abbreviation to *pre*; Meyer, van der Horst, and Galano print *primier.*

937 The line is long; Meyer prints *(a)trobares.*

938 Meyer prints *quel.*

939 Meyer prints *venr(r)a.*

940 Meyer prints *Adonc.*

941 Meyer prints *li* and *Pe[y]tavin.*

942 Meyer prints *m(i).*

943 Meyer prints *queus.*

944 Meyer prints *Adonc* and *intret.*

945 The line is long. Meyer prints *(lur) sivades.* Meyer suggests, alternatively, keeping *lur* and emending *donar* to *dar*; Galano prints *e sivades lur van donar.* The only reason to emend this line is to achieve an octosyllable; as *lur* has different functions in the sentence, its repetition is not, in itself, faulty.

946 Meyer prints *tornan.*

947 Meyer prints *au bas* for *aribas*; the word is the past participle, masc. s., of *arribar*, "to arrive."

948 The ms. reads *en sems.*

949 Van der Horst prints *mot.*

950 Van der Horst and Galano suggest *ausel[s]*; the Occitan declension system does not require an *-s* to mark the nominative case; see linguistic notes §4.1.

951 Meyer prints *bonne[s]*.

952 The line is long; Meyer prints *(si)*.

953 The line is short; Meyer prints *Blandin[et]*.

954 Meyer prints *Enmentre*; Galano omits *en* (her line 1750); Nelli and Lavaud start their next excerpt here.

955 The line is long; Meyer prints *(lur)*; Nelli and Lavaud print *E novellas*.

956 The line is short; Meyer prints *Blandin[et]*; Nelli and Lavaud print *Blandinet*.

957 The ms. shows *doncella* with the letter *z* under the letter *c*; Meyer prints *donzella*; van der Horst prints *donçella*; Galano prints *doncella*; Meyer and Nelli and Lavaud print *otramar*.

958 The line is short; Meyer prints *l'(en)avia*; Nelli and Lavaud print *che l'avia*.

959 The ms. reads *una damayssela* though *una* is hard to read; Meyer prints *una damoysella* without commentary; van der Horst prints *d'..a damayssela*, saying that the ms. was illegible (130n1740), but that *una* was the logical word; Galano prints *d'[un]a damaysela*.

960 The line is short; Meyer prints *[trop] gran*.

961 Nelli and Lavaud print *che-en*.

962 The marginal note refers to the theft of Blandin's horse, which story he is about to retell.

963 Meyer prints *iou*.

964 The ms. reads *vertat*; Meyer prints *veritat*, which van der Horst calls a desirable correction (131n1746).

965 Meyer prints *[An] che iou poghes*; Nelli and Lavaud print *An che iou poghes*; van der Horst prints *caval..r* claiming the ms. was illegible, but that *cavalcar* was the logical word as Meyer had supposed (131n1748). We see *cavalcar* in the ms.

966 Meyer and Nelli and Lavaud print *conpenssant*.

967 The line is long. Meyer prints *(iou)*; Nelli and Lavaud print *Mas ay jurat*.

968 The ms. reads *colray*; Meyer prints *iou, tolray*; Lavaud and Nelli print *Ch'iou non colray denguna*.

969 The ms. reads *len namenat*; Meyer, Nelli and Lavaud, van der Horst, and Galano print *l'en a menat*, with van der Horst noting the *n* in *n'a* must be an error (131n1754). We agree that there is a problem, though this issue may suggest either that the scribe heard the story as he transcribed it or that he was saying the story aloud to himself as he wrote.

970 Meyer prints *vera(i)ment*; Nelli and Lavaud print *verament*.

971 Meyer prints *Iou*.

972 The ms. reads *cavallier*; Meyer, Nelli and Lavaud, and van der Horst print *cavalier*.

973 The ms. reads *fach* with *i* inserted above the line.

[974] Meyer prints *chen*; Nelli and Lavaud print *che-m*; Galano prints *che.m*; we follow van der Horst, who prints *che.n* and adds "Dans *Che.n*, il y a *n* pour *m*" (131n1770).

[975] This is the last line in this Nelli and Lavaud excerpt.

[976] The ms. reads *vritat*; Meyer prints *veritat*.

[977] Meyer prints *Iou li perdone*.

[978] The line is short; Meyer prints *vos [be] che* and *pla(i)s*.

[979] Meyer prints *P(l)us*.

[980] Meyer prints *iou*.

[981] Meyer prints *iou*.

[982] The line is short; Meyer prints *quant [el]*.

[983] The line is long; Meyer prints *(A)donc*.

[984] The line is long; Meyer prints *(vos)*; Galano omits *vos*.

[985] The line is short; Meyer and Galano print *Blandin[et]*.

[986] Galano prints *d'aquestos*.

[987] The ms. offers two letters *p-*, each with a stroke through the staff. The first *p* is clearly *per*; we expand the second *p* in similar fashion, to *personniers*, consistent with our interpretation of this abbreviation throughout the text. The same pair of abbreviations is seen at line 1818. At line 2109, where the word is not shortened, it is spelled *presoner*. Here, Meyer prints *iou* and *presoniers*; van der Horst and Galano print *presonniers*.

[988] Meyer prints *plagra*; the ms. reads *deslieures*, which we emend to *deslieuren* for rhyme; van der Horst prints *deslieures*; Galano prints *deslieurem*.

[989] Meyer prints *mi*; Galano prints *faren*.

[990] The line is short; Galano prints *Adonc[has]*.

[991] We can only read this much of this marginal note.

[992] Meyer and Galano print *va[n]*.

[993] The ms. presents the same abbreviations here as at line 1808, though "prisoners" here is spelled with one *-n-*; Meyer prints *presoniers*; van der Horst and Galano print *presonniers*; we retain the scribe's orthography.

[994] Meyer prints *commandar*.

[995] The line is long; Galano omits *de*.

[996] Meyer prints *Respon[don]*.

[997] The ms. may read *e Peytavin* or *a Peytavin*. Meyer prints *e Peytavin*, whereas van der Horst saw *a Peytavin*; he suggests that *e* is a correction; we print *e Peytavin*, because no correction is needed.

[998] The ms. reads *am bellas*; Meyer, van der Horst, and Galano emend these words to *amb ellas*, and we follow suit, though to the ear, at least two interpretations are possible: *am bellas*, "play with the beauties" and *amb ellas*, "play with them."

[999] The line is long; Meyer prints *puys(ses)*; Galano prints *puys, mich*.

[1000] The line is short. Meyer prints *B. lo myen [car] senhor*; van der Horst prints *Bland ..., lo myen* saying several letters are illegible (132n1819); Galano prints *[a] Blandinet: "Lo myen senhor*. We believe all the letters can be read.

1001 The line is short; Meyer prints *Iou* and *[bon'] amor*.

1002 Van der Horst prints *c.stel*, claiming the *a* is illegible (132n1821); Galano prints *c[a]stel*. We believe the *a* of *castel* can be seen, albeit with difficulty.

1003 The line is short; Meyer prints *iou*.

1004 Meyer prints *iou*.

1005 Meyer prints *Ardidamen*; the ms. reads *non*; Meyer prints *non*; van der Horst prints *no.n*; Galano prints *nos*.

1006 Meyer prints *mentir*.

1007 Meyer prints *Cavalier*.

1008 Meyer prints *[vos] prengas d'aur*. The word "gold" is very hard to make out; we agree with van der Horst and Galano and print *aor*; Galano prints *che [vos] prengas d'aor*.

1009 Meyer prints *prennes*.

1010 Meyer prints *Cornoa(l)gla*.

1011 Meyer prints *[Na] Brianda, iou (vos) dich*—i.e. he suggests omitting the first *vos*; Galano prints *[na] Brianda jou dich vos ay*; we understand the repeated *vos* for emphasis.

1012 Meyer prints *Ni* and *al re*.

1013 Meyer prints *pla(y)s*; Galano prints *plas*.

1014 Meyer prints *iou*.

1015 Meyer prints *viuray*, an orthography close to today's spelling of the word *viurai*; van der Horst and Galano print *vivray*. We see no reason to emend.

1016 Meyer prints *Con(sy)*; Galano prints *con*.

1017 Meyer prints *iou*.

1018 Raynouard prints *comjat*; Galano prints *cumïat*.

1019 The ms. reads *aproppet*; Meyer read *aproppet* but printed *apropjet*; van der Horst prints *aproppet*; Galano prints *apropjet*; the infinitive is clearly *apropïar*, "to draw near."

1020 Meyer prints *(Adonc) Brianda se mete [a] p.*, silently emending; Bertoni ("Correzioni al testo," 411) suggests *mes* [*a*] *plorat*; Galano prints *[a] plorar*.

1021 Meyer prints *mot* and *menar*.

1022 *amas* for *amatz*.

1023 A space left in ms. suggests that the scribe knew something was missing; Meyer, van der Horst, and Galano also note this space.

1024 Meyer (ed., "Le roman de *Blandin*," 195n) thinks that two lines are missing at this point; Galano (ed., *Blandin*, 182n) refers to Meyer and van der Horst. Logically, Blandin would mention Guilhot by name in the missing lines.

1025 *dins en*, which appears to be a double preposition, is a fairly common usage, with multiple examples found in *COM*—e.g., Bernart de Ventadorn, PC 70, 35, line 31: "dins en mo cor"; Martin-Chabot, ed., *Chanson de la Croisade albigeoise*, laisse 168, line 39: "dins en la vila."

1026 Meyer prints *mont*.

1027 Van der Horst prints *vole*.

1028 Galano prints *vole*.

1029 The line is short; Meyer prints *[en] intren*; Galano prints *[E] nos intren*.

1030 Galano prints *cavalquant*.

1031 Meyer prints *foren*.

1032 Meyer prints *disia*; Galano prints *che [nos] dissïa*.

1033 The ms. reads *la ins*; Meyer prints *la jus*; van der Horst and Galano print *la ins*; *laïns*, "within, inside," is equally plausible.

1034 The line is long; Meyer prints *(a)vantura*; Galano omits *e*.

1035 Meyer prints *Adonc*.

1036 Meyer prints *cavalchem*.

1037 The first *e* of this line may have been added later, as it is actually in the margin.

1038 Meyer prints *tenghen*.

1039 Meyer prints *a nos a*.

1040 The ms. reads *no nos*; emendation to *no[s] nos* is grammatically necessary. The marginal note is perhaps a reference to line 1931.

1041 The ms. reads *vim*; following Meyer, Galano prints *non nos venguem*.

1042 Meyer prints *prenghem* and *couvenent*; Galano prints *prenghem*.

1043 Meyer prints *n(o)s trobassem*.

1044 Meyer prints *loch*.

1045 The ms. reads *sent* with a horizontal stroke over the *n*; Meyer prints *Sant*; van der Horst and Galano print *sent*.

1046 Meyer prints *sanssa*.

1047 Meyer prints *Senhor si vos pla(y)s*; van der Horst notes that *mi* was added above the line, making the line long (134n1919); Galano prints *si vos plas*.

1048 Meyer prints *almens*.

1049 The ms. reads *avres*; Galano prints *trobat*.

1050 We understand a future form of the infinitive *venir*.

1051 The line is long; Meyer prints *Blandin(et)* and *Iou*; Galano prints *Blandin*.

1052 Meyer prints *Dieu*.

1053 The line is short; Meyer prints *el [a]*; Galano prints *el [a] pres cumïat*.

1054 Meyer and Galano print *cavalchar*.

1055 Meyer prints *le*.

1056 Compare to line 283; Meyer prints *el cavalcheron*; van der Horst prints *es cavalcheron*; Galano prints *e[l]s cavalcheron*.

1057 Meyer prints *jorn*.

1058 Meyer and Galano print *descavalcar*.

1059 Meyer prints *El* and *Guilhot*.

1060 Meyer and Galano print *Che anc*; the spelling *aoc* is found again, at line 2036 of our text.

1061 Meyer prints *s'en* for *se*.

1062 Van der Horst prints *A quant*; Meyer prints *gran*.

1063 The line is short; Meyer prints *[ai]tal*; Galano prints *per [ay]tal*.

1064 The ms. reads *salve*; *salve* and *mal*, however, do not rhyme. In addition, the line is long. Meyer prints *(o) Prodom(e)* and *Dieus te sal(ve)*; Galano prints *"Prodom, Dieus te sal"*; emending to *sal* provides a clean rhyme.

1065 Galano prints *Cornoailha*.

1066 The line is long; Meyer prints *(son)*.

1067 Meyer prints *Guilhot*.

1068 Meyer prints *Iou*.

1069 Meyer prints *pla(y)s*; Galano prints *plas*.

1070 Meyer prints *Adonc*.

1071 Galano prints *Senhor*.

1072 Meyer prints *tems*.

1073 The line is short; Meyer and Galano print *puy[sas]*.

1074 Meyer prints *iou*.

1075 The line is short. Meyer prints *intret* and *per [lo] sandier*, proposing the emendation for reasons of meter; Galano prints *intret s'en per [lo] sandier*.

1076 Meyer and Galano print *A[n]* and *escudier*.

1077 The line is short; Meyer and Galano print *[va] serca[r]*.

1078 The line is long; Meyer prints *(et)*; Galano prints *desert ont*.

1079 Meyer prints *[a]quel*.

1080 Meyer prints *temps*.

1081 Galano prints *avïe*.

1082 Meyer prints *conpanh*.

1083 The ms. reads *Adonduns*, a likely error. Meyer prints *Adonc*; van der Horst prints *Adonduns* (his line 1993) but points to repetition of this line elsewhere (135n1993), where the spelling is *adonc* (our lines 867, 1121, 1975, 1993, 2029); Galano prints *Adonc*; the *FEW* offers an example of *ladonc(a)s* (*FEW* s.v. DUNC III 179a) which we use to justify our emendation, while recognizing the evidence of similar lines in the text.

1084 Meyer prints *pordom(e)*; Galano prints *prodom*.

1085 Meyer prints *gard(e)*; Galano prints *gard*; as van der Horst notes, the line is long because of the *-e* of *garde* (135n1996).

1086 The line is short; Meyer prints *[mi] vist*; Galano prints *[my] vist*.

1087 This line has several illegible letters; Meyer prints *Cornoalha, bon gherrier*; van der Horst prints *Cor...... ... guerrier*; Galano prints *Corn[oalha, bon gu]errier*.

1088 The line is long; Meyer prints *(son)*.

1089 The ms. reads *Miramal*; with Meyer and Galano, we emend to *Miramar* for rhyme (compare the rhymes at 11 : 12, 1981 : 1982, 2055 : 2056).

1090 Meyer prints *Iou*.

1091 Meyer prints *Adonc*.

1092 Meyer prints *jort*; Galano prints *jort[z]*; we do not emend but recognize the word should be plural.

1093 Meyer prints *tenq*.

1094 Meyer prints *iou*.

1095 Meyer prints *escudier*.

1096 Meyer prints *anc* and omits *ha*; Galano prints *anc novellas no atrobet*.

1097 Meyer prints *ven*.

1098 The line is short; Meyer prints *fon [ben]*.

1099 Meyer and Galano print *E[l]* for *e*.

1100 The line is short; Meyer prints *[mout] bel*.

1101 Meyer prints *a[c]* and *pauch (de) massage*; we follow Mistral, *Lou tresor dóu Felibrige*, s.v. *masage*, "réunion de fermes, groupe de maisons."

1102 The ms. reads *ribba*; Meyer and Galano print *ribeira*. The ms. reads *d'on*; Meyer and Galano print *d'un*; van der Horst prints *d'on*.

1103 Meyer prints *En (de)viron*.

1104 Meyer prints *descavalchet*.

1105 Galano prints *prodom*.

1106 The line is long and reads *dieus* with a dot below the *-s*; Meyer prints *Dieus, gard(e)*; Galano prints *Dieu vos gard*. The scribe tended to use *Dieu* (thirty-three times) more than *Dieus* (eighteen times), both as a subject and as an object in the sentence.

1107 Meyer prints *mi*.

1108 The line is long; Meyer prints *Che* and *(son) nom*.

1109 Meyer prints *Iou vos preghe(s)*.

1110 The ms. reads *sercan*; Meyer and Galano print *sercar*; van der Horst prints *sercan*; with Meyer and Galano, we emend for rhyme and for meaning.

1111 Meyer prints *pordom(e)*; metathesis for *prodome*; Galano prints *prodom*; the manuscript uses this spelling, *pordom* or *pordome* at lines 2013, 2050, and 2061, though the spelling *prodom* or *prodome* is more common (our lines 796, 799, 1972, 1977, 2051). The marginal note is covered by a strip of paper.

1112 Van der Horst prints *Iou vos say*.

1113 Meyer and Galano print *[ges] bonas*.

1114 Galano prints *avïe mort[s]*.

1115 Meyer prints *fort*.

1116 Meyer prints *Che*.

1117 Meyer and Galano print *vera[ya]ment*.

1118 The line is short; Meyer prints *Blandin[et]*; Galano prints *Adonch[as]*.

1119 Meyer prints *Iou vos prege(s)*.

1120 The ms. reads *vos meme nes*; Meyer, van der Horst, and Galano print *vos me menes*; we understand the verb *emmenar*, "to take with, to lead."

1121 The line is short. Meyer prints *[cert] parlar*; Galano prints *jou [li] vuelh*.

1122 Meyer prints *volontier*.

1123 Meyer prints *se partiron*.

1124 Meyer prints *anneron*.

1125 Meyer and Galano print *Blandin[et]*.

1126 Meyer prints *e li a*.

1127 Meyer prints *Iou* and *Cornoalha*; Galano prints *Blandin* in italics without explanation.

1128 Meyer and Galano print *preg[e]* and *Dieu*.

1129 The line is long; Meyer prints *(Che) digas*.

1130 The ms. reads *volho*; van der Horst and Galano agree with this reading; Meyer emends to *iou li volh* though he recognizes that *vole* might also be possible; Galano emends to *jou li vuelh*.

1131 Meyer prints *cavaller*.

1132 Meyer prints *(A)donc, senhor*; Galano prints *E lo sengnor*.

1133 The line is short. Meyer prints *cavallier* and *che [a] vos*; Galano prints *che [a] vos*.

1134 Meyer prints *Iou vene ayssi* and *aossit*.

1135 Meyer prints *Guillot*.

1136 The line is short; Meyer and Galano print *volgra [vos] mot*.

1137 Meyer prints *vos lo m(y) volghesses baylar*.

1138 The ms. reads *prec chel ami deslieures* with two dots below *ami*; Meyer prints *prech chel deslieures*; the scribe's deletion of *ami* maintains the octosyllabic meter.

1139 Van der Horst prints *Irradament*.

1140 Meyer prints *Iou tenc*; Galano prints *ten*.

1141 Meyer prints *Guilot*.

1142 Meyer, van der Horst, and Galano print *Si dons*; we believe a different word is used here; see Mistral, *Lou tresor dóu Felibrige*, s.v. *senoun*, with *sedoun*, "unless, otherwise."

1143 The line is long; Meyer prints *Iou vos met(e)ray Guillot*.

1144 Meyer prints *Ardidamen*; Meyer, van der Horst, and Galano print *l'en menes*; again we understand *emmenar*, "to lead or take away."

1145 The ms. reads *An*; Meyer prints *Ambe*.

1146 Meyer prints *li, cavalier*.

1147 Meyer prints *che[us]*; van der Horst proposes emending to *che vos* (137n2115); our reading concurs with that of Galano.

1148 The ms. reads *E Car*, with initial *E* crossed out.

1149 Meyer prints *gauch(s)*.

1150 Meyer prints *(A)donc*.

1151 Van der Horst prints *verayamant*.

1152 The ms. reads *aytrestal* with *y* inserted above the line; Meyer and van der Horst print *atrestal*; Galano prints *a[y]trestal*. Meyer prints *fes [tot]*; Galano prints *Blandin[et]*, two solutions to the metrical issue as the line is short.

1153 The line is long. Meyer prints *valent(e)ment*; Galano prints *come valen*.

1154 Van der Horst suggests *van* for *va* (138n2129); Galano prints *va[n]*.

1155 The line is long. Meyer prints *s(e)*; Galano omits *se*.

1156 Meyer proposes *grans*.

1157 The ms. reads *si tomberon* with a dot beneath *si*; Meyer prints *si tomberon*; van der Horst omits *si*, because it was expunged. The line is long unless *terra andous* elide.

1158 Meyer prints *tant*; Galano prints *gran[s]*.

1159 Meyer prints *la spassa* and *l[os] escut[z]*; Galano prints *sus l[os] escut*.

1160 The line is short. Meyer prints *Quels [en]brasses*; van der Horst prints *Que·ls*; Galano prints *que l[o]s*; van der Horst suggests reading *lor* for *los*; Galano prints *romput*.

1161 Meyer prints *tan gran*.

1162 Meyer prints *flamejan*.

1163 The ms. reads *dona*, though the infinitive *donar* is clearly the intended form.

1164 Meyer prints *Et mont*.

1165 The line is long; Meyer prints *(un) gran*; Galano prints *batalhon*.

1166 Meyer prints *convenh*.

1167 Van der Horst explains *alench* as a variant of *alen*, "breath," (*FEW* s.v. ANHELARE I 97a) as in line 2169. *Alench* is an *unicum* in *COM*.

1168 Meyer prints *estaboïtz*; van der Horst suggests reading *estaboritz*; Galano prints *estaboitz*.

1169 There is a hole in the ms., the size of one letter at the end of this line. Meyer prints *esbaïtz*; van der Horst prints *esbait* but admits it might have been *esbaitz* (138n2156); Galano prints *esbait[z]*, claiming the hole in the ms. makes the *-z* illegible (Galano, ed., *Blandin*, 202n). The tail of the *-z* is visible; Vitale-Brovarone reads *esbaicz* (personal communication). A comparison with the rhyme word makes *esbaitz* a good hypothesis.

1170 Meyer prints *del* for *de*.

1171 Meyer prints *dirai vos cumsi*; van der Horst prints *cunsi*.

1172 The ms. reads *fri*; Meyer prints *f[e]ri*; van der Horst prints *fri* and agrees with Meyer's suggestion; Galano prints *feri*.

1173 Meyer prints *Et mont*.

1174 Meyer, van der Horst, and Galano print *fon avissat*; we do not make sense of *fon* and propose *fo·n*, leading to our translation, "Blandin was alert to it."

1175 Meyer prints *vo(i)s*.

1176 The ms. reads *rende*; Meyer and Galano print *rende[s]*; van der Horst prints *rende*.

1177 Meyer prints *mor[r]es*.

1178 The ms. reads *aveir*, van der Horst prints *aueir* (his line 2176), suggesting the copyist wrote an *-e-* rather than the *-c-* of *aucir* (139n2176); Meyer and Galano print *aucir*.

1179 Meyer prints *se*.

1180 Meyer prints *Adonc* and *le fes*; Galano prints *Adon[c]*.

1181 The ms. reads *fesses* with dots below; *fes* is written above.

1182 Meyer prints *Guillot*.

1183 Meyer and Galano print *en apres e[l]*; van der Horst prints *en apres e.*

1184 Meyer prints *Guillot pensen.*

1185 The ms. reads *fam*; Meyer prints *faim*; van der Horst and Galano print *fam*, as do we, understanding the verb *faire*, 1st p. pl. present.

1186 Galano prints *tengron.*

1187 Meyer prints *van s'en*; Galano prints *va[n].*

1188 Meyer and Galano print *Tos tres ensems* (for both, line 2198); van der Horst reads *tros* (his line 2190) but says one should understand *tos*; we agree that *tos* is the logical emendation but chose not to emend. It is possible that the scribe's exemplar presented *trestos ensems*, similar to line 1740 in our text.

1189 Van der Horst says *lo* should be *los*; Galano prints *lo[s] deser[t]s.*

1190 Galano prints *bon[s].*

1191 Meyer and Galano print *cavalcavan*; Galano prints *lo[s].*

1192 Meyer prints *Guillot.*

1193 The line is short; Galano prints *[lo] conquistet.*

1194 Meyer prints *Et atressys Guillot.*

1195 Meyer prints *mort tam bon guerriers*; *guerries* obviously represents *guerriers.*

1196 Meyer prints *tot.*

1197 Meyer prints *donzel.*

1198 The ms. reads *ten da anar*; Meyer prints *d'anar*; Galano prints *Pe[y]tavin* and *d'anar.*

1199 The line is long. Meyer prints *(a)*; Galano emends *dicas* to *di.*

1200 Galano prints *jeu.*

1201 The ms. reads *s'an nasset* which Meyer prints, though he suggests a correction to *s'avisset*; van der Horst prints *s'anvasset* and suggests metathesis of *s'avansset* (139n2213); Galano prints *s'avansset*. We propose the infinitive *s'en assar*, "to become calm, to compose (oneself)," building on the suggestion of the *FEW* s.v. SĔRĒSCĔRE XI 511, of a Catalan form *assarirse.*

1202 The line is short; Meyer prints *[E] tantost*; Galano prints *[a]trobet.*

1203 This rhyme pair *donzel* : *castel* offers assonance at best.

1204 The line is short. The ms. reads *avenent donzel* with *avenent* expunged; Meyer and Galano print *donzel[et].*

1205 Meyer prints *Guillot.*

1206 Meyer prints *mi.*

1207 The line is long; Meyer prints *(A)donc* and *(a)culhir*; Galano omits *Adonch.*

1208 Meyer prints *Ambe* and *ganch.*

1209 Meyer prints *dire.*

1210 Meyer prints *Adonc*; Galano prints *gratïossa.*

1211 The line is short. Meyer prints *[mot] allegra*; Galano prints *[mot] alegra.*

1212 Meyer prints *Quan.*

1213 The line is long; Meyer prints *nov(ell)as.*

1214 The line is short; Meyer prints *[mot] alegrament.*

1215 Galano prints *anar*.

1216 Meyer prints *la[s] sella[s]* for reasons of rhyme.

1217 Meyer prints *montant*.

1218 Meyer prints *vers, veray[a]ment*.

1219 The line is long; Meyer and Galano print *quant son*.

1220 The ms. reads *vistiz*; Meyer and Galano print *vistz*; van der Horst prints *visttz*, describing Meyer's correction to *vistz* as good (140n2242); we chose not to emend.

1221 The ms. reads *anar* with a horizontal stroke over the *a-*; Meyer prints *annar*; van der Horst and Galano print *anar*.

1222 Meyer prints *Ver[s]*.

1223 Galano prints *el*; Meyer prints *va[n]*.

1224 The ms. reads *e rissant* with a dot under the *e*; Meyer and Galano print *rissent*; van der Horst prints *rissant* but recognizes that *rissent* is needed for the rhyme (140n2252).

1225 The line is short. Meyer and Galano print *desca[va]lchas*, an emendation that makes the line octosyllabic.

1226 Galano prints *va[n]*.

1227 Meyer prints *apparelhadas*.

1228 The ms. reads *vanti*; Meyer and all subsequent editors emend to *van si*.

1229 Meyer, van der Horst, and Galano print *verament*. We see not one, but two abbreviation signs, which lead us to expand the word further.

1230 The line is short; Meyer prints *[Tras]tos ensems allegrament*.

1231 Meyer prints *sopat(z)*; Galano prints *sopat*.

1232 Meyer prints *dit*.

1233 Meyer prints *homme, pens(e)* and *co[l]car*; Galano prints *hom* and *co[l]car*.

1234 The line is long. Meyer prints *(tos en)tro*. We see clearly that the scribe wrote *panssen* and then emended it to *paussen*.

1235 Meyer and Galano print *doman*.

1236 The ms. reads *no nos*; Meyer prints *nos nos governerem*; Galano prints *nos nos governarem*.

1237 Galano prints *co[l]char*.

1238 Meyer prints *Guillot*.

1239 The line is long. Galano omits *E*; Meyer prints *(la) nuich*; Meyer emends *li* to *si*.

1240 Meyer prints *quan*.

1241 The line is long. Meyer prints *Blandin(et), Guilot* and *annatz*; Galano prints *Blandin*.

1242 Meyer prints *teng(he)ron*.

1243 The line is short. Meyer prints *Adonc [lo bon]*; Galano prints *Adonch[as] Blandin[et]*.

1244 The line is long. Meyer prints *Che conseillas, Guillot*; van der Horst prints *me conselhas vos, Guilhot* (his line 2282) (*me* is added above the line) and argues that the *v-* of *vos* is written over another letter (perhaps a *g-*) (141n2282); Galano prints *Che·m conselhas Guilhot*. Alternatively one can read the obscured word as *gras* for *gratz*, "pleasing."

1245 The line is short. Meyer prints *[mot] francha*; Galano prints *[tant] humil*.

1246 Meyer prints *iou*.

1247 The line is short. Meyer prints *pansar [nul]*; Galano prints *[ges] point* to correct meter.

1248 Meyer prints *iou*.

1249 Meyer prints *Guillot*.

1250 Galano prints *fermasses*.

1251 Meyer prints *presseses*.

1252 Meyer prints *chens*.

1253 Meyer prints *ensems*, *p(l)us* and *podem*; Galano prints *andous*.

1254 Meyer prints *li dich*.

1255 Galano understands *Don* as part of Blandin's speech.

1256 This is the first line in the final Nelli and Lavaud excerpt.

1257 The ms. reads *aron*; Meyer and Nelli and Lavaud print *aneren*; Galano prints *a[ne]ren*; we emend the conjugation for sense but keep the verb ending proposed by the scribe.

1258 Nelli and Lavaud print *E-a*.

1259 Meyer and Nelli and Lavaud print *ly* and *sapjas*.

1260 Meyer prints *iou*; Nelli and Lavaud print *vole se a*.

1261 The line is long. Meyer prints *vostre sor(re)*; Nelli and Lavaud and Galano print *sor*.

1262 The line is short. Meyer and Nelli and Lavaud print *conpanhon*; Galano prints *companh[o]n*.

1263 Meyer and Nelli and Lavaud print *cortes*.

1264 Meyer prints *preg[e]* and *pla(y)s*; Nelli and Lavaud and Galano print *prege* and *plas*.

1265 Meyer prints *com*; Nelli and Lavaud print *veramen*.

1266 Meyer and Nelli and Lavaud print *mi*.

1267 Meyer prints *fe* and *mon*; Nelli and Lavaud print *fe*; van der Horst prints *men*.

1268 Van der Horst and Galano print *tos temps*.

1269 The ms. reads *viray*; Meyer and Nelli and Lavaud print *viuray*; van der Horst says one should read *vivray* for *viray* (his line 2320); Galano prints *vi[u]ray*; these words are also found at line 1864 where the word is *viuray*. Exceptionally, we emend.

1270 Meyer and Nelli and Lavaud print *Adonc*.

1271 The ms. reads *vritat*; Meyer prints *veritat*; van der Horst prints *vritat*; Galano prints *v[e]ritat*.

1272 Meyer prints *iou*.

1273 Meyer and Nelli and Lavaud print *Non*.

1274 The line is long. Meyer prints *iou* and *com*; Nelli and Lavaud print *Ch'iou* and *com*; van der Horst prints *come*; Galano prints *com*.

1275 The line is short; Meyer and Nelli and Lavaud print *ambe*.

1276 Meyer prints *p(l)us*; Nelli and Lavaud print *pus che-a*; Galano prints *pla[i]s*. This couplet does not rhyme, and there are several possible corrections, that of Galano, for example, or changing line 2348 to *faray[s]*; we accept this pair as indicative of the author's pronunciation.

1277 Meyer prints *iou*.

1278 The ms. reads *prec*; Meyer prints *preg(e)*; Nelli and Lavaud print *prege*; Galano prints *preg[e]*.

1279 Meyer prints *(aqu)est*; Nelli and Lavaud print *appelat* and *quest*.

1280 The line is long; Meyer prints *(A)donc*; Nelli and Lavaud print *Donc*.

1281 Meyer prints *pla(i)s*; Nelli and Lavaud and Galano print *plas*.

1282 The line is long; Meyer prints *[el] van*; Galano prints *[els] van*.

1283 Meyer prints *sor[r]e*; Nelli and Lavaud print *sorre*.

1284 The line is short. Meyer prints *Guillot* and *va [donc]*; Nelli and Lavaud print *Guillot la va donc*.

1285 Meyer prints *trestoz*.

1286 The line is short. Meyer prints *Blandin[et]*; Nelli and Lavaud print *Blandinet*.

1287 Meyer and Nelli and Lavaud print *Dieus*.

1288 The ms. reads *juraz*; Meyer and Nelli and Lavaud print *juratz*; van der Horst and Galano print *juras*; Levy (*Petit dictionnaire provençal-français*) offers "fiancer," "to betroth," as one meaning of *jurar*.

1289 The line is short. Meyer and Galano print *[na] Brianda*; Nelli and Lavaud print *na Brïanda*.

1290 Meyer prints *Antoni*; Nelli and Lavaud print *Che-al, Antoni*.

1291 Meyer prints *Se fes[es]sa, matrimoni*; Nelli and Lavaud print *S fes[es]sa, matrimoni*; Galano prints *fassa*.

1292 Meyer and Nelli and Lavaud print *puys*.

1293 Meyer prints *conpanh*.

1294 Meyer and Nelli and Lavaud print *Guillot*.

1295 Meyer and Nelli and Lavaud omit *a*; Meyer prints *hom[e]*; Nelli and Lavaud print *home*.

1296 The line is short. Meyer and Galano print *iou vera[ya]ment*; Nelli and Lavaud print *verayament*.

1297 Meyer and Nelli and Lavaud print *tot*; this is the final line in this Nelli and Lavaud excerpt.

1298 The line is long; Meyer prints *cum (o)*; Galano prints *fan*.

1299 The ms. has *iustas*; Galano prints *fan*.

1300 Meyer prints *vent*.

1301 The line is short; Meyer prints *el[a]s*.

1302 The line is long. Meyer prints *Veng(he)ron* and *cavalliers*; Galano prints *vengron*.

1303 Meyer prints *escudiers*.

1304 The line is short. Meyer prints *onor* and *[na] Brianda*; Galano prints *[na] Brianda*.

1305 Meyer prints *[Tres]totz ensems*; van der Horst omits *e* which he says was wrongly expunged (142n2368). We agree there is a dot beneath *e*; we keep the word for the sense of the line which would be very short otherwise. Galano prints *[e] ben e honesta* to solve the metrical issue.

1306 The ms. reads *iustas*; Galano prints *biorts*.

1307 Meyer prints *ben*.

1308 Meyer prints *(E)*.

1309 The line is short; Meyer and Galano print *Blandin[et]*.

1310 Meyer prints *Guillot*.

1311 Meyer prints *cavalers*.

1312 Meyer prints *vogron* and *g[u]era*.

1313 Meyer prints *Gulhot*.

1314 Raynouard prints *Che troberon*; Meyer prints *molhers*.

1315 The line is long; Meyer prints *com(a)*; Galano prints *com*.

1316 Raynouard and Meyer print *Dieu*; Raynouard prints *prenha*; van der Horst reproduces the text as presented in the ms.: *E pregas Dieus che ayssi vos prenna, / E che ve don a tut e a tute la bonna strenna*. Meyer prints *E che vos don (a tut e a tute) la bona strenna*; Galano re-orders the text as we have, but omits *a tut et a tute*. Re-ordering the last words of the text makes the final rhyme clear, offers octosyllabic lines, and allows for a clean ending, along with good wishes for the audience.

Bibliography

Manuscripts

Paris, Bibliothèque nationale de France, Doat 202 and 211.
Paris, Bibliothèque nationale de France, latin 6489.
Paris, Bibliothèque nationale de France, nouv. acq. fr. 5087.
Torino (Turin), Biblioteca nazionale ed universitaria, G II 34.

Dictionaries

Alcover i Sureda, Antoni Maria and Francesch de Borja Moll y Casasnovas, eds. *Diccionari català-valencià-balear.* 10 vols. Palma de Mallorca: Impr. de M. N. Alcover, 1928–1962.

Dictionnaire de l'Occitan médieval. DOM en ligne. Directed by Wolf-Dieter Stempel and Maria Selig. Munich: Bayerische Akademie der Wissenschaften. http://www.dom-en-ligne.de/.

Faure, Andrieu, ed. *Diccionari d'alpin d'oc.* www.locongres.org/fr/applications/dicodoc-fr/ and www.espaci-occitan.com/asso/file/diccionari_alpin_oc.pdf.

Grosclaude, Miquèu, Gilabèrt Nariòo and Patric Guilhemjoan. *Dictionnaire français occitan (gascon).* 2 vols. Orthez: Per Noste, 2007.

Honnorat, Simon-Jules, ed. *Dictionnaire provençal-français, ou Dictionnaire de langue d'oc ancien et moderne.* 4 vols. Digne: Repos, 1846. http://gallica.bnf.fr/ark:/12148/bpt6k5816077m.r=dictionnaire+honnorat.langFR.

Levy, Émile, ed. *Petit dictionnaire provençal-français.* Heidelberg: C. Winter, 1961.

Mistral, Frédéric, ed. *Lou tresor dóu Felibrige.* 2 vols. 1879; rpt. 13280 Raphèle-lès-Arles: Marcel Petit, Culture provençale et méridionale, 1979 and 2005.

Oxford English Dictionary. http://www.oed.com.

Pansier, P[ierre]. "Lexique provençal-français." Vol. 3 in *Histoire de la langue provençale à Avignon du XIIe au XIXe siècle.* 4 vols. Avignon: Librairie Aubanel, 1927.

Raynouard, François-Just-Marie, ed. *Lexique roman ou Dictionnaire de la langue des troubadours comparée avec les autres langues de l'Europe latine.* 6 vols. Paris: Chez Silvestre, 1838–1844; rpt. Geneva: Slatkine Reprints, 1977.

Rei Bèthvéder, Nicolau. *Dictionnaire français/occitan: gascon toulousain.* Toulouse: IEO, 2004.

Wartburg, Walter von, ed. *Französisches etymologisches Wörterbuch: eine Darstellung des galloromanischen Sprachschatzes.* Tübingen: Mohr, 1948–.

Primary Sources

Andreas Capellanus. [*De amore*], *Andreas Capellanus on Love*, edited and translated by P. G. Walsh. London: Duckworth, 1982.

Arthur, Ross G., tr. *Blandin de Cornoalha e Guilhot de Miramar: A Generic Medieval Adventure Romance*. Toronto: Alektryaina Press, 1988.

Arthur, Ross G., tr. *Jaufre: An Occitan Arthurian Romance*. New York: Garland, 1992.

Aucassin et Nicolette, chantefable du XIIIe siècle, edited by Mario Roques. CFMA 41. Paris: Librairie ancienne Edouard Champion, 1925.

Bernart de Ventadorn. *Bernard de Ventadour, troubadour du XIIe siècle*, edited by Moshé Lazar. Paris: Klincksieck, 1966.

Breuer, Hermann, ed. *Jaufre: Ein altprovenzalischer Abenteuerroman des XIII. Jahrhunderts*. Halle a. S.: Max Niemeyer, 1925.

Burrell, Margaret A. "A Critical Edition of the Provençal Romance *Blandin de Cornouailles*." PhD diss. Toronto: University of Toronto, 1974.

Careri, Maria, Christine Ruby and Ian Short, eds., with Terry Nixon and Patricia Stirnemann. *Livres et écritures en français et en occitan au XIIe siècle. Catalogue illustré*. Rome: Viella, 2011.

Cerveri de Girona. *Obras completas del trovador Cerveri de Girona*, edited by Martín de Riquer. Barcelona: Horta, 1947.

Chiesa, Paolo. "Iacopo da Acqui." *Dizionario Biografico degli Italiani*. Rome: Treccano, 2004. https://www.treccani.it/enciclopedia/iacopo-da-acqui_(Dizionario-Biografico)/.

Chrétien de Troyes. *Cligès*, edited by Alexandre Micha. Paris, 1957; rpt. Paris: Champion, 1965.

Chrétien de Troyes. *Erec et Enide*, edited by Mario Roques. Paris, 1954; rpt. Paris: Champion, 1970.

Chrétien de Troyes. *Lancelot or, The Knight of the Cart (le Chevalier de la Charrete)*, edited and translated by William W. Kibler. New York: Garland, 1981.

Chrétien de Troyes. *Le roman de Perceval ou le Conte du Graal*, edited by Keith Busby. Tübingen: Max Niemeyer Verlag, 1993.

Chrétien de Troyes. *Yvain (le Chevalier au lion)*, edited by T. B. W. Reid. Manchester: Manchester University Press, 1942.

Combarieu du Grès, Micheline de and Gérard Gouiran, eds. and trs. *La chanson de Girart de Roussillon*. Paris: Librarie générale française, 1993.

Delorenzi, Lorenzino. "Il poemetto provenzale 'Blandin de Cornovalha' Ms. G II 34 della Biblioteca nazionale di Torino." Thesis in Romance Philology. Torino: Regia Università di Torino, 1926.

Fasseur, Valérie, tr., François Zufferey, ed. *Flamenca*. Paris: Livre de poche, 2014.

Galano, Sabrina, ed. *Blandin di Cornovaglia*. Alessandria: Edizioni dell'Orso, 2004.

Guilhem IX. *The Poetry of William VII, Count of Poitiers, IX Duke of Aquitaine*, edited and translated by Gerald A. Bond. New York: Garland, 1982.

Guillaume, Paul, ed. "Istorio de Sainct Poncz." *RlaR* 31 (1887): 461–553.

Guiraut Riquier. *Les épîtres de Guiraut Riquier, troubadour du XIIIe siècle*, edited by Joseph Linksill. Liège: A.I.E.O., 1985.

Guisado, Maite, ed. *Blandín de Cornoalla: Conte d'amor i de caballeria (segle XIV)*. Barcelona: La Magrana, 1997.

Hershon, Cyril P., Peter T. Ricketts, et al., eds. *Elucidari de las proprietatz de totas res naturals*. Cahiers de Ventadour. [Egletons]: Carrefour Ventador, 2018.

Horst, Cornelius H. M. van der, ed. *Blandin de Cornouaille, introduction, édition diplomatique, glossaire*. The Hague: Mouton, 1974.

Huchet, Jean-Charles, tr. *Blandin de Cornouaille*. In *La légende arthurienne. Le Graal et la Table ronde*, edited by Danielle Régnier-Bohler, 923–56. Paris: Laffont, 1989.

Jeanroy, Alfred, ed. *Les joies du gai savoir, recueil de poésies*. Toulouse: Privat, 1914.

Lee, Charmaine, ed. *Daurel e Beton*. Parma: Pratiche Editrice; Rome: Carocci, 1991.

Lee, Charmaine, ed. *Jaufre*. Rome: Carocci, 2006.

Limentani, Alberto, ed. *Las novas de Guillem de Nivers ("Flamenca")*. Padua: Editrice Antenore, 1965.

Lods, Jeanne, ed. *Le roman de Perceforest*. Geneva: Droz, 1951.

Marie de France. *Lais*, edited by A[lfred] Ewert. Oxford, 1944; rpt. Oxford: Blackwell, 1960.

Marshall, J. H., ed. *The* Razos de trobar *of Raimon Vidal and Associated Texts*. Oxford: Oxford University Press, 1972.

Martin-Chabot, Eugène, ed. *Chanson de la Croisade albigeoise*, translated by Henri Gougaud. Paris: Livre de poche, 1989.

Meyer, Paul. "Quatrains sur l'avarice." *Rom* 1 (1872): 417–19.

Meyer, Paul, ed. "Le roman de *Blandin de Cornouailles et de Guillot Ardit de Miramar*, publié pour la première fois d'après le ms. unique de Turin." *Rom* 2 (1873): 170–202.

Molinier, Guilhem. *Las Leys d'amors, manuscrit de l'Académie des Jeux floraux*, edited by Joseph Anglade. Toulouse: Edouard Privat, 1919–1921.

Molinier, Guilhem. *Las Leys d'amors, redazione lunga in prosa*, edited by Beatrice Fedi. Florence: Edizioni dell Galluzzo per la Fondazione Ezio Franceschini, 2019.

Mondschein, Ken. *The Knightly Art of Battle*. Los Angeles: J. Paul Getty Museum, 2011.

Morawski, Joseph, ed. *Proverbes français antérieurs au XVe siècle*. Paris: Édouard Champion, 1925.

Nelli, René and René Lavaud, eds. and trs. *Blandin de Cornouailles*. In *Les troubadours: Le trésor poétique de l'Occitanie*, edited by René Nelli and René Lavaud, 2:450–73. Bruges: Desclée de Brouwer, 1966.

Nelli, René and René Lavaud, eds. and trs. *Le roman de Jaufre*. In *Les troubadours: Le trésor poétique de l'Occitanie*, edited by René Nelli and René Lavaud, 1:17–618. Bruges: Desclée de Brouwer, 1960.

Nostredame, Jehan de. *Les vies des plus célèbres et anciens poëtes provensaux*, edited by C[amille] Chabaneau and J[oseph] Anglade. Paris: H. Champion, 1913.

Pacheco, Arseni, ed. *Blandín de Cornualla i altres narracions en vers dels segles XIV i XV*. Barcelona: Edicions 62, 1983.

Paden, William D., ed. and tr. *The Medieval Pastourelle*. 2 vols. New York: Garland, 1987.

Paden, William D., Tilde Sankovitch and Patricia H. Stablein, eds. *The Poems of the Troubadour Bertran de Born*. Berkeley: University of California Press, 1989.

Portet, Pierre. *Bertrand Boysset, la vie et les œuvres techniques d'un arpenteur médiéval (v.1355–v.1416): Édition et commentaire du texte provençal de* La siensa de destrar *et de* La siensa d'atermenar. 2 vols. Paris: Le Manuscrit, 2004.

Raimond Feraud,. *La vida de sant Honorat*, edited by Peter T. Ricketts and Cyril P. Hershon. Turnhout: Brepols, 2007.

Renaut de Bâgé. *Le Bel Inconnu (li Biaus Descouneüs, The Fair Unknown)*, edited by Karen Fresco, translated by Colleen P. Donagher, music edited by Margaret P. Hasselman. New York: Garland, 1992.

Ricketts, Peter T., dir. *Concordance de l'occitan médiéval (COM) 1 and 2*. Turnhout: Brepols, 2005. CD-ROM.

Riquer, Martín de. *Història de la literatura catalana: Part antiga*. 3 vols. Barcelona: Editorial Ariel, 1980.

Roussineau, Gilles, ed. *Perceforest, troisième partie*. 2 vols. Geneva: Droz, 1988–1993.

Russell-Gebbett, Paul, ed. *Medieval Catalan Linguistic Texts*. Oxford: Dolphin Press, 1965.

Segre, Cesare, ed. *La chanson de Roland, nouvelle édition refondue*, translated from the Italian by Madeleine Tyssens. 1971; rpt. Geneva: Droz, 2003.

Stuip, René Ernst Victor, ed. *La chastelaine de Vergi, édition critique du ms. B.N. fr. 375 avec introduction, notes, glossaire et index, suivie de l'édition diplomatique de tous les manuscrits connus du XIIIe et du XIVe siècle*. The Hague: Mouton, 1970.

Suchier, Hermann, ed. *Diététique, d'après l'Epistola Aristoteli ad Alexandrum. Denkmäler provenzalischer Literatur und Sprache*. 201–13, 473–80. Halle: Niemeyer, 1883.

Taylor, Jane H. M., ed. *Le roman de Perceforest, première partie*. Geneva: Librairie Droz, 1979.

Thiolier-Méjean, Suzanne, ed. *Une belle au bois dormant médiévale: Frayre de Joy et Sor de Plaser*. Paris: Centre d'enseignement et de recherche d'Oc, Université de Paris IV, 1996.

Tiñena, Jordi, tr. *Blandín de Cornualla, anònim. Narració en vers del s. XIV*. Barcelona: Edicions Bromera, 1987; rpt. 1988.

Trésor manuscrit de l'ancien occitan. http://tmao.aieo.org/.

Vidal Lloret, Vicent, tr. "*Blandín de Cornualla*: Versió al català actual i traducció al castellà." MA thesis. Alicante: University of Alicante, 2011–2012.

Villeneuve, Louis-François de. *Lyonnel ou la Provence au XIIIe siècle, roman historique*. 3 vols. Paris: J.-J. Blaise, 1824.

Walter Map. *Master Walter Map's Book, De nugis curialium (Courtier's Trifles)*, translated by Frederick Tupper and Marbury Bladen Ogle. London: Chatto & Windus, 1924.

Whitehead, Frederick, ed. *La châtelaine de Vergy*. Manchester: Manchester University Press, 1961.

Secondary Sources

Adams, Edward L. *Word-Formation in Provençal*. New York: Macmillan, 1913.

Adams, Tracy. *The Life and Afterlife of Isabeau of Bavaria*. Baltimore: Johns Hopkins University Press, 2010.

Adler, Alfred. "Sovereignty as the Principle of Unity in Chrétien's *Erec*." *PMLA* 60 (1945): 917–36.

Adler, Alfred. "Sovereignty in Chretien's *Yvain*." *PMLA* 62 (1947): 281–305.

Alart, Julien-Bernard. "Observations sur la langue du roman du *Blandin de Cornouailles et Guillot Ardit de Miramar*." *RlaR* 5 (1874): 275–304.

Anglade, Joseph. *Grammaire de l'ancien provençal*. Paris: Klincksieck, 1921.

Ashdown, Charles Henry. *European Arms and Armor*. Rpt. New York: Barnes & Noble, 1995.

Asperti, Stefano. "Bacinetti e berroviere: Problemi di lessico e di datazione nel *Blandin de Cornoalha*." In *Studia in honorem prof. M. de Riquer*, edited by Carlos Alvar, Lola Badia, Pedro Cátedra and Jaume Vallcorbal Plana, 1:11–35. 3 vols. Barcelona: Quaderns Crema, 1986.

Autrand, Françoise. *Jean de Berry: L'art et le pouvoir*. Paris: Fayard, 2000.

Badel, Pierre-Yves. *Introduction à la vie littéraire du Moyen Âge*. Paris: Bordas, 1969.

Barchilon, Jacques. "L'histoire de *La belle au bois dormant* dans le *Perceforest*." *Fabula* 31 (1990): 17–23.

Bazin-Tacchella, Sylvie, Laurence Hélix and Muriel Ott, eds. *Le livre du voir dit de Guillaume Machaut*. Neuilly: Atlande, 2001.

Becker, Georges. "Guillaume de Machaut." In *Dictionnaire des lettres françaises: Le Moyen Âge*, edited by Robert Bossuat with Guy Reynaud de Lage, Georges Grente and Louis Pichard, 353–358. Paris: Librairie Artheme Fayard, 1964.

Bertoni, Giulio. "Correzioni al testo di *Blandin de Cornouailles*." *Archivum Romanicum* 5 (1921): 408–12.

Bohigas, Pere. "La matière de Bretagne en Catalogne." *Bulletin bibliographique de la Société internationale arthurienne* 13 (1961): 81–98.

Bourciez, Édouard. *Éléments de linguistique romane*. 5th ed. Paris: Klincksieck, 1967.

Bourciez, Jean and Édouard Bourciez. *Phonétique française: Étude historique*. Paris: Klincksieck, 1967.

Bradbury, Jim. *The Routledge Companion to Medieval Warfare*. London: Routledge, 2004.

Bras, Miriam and Jean Sibille. "Lo futur perifrastic de tipe *anar +infinitiu* en occitan." In *Fidelitats e dissidéncias: Actes du XII*[e] *Congrès de l'Association internationale d'études occitanes*, edited by Jean-François Courouau and David Fabié. 2 vols. 1:157–68. Toulouse: SFAIEO, 2020.

Brault, Gerard J. *Early Blazon: Heraldic Terminology in the Twelfth and Thirteenth Centuries with Special Reference to Arthurian Heraldry*. 2nd ed. Woodbridge, Suffolk: Boydell Press, 1997.

Briquet, Charles Moïse. *Les filigranes. Dictionnaire historique des marques du papier dès leur apparition vers 1282 jusqu'en 1600*. 4 vols. Paris, 1907.

Brodeur, Arthur Gilchrist. "The Grateful Lion." *PMLA* 39 (1924): 485–524.

Brown, Arthur C. L. *Iwain: A Study in the Origins of Arthurian Romance*. 1903; rpt. New York: Haskell House, 1968.

Bruchet, Max. *Le chateau de Ripaille*. Paris: Librairie Ch. Delagrave, 1907.

Bueno de Mesquita, D. M. *Giangaleazzo Visconti, Duke of Milan (1351–1402): A Study in the Political Career of an Italian Despot*. Cambridge: Cambridge University Press, 1941.

Burrell, Margaret A. "*Blandin de Cornouailles*, a Late Example of *conjointure* between *sens* and Structures." *New Zealand Journal of French Studies* 5, no. 2 (1984): 33–50.

Burrell, Margaret A. "The Classification of *Blandin de Cornouailles*: The Romance within and Without." *Florilegium* 20 (2001): 1–9.

Busby, Keith. "*Blandin de Cornoalha* and Romance Tradition." *Tenso* 8, no. 1 (1992): 1–25.

Busby, Keith. *Codex and Context: Reading Old French Verse Narrative in Manuscript*. 2 vols. Amsterdam: Rodopi, 2002.

Busby, Keith. *Gauvain in Old French Literature*. Degré second 2. Amsterdam: Rodopi, 1980.

Cabié, Edmond. "Notes et documents sur les différends des comtes de Foix et d'Armagnac en 1381." *Annales du Midi* 13 (1901): 500–529.

Cabré, Miriam and Anton Espadaler. "La narrativa en vers." In *Història de la literatura catalana*, vol. 1, *Dels orígens al segle XIV*, edited by Àlex Broch, 297–372. Barcelona: Enciclopèdia catalana, Editorial Barcino, and Ajuntament de Barcelona, 2013.

Calin, William. *A Poet at the Fountain: Essays on the Narrative Verse of Guillaume de Machaut*. Lexington: University Press of Kentucky, 1974.

Caluwé, Jacques de. "Le roman de *Blandin de Cornouailles et de Guillot Ardit de Miramar*: Une parodie de roman arthurien?" *Actes du VII*[e] *Congrès international de langue d'oc et d'études franco-provençales, Cultura neolatina* 38 (1978): 55–66.

Camproux, Charles. *Histoire de la littérature occitane*. Paris: Payot, 1971.

Camus, J. "La maison de Savoie et le mariage de Valentine Visconti." *Bollettino storico-bibliografico subalpino* 4 (1899): 113–26.

Cerquiglini, Jacqueline. "Le clerc et l'écriture: Le *voir dit* de Guillaume de Machaut et la définition du *dit*." In *Literatur in der Gesellschaft des Spätmittelalters*, edited by Hans Ulrich Gumbrecht, 151–68. Heidelberg: Carl Winter, 1980.

Chabaneau, Camille. "Notes critiques sur quelques textes provençaux. II: *Blandin de Cornouailles*." *RlaR* 8 (1877): 31–47.

Chamberlin, E. R. *The Count of Virtue: Giangaleazzo Visconti, Duke of Milan*. New York: Charles Scribner's Sons, 1965.

Chambers, Frank M. *An Introduction to Old Provençal Versification*. Memoirs of the American Philosophical Society 167. Philadelphia: American Philosophical Society, 1985.

Cingolani, Stefano. "Il *Blandin de Cornualha* e la letteratura populare fra Provenza e Catalogna." In *La narrativa in Provenza e Catalogna nel XIIIe e XIV secolo. Colloquio organizzato dal Dipartimento di lingue e letteratura ... Roma, 12–14 maggio 1993*, edited by Fabrizio Beggiato and S. Cingolani, 145–59. Pisa: ETS, 1995.

Cognasso, Francesco. "IV. L'influsso francese nello Stato sabaudo durante la minorità di Amedeo VIII—Note e documenti inediti." *Mélanges d'archéologie et d'histoire* 35 (1915): 257–326. doi: 10.3406/mefr.1915.7125.

Colby, Alice M. *The Portrait in Twelfth-Century French Literature: An Example of the Stylistic Originality of Chrétien de Troyes*. Geneva: Droz, 1965.

Cordey, Jean. *Les comtes de Savoie et les rois de France pendant la Guerre de Cent ans (1329–1391)*. Paris: Honoré Champion, 1911.

Cormier, Raymond J. "Indications d'oralité dans l'expression poétique du *Roman d'Éneas*." *Rom* 133 (2015): 311–27.

Creton, Rosa Thea. *Bonne de Bourbon, comtesse de Savoie*. Yens sur Morges: Editions Cabédita, 2003.

Demotz, Bernard. *Le Comté de Savoie du XIe au XVe siècle. Pouvoir, château et état au Moyen Âge*. Geneva: Slatkine, 2000.

Durrieu, Paul. "Bernard VII, comte d'Armagnac, connétable de France, 136?–1418." Thesis. Paris: L'École des chartes, 1878; rpt. Villemomble: Arnaud de Solanges, 2001–2003.

Durrieu, Paul. *Les Gascons en Italie*. Auch: G. Foix, 1885.

Eckhardt, Caroline D. "Reading *Jaufré*: Comedy and Interpretation in a Medieval Cliff-Hanger." *The Comparatist* 33 (2009): 40–62. https://www.jstor.org/stable/26237208.

Egedi-Kovács, Emese. *La "morte vivante" dans le récit français et occitan du Moyen Âge*. Budapest: Elte Eötvös Kiadó, 2012.

Espadaler, Anton. "El meravellós com a luxe i pedagogia." In *El món imaginari i el món meravellós a l'edat mitjana*, edited by Victor Hurtado and Marcel La Matheu, 137–49. Barcelona: Fundació Caixa de pensions, 1986.

Espadaler, Anton. "Las *novas*, un territorio sin fronteras." In *De los orígenes de la narrativa corta en Occidente*, edited by Reinhard Huamán Mori and Helena Roig Torres, 103–17. [Lima, Peru]: Ginebra Magnolia, 2007.

Fasseur, Valérie. "La matière bretonne dans la littérature d'oc." In *La matière arthurienne tardive en Europe 1270–1530*, edited by Christine Ferlampin-Acher, 311–29. Rennes: Presses universitaires de Rennes, 2020.

Fauriel, Claude. *Histoire de la poésie provençale*. 3 vols. 1846; rpt. Paris: Classiques Garnier, 2011.

Fernández González, José Ramón. *Gramática histórica provenzal*. Oviedo: Universidad de Oviedo, 1985.

Finó, J.-F. "Les armées françaises lors de la Guerre de cent ans." *Gladius* 13 (1977): 5–23.

Fleischman, Suzanne. "'Jaufre' or Chivalry Askew: Social Overtones of Parody in Arthurian Literature." *Viator* 12 (1981): 101–29.

Fouché, Pierre. *Phonétique historique du roussillonnais*. Toulouse: Edouard Privat, 1924.

Foulet, Alfred and Mary Blakely Speer. *On Editing Old French Texts*. Lawrence: The Regents Press of Kansas, 1979.

Frappier, Jean. "The Vulgate Cycle." In *Arthurian Literature in the Middle Ages: A Collaborative History*, edited Roger Sherman Loomis, 295–318. Oxford: Oxford University Press, 1959.

Fraser, Veronica. "Humour and Satire in the Romance of *Jaufre*." *Forum for Modern Language Studies* 31 (1995): 223–33.

Frazer, J. G. *The Golden Bough: A Study in Magic and Religion*, abr. ed. London: Macmillan, 1922.

Galano, Sabrina. "Il *Blandin de Cornoalha*: Riflessioni sulla lingua." In *Studi di letteratura*, edited by Michele Bottalico and Maria Teresa Chialant, 201–24. Naples: Scientifiche Italiane, 2003.

Galano, Sabrina. "Indizi di oralità nel *Blandin de Cornoalha*." *Romanica Vulgaria Quaderni* 16–17 = *Studi provenzali* 98–99 (1999): 199–239.

Galano, Sabrina. "Nuove congetture sulla lingua del *Blandin de Cornoalha*." In *Actas del XXIII Congreso internacional de lingüística y filologia románica, Salamanca, 24–30 septiembre 2001*, edited by Fernando Sànchez Miret, 4:99–110. 5 tomes in 6 vols. Tübingen: Niemeyer, 2003.

Gorrini, Jean. *L'incendie de la Bibliothèque nationale de Turin*. Preface by Pascal Villari. Turin: Editori Renzo Streglio, 1904.

Grandeau, Yann. "De quelques dames qui ont servi la reine Isabeau de Bavière." *Bulletin philologique et historique (jusqu'à 1610) année 1975*, 129–238. Paris: Comité des travaux historiques et scientifiques / Bibliothèque nationale, 1977.

Gravdal, Kathryn. *Ravishing Maidens: Writing Rape in Medieval French Literature and Law*. Philadelphia: University of Pennsylvania Press, 1991.

Graves, Robert. *The White Goddess: A Historical Grammar of Poetic Myth*. London: Faber and Faber, 1961.

Grévisse, Maurice. *Le bon usage: Grammaire française*. 13th ed. Paris: Duculot, 1994.

Grossel, Marie-Geneviève. "Conclure le roman en terre d'oc: L'exemple de *Jaufre*." *Pris-Ma: Recherches sur la littérature d'imagination au Moyen Âge* 14 (1998): 117–34.

Hasenohr, Geneviève. "Le rythme et la versification." In *Mise en page et mise en texte: Du livre au manuscrit*, edited by Henri-Jean Martin and Jean Vezin, 235–38. Paris: Editions du Cercle de la Librarie-Promodis, 1990.

Heap, David. *La variation grammaticale en géolinguistique: Les pronoms sujet en roman central*. Munich: Lincom Europa, 2000.

Henrichsen, Arne-Johan. "La périphrase anar + infinitif en ancien occitan." In *Omagiu lui Alexandru Rosetti, la 70 de ani*, 357–63. Bucharest: Editura Academiei Republicii Socialiste România, 1965.

Hewitt, John. *Ancient Armour and Weapons in Europe: From the Iron Period of the Northern Nations to the End of the Thirteenth Century*. Oxford and London: J. Henry and J. Parker, 1855–1860.

Holmes, Urban Tignor. *A History of Old French Literature*, rev. ed. New York: Russell and Russell, 1962.

Honeggar, Thomas. *Introducing the Medieval Dragon*. Cardiff: University of Wales Press, 2019.

Huchet, Jean-Charles. "*Jaufré* et *Flamenca*, *novas* ou romans?" *RlaR* 96, no. 2 (1992): 275–300.

Huchet, Jean-Charles. *Le roman occitan médiéval*. Paris: Presses universitaires de France, 1991.

Jarry, Eugène. *La vie politique de Louis de France duc d'Orléans 1372–1407*. 1889; rpt. Geneva: Slatkine-Megariotis Reprints, 1976.

Jeanroy, Alfred. *Histoire sommaire de la poésie occitane des origines à la fin du XVIIIe siècle*. Toulouse: Privat, 1945.

Jeay, Madeleine. *Le commerce des mots. L'usage des listes dans la littérature médiévale (XIIe–XVe siècles)*. Geneva: Droz, 2006.

Jewers, Caroline. "The Name of the Ruse and the Round Table: Occitan Romance and the Case for Cultural Resistance." *Neophilologus* 81 (1997): 187–200.

Jiménez Mola, Zulema. "Un género para 'Un bel dictat': *Blandin de Cornualles*." In *Actas del VIII Congreso internacional de la Asociación de literatura medieval: Santander, 22–26 septiembre de 1999, Palacio de La Magdalena, Universidad Internacional Menéndez Pelayo*, edited by Margarita Freixas and Silvia Iriso, 2:1031–38. 2 vols. Santander: Consejería de cultura del Gobierno de Cantabria, 2000.

José, Marie. *La maison de Savoie*, vol. 1, *Les origines, le comte vert, le comte rouge*. Preface by Benedetto Croce. Paris: Albin Michel, 1956.

Kelly, Douglas. *Sens and conjointure in the Chevalier de la Charrette*. The Hague: Mouton, 1966.

Lacy, Norris. "Halfway to Quixote: Humor in *Blandin de Cornoalha*." In *Risus mediaevalis: Laughter in Medieval Literature and Art*, edited by Herman Braet, Guido Latré and Werner Verbeke, 173–80. Leuven: Leuven University Press, 2003.

Lacy, Norris. "On Customs in Medieval French Romance." *Revue belge de philologie et d'histoire* 83 (2005): 977–86. https://www.persee.fr/doc/rbph_0035-0818_2005_num_83_3_4953.

Lafont, Robert and Christian Anatole. *Nouvelle histoire de la littérature occitane*. 2 vols. Paris: Presses universitaires de France, 1970.

Lazzerini, Lucia. *Letteratura medievale in lingua d'oc*. Modena: Mucchi, 2001.

Lee, Charmaine. "'Versi d'amore e prose di romanzi': The Reception of Occitan Narrative Genres in Italy." *Tenso* 28 (2013): 18–32.

Léglu, Catherine. *Multilingualism and Mother Tongue in Medieval French, Occitan and Catalan Narratives*. University Park: Pennsylvania State University Press, 2010.

Léonard, Monique. *Le* dit *et sa technique littéraire des origines à 1340*. Paris: Honoré Champion, 1996.

Leverage, Paula. *Reception and Memory: A Cognitive Approach to the Chansons de geste*. Amsterdam: Rodopi, 2010.

Lewent, Kurt. "Three Little Problems of Old Provençal Syntax." In *French and Provençal Lexicography: Essays Presented to Honor Alexandre Herman Schutz*, edited by Urban T. Holmes and Kenneth R. Scholberg, 164–82. Columbus: Ohio State University Press, 1964.

Lewis, Charles Bertram. *Classical Mythology and Arthurian Romance: A Study of the Sources of Chrestien de Troyes'* Yvain *and Other Arthurian Romances*. 1932; rpt. Geneva: Slatkine, 1974.

Limentani, Alberto. *L'eccezione narrativa: La Provenza medievale e l'arte del racconto*. Turin: Einaudi, 1977.

Loomis, Roger Sherman. *Arthurian Tradition and Chrétien de Troyes*. New York: Columbia University Press, 1949.

Loomis, Roger Sherman. "Morgain la Fée and the Celtic Goddesses." *Speculum* 20 (1945): 183–203.

Lote, Georges. *Histoire du vers français*. 3 vols. Paris: Boivin, 1949–1955.

Marinis, Tammaro de. *La legatura artistica in Italia nei secoli XV e XVI. Notizie ed elenchi*. 3 vols. Florence: Fratelli Alinari, 1960.

Marjorossy, Imre Gabor. "Aventures en deux directions: Allusions chrétiennes dans *Blandin de Cornualla*." In *L'Occitan invitée de l'Euregio. Liège 1981 – Aix-la-Chapelle 2008: Bilan et perspectives*, edited by Angelica Rieger, 461–70. 2 vols. Aachen: Shaker Verlag, 2011.

Marquèze-Pouey, Louis. "Les 'grands vers' dans la poésie occitane des XIIe et XIIIe siècles." *Hommage à Jean Séguy*, vol. 1, *Via Domitia* 14 (1978): 281–90.

Martínez, Vicent. "'Blandin de Cornualla': Cap a la novel.la cavalleresca." In *Actes del vuitè Col.loqui internacional de llengua i literatura catalanes. Tolosa de

Llenguadoc, 12–17 de setembre de 1988, edited by Antoni M. Badia et al., 1:435–48. 2 vols. Associació internacional de lengua i literatura catalanes. Barcelona: Publicacions de l'Abadia de Montserrat, 1989.

Martínez, Vicent. "Una entesa ben interessada entre la realitat i la fantasia: *Blandin de Cornualla*." *Caplletra* 5 (1988): 39–49.

Martínez Pérez, Antonia. "Consideraciones sobre la estructuración narrativo-literaria del *Blandin de Cornualla*." In *Actas del VI Congreso internacional de la Asociación hispánica de literatura medieval (Alcalá de Henares, 12–16 de septiembre de 1995)*, edited by José Manuel Lucía Megías, 2:1009–22. 2 vols. Alcalá: Universidad de Alcalá, 1997.

Massó Torrents, Jaume. *Repertori de l'antiga literatura catalana*. Barcelona: Editorial Alpha, 1932.

McCulloch, Florence. *Medieval Latin and French Bestiaries*. Chapel Hill: University of North Carolina Press, 1960.

Meliga, Walter. "Osservazioni sulle grafie della tradizione trobadorica." In *Atti del secondo Congresso Internazionale della Association internationale d'études occitanes, Torino, 31 agosto–5 settembre 1987*, edited by Giuliano Gasca Queirazza, 763–97. 2 vols. Turin: Dipartimento di scienze letterarie e filologiche, Università di Torino, 1993.

Muhlberger, Steven. *Deeds of Arms: Formal Combats in the Late Fourteenth Century*. Highland Village, TX: The Chivalry Bookshelf, 2005.

Neemann, Harold. "Schlafende Schönheit (AaTh/ATU 410)." *Enzyklopädie des Märchens Online: Handwörterbuch zur historischen und vergleichenden Erzählforschung*. Berlin: De Guyter, 2007. Online edition 2016. http://db.degruyter.com/view/emo.

Newstead, Helaine. "The Besieged Ladies in Arthurian Romance." *PMLA* 63 (1948): 803–30.

Newstead, Helaine. *Bran the Blessed in Arthurian Romance*. New York: AMS Press, 1966.

Nitze, William A. "A New Source of the *Yvain*." *Modern Philology* 3 (1905): 269–80.

Nitze, William A. "The Waste Land: A Celtic Arthurian Theme." *Modern Philology* 43 (1945–1946): 58–62.

Nixon, Terry. "Romance Collections and the Manuscripts of Chrétien de Troyes." In *Les manuscrits de Chrétien de Troyes / The Manuscripts of Chrétien de Troyes*, edited by Keith Busby, Terry Nixon, Alison Stones and Lori Walters, 1:17–25. 2 vols. Amsterdam: Rodopi, 1993.

Northrup, George Tyler. *An Introduction to Spanish Literature*. Chicago: University of Chicago Press, 1925.

Oster, Patricia. "Les six réveils de la Belle au bois dormant." In *Livres anciens, lectures vivantes: Ce qui passe et ce qui demeure*, edited by Michel Zink with Odile Bombarde, 229–61. Paris: Odile Jacob, 2010.

Pacheco, Arseni. "El Blandin de Cornualha." In *Catalan Studies (estudis sobre alá). Volume in Memory of Josephine de Boer*, edited by Joseph Gulsoy and J. Maria Sola-Solé, 149–61. Barcelona: Borràs, 1977.

Paden, William D. *An Introduction to Old Occitan*. New York: Modern Language Association of America, 1998.

Pailhès, Claudine. *Gaston Fébus: Le prince et le diable*. Paris: Perrin, 2007.

Paradisi, Gioia. "La Bella Addormentata nel *Blandin de Cornoalha* e in *Frayre de Joy et Sor de Plaser.*" *Le Forme e la storia* n.s. 8.2 (2015): 751-74.

Pasini, Giuseppe, with Francesco Berta and Antonio Rivautella. *Codices manuscripti bibliothecae regii taurinensis athenaei*. 2 vols. Turin, 1749.

Pastoureau, Michel. *Black: The History of a Color*, translated by Jody Gladding. Princeton, NJ: Princeton University Press, 2009.

Pastoureau, Michel. *Rouge: Histoire d'une couleur*. Paris: Seuil, 2016.

Patch, Howard R. *The Other World according to Descriptions in Medieval Literature*. 1950; rpt. New York: Octagon Books, 1970.

Paton, Lucy Allen. *Studies in the Fairy Mythology of Arthurian Romance*. 1903; rpt. New York: Burt Franklin, 1960.

Pellegrin, Elisabeth. *La bibliothèque des Visconti et des Sforza ducs de Milan, au XVe siècle*. Paris: Service des publications du CNRS, 1955.

Pfeffer, Wendy. "À la marge d'un roman à la marge: Le cas de *Blandin de Cornoalha*." In *Fidelitats e dissidéncias. Actes du XIIe Congrès international de l'Association internationale d'études occitanes*, edited by Jean-François Courouau with David Fabié, 2:541–51. 2 vols. Toulouse: SFAIEO, 2020.

Pfeffer, Wendy. "*Blandin de Cornoalha*, Yet Another Look." *Encomia* 36–37 (2012–2013) [2018]: 37–49.

Pfeffer, Wendy. "Canes virumque cano: *Blandin de Cornoalha*." In *Occitània en Catalonha: De tempses novèls, de novèlas perspectivas: Actes de l'XIen Congrès de Associacion internacionala d'estudis occitans (Lleida 2014)*, edited by Aitor Carrera and Isabel Grifoll, 593–601. Lleida: Generalitat de Catalonha, Departament de la Cultura, 2017.

Pfeffer, Wendy. *Proverbs in Medieval Occitan Literature*. Gainesville: University Press of Florida, 1997.

Pfeffer, Wendy. "The Birds and the Bees and *Blandin de Cornoalha*." Paper presented at (Un)Expected Animals in (Un)Expected Places in the Middle Ages and Early Modern Period, Third International Meeting of the Medieval Animal Data-Network, Louisville, KY, May 6, 2014.

Pfister, Max. "La localisation d'une scripta littéraire en ancien occitan." *Travaux de linguistique et de littérature* 19 (1972): 253–91.

Philipot, Emmanuel. "Un épisode d'*Erec et Enide*: La 'Joie de la Cour'." *Rom* 25 (1896): 258–94.

Philipot, Emmanuel. Review of *Studies on the Libeaus Desconus* by William Henry Schofield. *Rom* 26 (1897): 290–305.

Pillet, Alfred and Henry Carstens. *Bibliographie der Troubadours*. Halle: Max Niemeyer, 1933.

Poirion, Daniel. "Traditions et fonctions du *dit poétique* au XIVe et au XVe siècle." In *Literatur in der Gesellschaft des Spätmittelalters*, edited by Hans Ulrich Gumbrecht, 147–50. Heidelberg: Carl Winter, 1980.

Pope, M. K. *From Latin to Modern French with Especial Consideration of Anglo-Norman*. Manchester: Manchester University Press, 1934; rpt. 1952.

Renier, Rudolfo. "Una vecchia memoria sul 'Blandin de Cornoalha'." *Giornale storico della letteratura italiana* 6 (1885): 476.

Ribera Llopis, Juan Miguel. "*Blandin de Cornualla* (f. s. XII–s. XIV) y la modificación irónica del código caballeresco." In *Actes du XVIIIe Congrès international de linguistique et philologie romanes, Université de Trèves (Trier) 1986*, edited by Dieter Kremer, 6:355–61. 7 vols. Tübingen: Max Niemeyer, 1988.

Richter, Elise. "Altprovenzalisch *barra*, 'Kiefer'?" *Zeitschrift für romanische Philologie* 31 (1907): 610–11.

Romano, C. "Gian Galeazzo Visconti e gli eredi di Bernabò." *Archivio storico lombardo*, 2nd ser., 8 (1891): 5–59, 291–341.

Ronjat, Jules. *Grammaire istorique des parlers provençaux modernes*. 4 vols. Montpellier: Société des langues romanes, 1930–1941.

Roussineau, Gilles. "Tradition littéraire et culture populaire dans l'histoire de Troïlus et de Zellandine (*Perceforest*, Troisième partie), version ancienne du conte de la Belle au bois dormant." *Arthuriana* 4, no. 1 (Spring 1994): 30–45.

Saintsbury, George. *A Short History of French Literature (from the Earliest Texts to the Close of the Nineteenth Century)*. Oxford: Oxford University Press, 1882.

Savli d'Igliano, Ludovico. "Del cavaliere errante, romanzo di Tommaso III, marchesse di Salvazzo." *Memorie della Reale accademia delle scienze di Torino* 27, *Memorie della classe di Scienze morali, storiche e filologiche* (1823): 1–71. http://www.biodiversitylibrary.org/item/32621#page/442/mode/1up.

Short, Ian. "L'avènement du texte vernaculaire: La mise en recueil." In *Théories et pratiques de l'écriture au Moyen Âge, actes du Colloque, Palais du Luxembourg-Sénat, 5 et 6 mars 1987*, edited by Emmanuèle Baumgartner and Christiane Marchello-Nizia, 11–24. *Littérales* 4 (1988).

Sibille, Jean. "Fidelitat a la lenga vernaculara e escritura literària: L'emplec de *p(l)us* e *mai* per la gradacion dels adjectius e la quantificacion dels substantius a cò de qualques autors roergasses … emai maites." In *Fidelitats e dissidéncias: Actes du XIIe Congrès de l'Association internationale d'études occitanes*, edited by Jean-François Courouau with David Fabié. 2 vols. 1: 285–97. Toulouse: SFAIEO, 2020.

Smith, Nathaniel B. and Thomas G. Bergin, eds. *An Old Provençal Primer*. New York: Garland, 1984.

Snell, Frederick John. *Periods of European Literature*, vol. 3, *The 14th Century*. New York: Scribner, 1899. http://books.google.com/books?id=bBk2yYiY9RsC&pg=PA24&lpg=PA24&dq="blandin+de+cornoalha"&source=bl&ots=8Ud2eoDbyK&sig=xaNM911EPHigRzUxehTgWVdS5Hk&hl=en&sa=X&ei=PtF6UZiHDOPh4APV64DYCQ&ved=0CC0Q6AEwADgK#v=twopage&q&f=false.

Soriano, Marc. *Les contes de Perrault: Culture savante et traditions populaires*. Paris: Gallimard, 1969.

Thompson, Stith. *Motif-Index of Folk-Literature: A Classification of Narrative Elements in Folktales, Ballads, Myths, Fables, Mediaeval Romances, Exempla, Fabliaux, Jest-Books, and Local Legends*, rev. ed. 6 vols. Bloomington, IN: Indiana University Press, 1955–1958.

Uther, Hans-Jörg. *The Types of International Folktales: A Classification and Bibliography, Based on the System of Antti Aarne and Stith Thompson*. Helsinki: Suomalainen Tiedeakatemia, Academia Scientiarum Fennica, 2004.

Varvaro, Alberto. *La tragédie de l'histoire: La dernière oeuvre de Jean Froissart*. Paris: Classiques Garnier, 2011.

Vernier, Richard. *Lord of the Pyrenees: Gaston Fébus, Count of Foix (1331–1391)*. Woodbridge, Suffolk: Boydell Press, 2008.

Vitale-Brovarone, Alessandro. Multiple emails to Pfeffer, between November 2013 and March 2017.

Vondra, Sylvain. "Le bacinet de Banyuls." *Bulletin de l'Association archéologique des Pyrénées-Orientales* 20 (2005): 107–10.

Wehowski, Else. *Die Sprache der Vida de la benaurada sancta Doucelina. Lautstand, Formen und einige syntaktische Erscheinungen. Eine Studie zum Dialekt von Marseille*. Berlin: E. Ebering, 1910.

Zago, Esther. "Some Medieval Versions of Sleeping Beauty: Variations on a Theme." *Studi francesi* 23 (1979): 417–31.

Zufferey, François. *Recherches linguistiques sur les chansonniers provençaux*. Geneva: Droz, 1987.

Index

TEAMS

VARIA SERIES

The Study of Chivalry: Resources and Approaches, edited by Howell Chickering and Thomas H. Seiler (1988)

Studies in the Harley Manuscript: The Scribes, Contents, and Social Contexts of British Library MS Harley 2253, edited by Susanna Fein (2000)

The Liturgy of the Medieval Church, edited by Thomas J. Heffernan and E. Ann Matter (2001; second edition 2005)

Johannes de Grocheio, *Ars musice*, edited and translated by Constant J. Mews, John N. Crossley, Catherine Jeffreys, Leigh McKinnon, and Carol J. Williams (2011)

Aribo, "De musica" and "Sententiae," edited and translated by T. J. H. McCarthy (2015)

Guy of Saint-Denis, *Tractatus de tonis*, edited and translated by Constant J. Mews, Carol J. Williams, John N. Crossley, and Catherine Jeffreys (2017)

Anthony Munday, *The Honourable, Pleasant and Rare Conceited Historie of Palmendos,* edited by Leticia Álvarez-Recio (2022)

Typeset in Garamond Premier Pro

Medieval Institute Publications
College of Arts and Sciences
Western Michigan University
1903 W. Michigan Avenue
Kalamazoo, MI 49008-5432
http://wmich.edu/medievalpublications